WILLIAM ALLEN WHITE

Maverick on Main Street

John DeWitt McKee

Contributions in American Studies, Number 17

GREENWOOD PRESS

Westport, Connecticut • London, England

Library of Congress Cataloging in Publication Data

McKee, John DeWitt, 1919-
William Allen White: maverick on main street.

(Contributions in American studies; no. 17)
Bibliography: p.
Includes index.
1. White, William Allen, 1868-1944.
PN4874.W52M3 818'.5'209 [B] 74-5991
ISBN 0-8371-7533-X

Library of Congress Catalog Card Number: 74-5991
ISBN: 0-8371-7533-X

First published in 1975

Greenwood Press, a division of Williamhouse-Regency Inc.
51 Riverside Avenue, Westport, Connecticut 06880

Manufactured in the United States of America

TO MY WIFE JEANNETTE

A True Partner in This Enterprise

Acknowledgment is given to the publishers listed below for permission to reprint:

From Robert Sherwood and Wendell Willkie on pages 186, 188, and 191 © 1940 by The New York Times Company. Reprinted by permission.

From Elting E. Morison, ed., *The Letters of Theodore Roosevelt,* © 1951 by Harvard University Press. Reprinted by permission of Harvard University Press.

From Walter Johnson, *Selected Letters of William Allen White, 1895-1943,* © 1947 by Walter Johnson. Reprinted by permission of Walter Johnson.

From William L. White *The Autobiography of William Allen White,* copyright 1946 by Macmillan Publishing Co., Inc., renewed 1974 by Macmillan Publishing Co., Inc., and W. L. White by permission of Macmillan Publishing Co., Inc., and Mrs. William L. White.

From *William Allen White: In Memoriam,* contributions by Henry Seidel Canby, Dorothy Canfield (Fisher), Harry Scherman, and others by permission of Book-of-the-Month Club, Inc.

From *FDR: His Personal Letters:* Reprinted by permission of Hawthorn Books, Inc. from *FDR: His Personal Letters* by Elliott Roosevelt, ed. Copyright © 1950 by Elliott Roosevelt.
All rights reserved.

From the William Allen White Collection, Library of Congress and the William Allen White Collection, William Allen White Memorial Library, Kansas State Teachers College, Emporia, by permission of Mrs. William L. White.

From Oswald Garrison Villard, "A Long and Foolish Life," *The Nation* © 1937 by *The Nation.* Reprinted by permission.

Contents

Acknowledgments

It is a pleasure to acknowledge the assistance and encouragement given me in the preparation of this work by George Arms, professor of English; T. M. Pearce, professor emeritus of English; the late Howard J. McMurray, who was professor of government; and the late Charles B. Judah, former professor of government, all of the University of New Mexico.

I would like also to acknowledge the invaluable assistance of the staff of the Manuscript Division of the Library of Congress and to thank them for their cooperation in my work with the library's White Collection. Thanks are also due to Professor Everett Rich, then of Kansas State Teachers College, Emporia, and to the late W. L. White, who was publisher of *The Emporia Gazette,* for their kindness in opening doors for me and for sharing with me their memories of William Allen White; to the staff of the William Allen White Memorial Library at Kansas State Teachers College; to Dean Burton W. Martin of the William Allen White School of Journalism and Public Information, director of the William Allen White Foundation, Lawrence, Kansas, for supplying copies of the annual William Allen White Memorial Lectures; to Professor Walter Johnson, of the University of Chicago, for supplying me with a copy of his bibliography of the published works of William Allen White; to Carol Reser, of the Kansas State Historical Library, Topeka, for supplying me with important statistical information; to the staff of the Zimmerman Library, University of New Mexico, and especially to Zanier Lane, for locating an obscure congressman; to Gene Clevenger and Beverly Hawks of the W. Martin Speare Memorial Library, New Mexico Tech, for numerous searches and retrievals; to Dorothy Holmes and the staff of the Socorro Public Library; to the New Mexico Easter Seal Society through whose arrangements the travel incident to research was made possible; to Mrs. W. L. White, without whose kindness and concern, I would have been guilty of some errors of fact; and finally, to the Research Foundation of the New Mexico Institute of Mining & Technology for the grant that gave me a summer in which to put this book together.

March 1974

William Allen White

1

Prairie Princeling

"Of all the American Liberals," wrote Oswald Garrison Villard, "Bill White of Emporia is the most pernickety, perverse, pernicious, and periodic. He is the most often mistaken, inconstant, inconsistent, unwise, short-sighted, percipient, emotional, banal, self-righteous, self-critical, partisan and independent, generally maddening and altogether loveable conservative in the whole country. . . ."[1]

The occasion for this outburst of adjectives was a review of William Allen White's *Forty Years on Main Street,* a compilation of *Emporia Gazette* editorials that illustrated every adjective Villard had used and then some.[2] There was in the review the sort of indulgent irritation usually reserved for a winsome but willful child. But if anybody thought that such an appraisal put White in an awkward position, he had another thought coming. Chances are that White agreed with the evaluation entirely. He had spent his life fostering just the image that Villard had outlined, though he would have insisted that he was a liberal among liberals, even a radical at times. Neither his friends nor his enemies—and in his seventy-six years White managed to gather an assortment in both categories—knew quite what to make of this ebullient Kansan who made an international career out of a strong, pervasive, mercurial personality and a newspaper whose circulation never went above seven thousand subscribers.

As Villard went on to say, "'A long and foolish life,' he terms his existence, heaven bless him! But it has been a foolishness for which men and women innumerable have loved him; which has made him an American institution, as variable as a weather vane but as serene and happy as the leadenest rooster perched on any Kansas barn; a source of infinite betting as to which side he will jump to whenever an issue comes up; a joy forever."[3]

It was just this sort of kewpie doll loveableness, this sly innocence, that was part of White's fascination for his contemporaries. And he gloried in it. He reported with obvious relish the overheard comment of a political enemy: "Look at that face! As round and innocent as a baby's bottom—but watch out!" He insisted on his inconsistency, and his contemporaries ran themselves ragged at the base line, trying to return his volleys, now to the right of them, now to the left. He wouldn't be pigeon-holed; he wouldn't stay put.

This was part of the legend of William Allen White, a legend that White himself planted, consciously or unconsciously, and nurtured from the day he wrote his first editorial in the *Gazette.* But it was not all of the legend. White became synonymous with political sagacity and journalistic acumen to the extent that Rolla A. Clymer, who had started his newspaper career as a reporter for White and had gone on to edit the *Eldorado Republican,* could call his mentor a "colossus of the prairie."[4]

It was a legend which was to make White the Sage of Emporia, a rustic oracle expounding gnomic wisdom from his cracker-barrel perch on the plains. The picture is sentimentally false, false because it presents only one side of the man, the side most easily caught. For William Allen White was a man of many facets. He was at the same time, for instance, the most cosmopolitan of the provincials and the most parochial of the cosmopolites. He was editor, reporter, author, politician, and diplomat; but he himself realized that the swath he cut would soon grow over. He was a sentimental idealist and the driver of some of the toughest bargains in the history of American grass-roots politics. He was a man who preached education all his life and picked up most of his own considerable learning from his own reading, from the copy desk, and from travel and conversation with the great and near-great of his time. He was a man who knew that he was good at his craft, who used his editorial page as much for self-fulfillment and self-revelation as for discussion of issues; yet he was a truly modest man, sometimes to the point of almost stammering self-effacement. If he was somewhat less than Clymer's "colossus of the prairies," if he was somewhat less than the Sage of Emporia whom many Kansans venerate as a sort of minor saint, he was also a good deal more than the Foxy Grampa of Midwestern grass-roots politics that many of his friends and enemies have painted.

Nor was he as inconsistent as a day-to-day examination of his activities might indicate. William Allen White performed his dance of apparent inconsistencies upon a stage of beliefs and principles which remained constant throughout his long public career. The stage he built for his performance was broad, and there was room for many seeming inconsistencies within the pattern of the dance; but the dance did have a pattern, and the success or failure of the performance depended on it.

Of course, White had nothing to do with laying the foundations of his stage. That was the accident of time, place, and parentage. The Kansas Willie White was born into in 1868 in Emporia was the green eastern Kansas of rural villages planted in the midst of surrounding farms. These little dots of civilization that punctuated the prairie horizon were only just removed temporally from the frontier. In White's boyhood there was still the danger of prairie fires.[5] It was even possible for him on at least one occasion to ride on the saddlebow in front of an Indian squaw and to guide her and her party into town.[6] And he met and became a playmate of a little boy who had been captured by the Indians, had lived with them and learned their ways, and had been rescued and brought home. He recorded in his autobiography that the boy died after being returned to the white man's ways. And he speculated on the effect of civilization on the reconverted noble savage.[7]

A good part of White's early education, the part he was to insist was of most importance to him, he gathered in the dusty road that meandered past the house, in the woods, along the streams, and in the improvised gymnasium in the loft of his father's barn.[8] He watched "one of the town's most distinguished artists . . . a wagon painter who striped buggy wheels and painted the elaborate designs . . . on the sides of the wagons."[9] His nose wrinkled in boy-like perverse pleasure at the stink of the tannery and the slaughterhouse. And when his feet were not bare and splayed in the velvety warm summer dust of the road or dangling in the stream, they were encased in the long stockings that his mother knitted for him and in the shoes which the village cobbler had made for him from the last up.[10]

Willie White's father was Dr. Allen White, "Old Doc" White, whom his son remembered as a real "somebody" in the village–doctor, druggist, storekeeper, politician, leading citizen–and he had merchandise shipped in from St. Louis. He ordered his own shoes from St. Louis, too, and sometimes material for a dress for Mrs. White or a suit for himself. For the most part, however, the Whites lived a self-sufficient existence, as did Eldorado, where Willie spent his boyhood, and as did all the other little farming towns around. For when William Allen White was a boy, the agrarian society which the Civil War had laid waste in the South remained strong in the states of the Midwest. The villages no less than the farms themselves were self-sufficient entities. Because the farms as well as the towns were isolated from each other, the farmers still lived in the enforced independence of frontier days. The country had not yet been knitted together, though the war that had just ended had begun the process and the great railroad boom of the 1880s would complete it.

A change was coming, however, while Willie White grew. Homesteaders had begun to move in on the vast, uncut prairie, and White was to write wonderingly about the scores of young ex-soldiers and their wives who came into the Walnut Valley in those days, either to settle in the village or to homestead their share of the prairie surrounding it.[11] Along with the homesteaders, the Midwest had its quota of those who dreamed of great cities on the plains, of railroad centers and packing centers, and of cities which came no nearer to realization than the prospectus for them. When the dream cities did get beyond realtor's rhetoric, they often baked out their short lives waiting for rain in the western short grass land. There were those who went west to the sand hills of Kansas and came back two or three, or sometimes ten years later, bent and gnarled by the savage impersonality of the elements.

These were the people White knew or knew about in his boyhood and youth, the boomers and the beaten farmers–these and the prosperous farmers of the eastern side of the state, the small businessmen and the professional men. And this was the yeasty, in-between time when the country rode a boom and projects sprouted like weeds on the prairie, when, as White was to remember, "the mortgage to buy farm machinery was being plastered all over the new state."[12] All the gamblers were not in the grain market pits. Some were on the prairies of the Midwest, floating bonds for streets, for street railways, for electric lights. Farmers went west and mortgaged unplanted crops to pay for machinery with which to work the crops. More times than not, in a land of submarginal rainfall and grasshoppers, they waited in vain for the harvest. One seed that was planted in the mid-seventies, however, was beginning to burgeon into bitter fruit, and the Panic of 1873 was a foretaste. The post-Civil War centralization of capital had begun, the farmers were beginning to feel the squeeze, and the seeding of revolt was showing green above the prairie loam.[13]

This was the cosmos of White's boyhood and youth, small-town, agrarian, self-sufficient. This was his land, and although he became a world traveler, it was to remain his land. Although what he wrote in his lifetime helped bridge the gap between the simple, small-town society of his boyhood and the intricacies of urban industrial civilization, Kansas and Emporia remained the center of his universe. Kansas was to be all things for him, various as a woman, tender and savage, beautiful and scarred, rolling green, with seas of summer gold in the wheatfields and moaning, wind-blasted loneliness in the western sand hills. It was to be the nation's conscience, its low barometer, a state of mind, and the furtherest reaches of the lava flow of New England Puritanism.[14]

Three threads run through *The Autobiography of William Allen White* and through much of White's fiction: the fact of his Yankee ancestry, the fact that he belonged to the village elite, and a deep nostalgia for things as they had been when he was growing up. It was not only for economic reasons that the railroads were to be his black beast, as they were to be the black beast of the Progressives with whom he became associated. The coming of the railroads to the little country villages dried up the home industries, the harness shops, the tannery, the furniture factory.

"Then the railroads came," he wrote, "and everything changed. I did not know that the smell of coal smoke, which greeted my nostrils with the railroad engine, was to be the sign and signal for the decay of a town and indeed of pioneer times, when men made things where they used them—all the things necessary to a rather competent civilization."[15] This reaching back for things of the past—something that White did not only at the end of his life, when the things of childhood could be expected to wear a golden haze, but throughout his career—seems a strange occupation for a man who made a reputation as one of the most militant of the Progressives. But it was William Allen White's occupation a good deal of the time, and it is one of the many seeming paradoxes in his life. For he remembered the other side of that life, too, the movers optimistically going west to start a new life, only to return by the same road a few years later broken, embittered, driven from their dreams by fruitless labor, endless droughts, and an ever-tightening credit.[16] He saw both sides, and later he recorded both sides, but the happy times are the times one remembers best, and, except for an "if I had only known" confession that runs through the autobiography, this was the world that White wanted for his own.

That he was a member of the ruling class of his society he had no doubt. His father was Dr. Allen White, and Dr. Allen White was not only a physician, he was also a druggist, a merchant, a dealer in real estate, and a man who lost money by operating a boarding house on the principle that good food and good company were worth more than profit. In addition, he was a member of the town council, who once got himself elected street commissioner so that he could see to it that Eldorado's main street was macadamized.[17] He was an odd fish in post-Civil War Kansas, when the politics of the whole Midwest was dominated by returned Union veterans who were at one and the same time members of the Grand Army of the Republic and of the Republican party. Allen White was a successful anti-slavery, prohibitionist, Copperhead, "still unwashed, still voting for Jackson," Democrat.[18] He was a leading member of his party in Kansas and a leading citizen in Eldorado, where he was mayor at the time of his death.

Allen White was also a peculiar combination of self-deprecation and self-dramatization. A short, round man with whiskbroom whiskers, he strutted a bit, as short round men are wont to do, sported a plug hat and a walking stick, and wore nankeen suits in the summertime. He traced his Yankee ancestry beyond the American Revolution. And, though he was never elected to state office, he was a power in Kansas politics, sometimes, according to his son's recollection, representing the town in the state capital when the issues transcended party lines.[19] And yet, though his son remembered him defending his point of view "courageously but not cantankerously," he remembered, too, that Dr. Allen White would go to great lengths to avoid an argument, and that he was "above all, self deprecating."[20] What he wrote about his father would do for a portrait of the son. William Allen White developed the same paradoxical love of the limelight and penchant for self-deprecation.

That was a good house to grow up in, that house kept by Dr. Allen White and Mary Ann Hatten White. There were books, and there was music, and the good food and conversation drew some of the greats of the day to the White table. Young Willie White met Elizabeth Cady Stanton, a friend of his mother, and "it was a tradition of family pride," White remembered, "that we entertained Susan B. Anthony in the sixties when she was campaigning in Kansas for woman suffrage."[21] Obviously, only the family tradition was in White's memory, since he did not arrive in the world until 1868. He also remembered the tradition, and perhaps the event, too, since it happened in the seventies when Prohibition was an issue in Kansas, of entertaining John P. St. John, "the Kansas Republican hero of Prohibition."[22] With these house guests and others, and considering his father's position in the community, it would not be a wonder if Willie White became imbued with the idea that he was a member of the ruling class, and no surprise if he had developed into a little snob, as he was later to suspect he had.[23]

Such conversation as must have made its way around and across the White dining table would be heady stuff for a boy to hear, if he understood it. And he probably did understand it, because politics was in the air in the White household most of the time. If his father was a "Stephen Douglas Copperhead Democrat,"[24] his mother was a "black abolitionist Republican,"[25] and it was here, he remembered, "in their politics, that these two began to live in my traditions and in my consciousness."

Dr. White took his son to the state capital at Topeka a number of times when he had business there. He imbued his son with the vision of politics as a means to social and economic betterment for the people. He impressed upon the boy a sense of *noblesse oblige,* reinforcing the idea of the ruling class. He believed that boys should work, but on one occasion he marched young Willie home with his shoe-shine box under his arm because he wanted his son to polish no man's shoes.[26] He also had great courage, with which, and with little else but his voice and his prestige in the community, he averted armed conflict over whether Eldorado or Augusta should be the county seat of Butler County.[27] He was skeptical, whimsical, a highly practical politician who could still give his allegiance quixotically to a party which in that time and place had the chance of a snowball in a Kansas July.

The characterisitics of the son begin to emerge in the study of the father, at least as the son tells the story, and the son would use this to illustrate the importance of heredity, the importance of the Yankee characteristics he inherited. But it was not only inheritance. It was also instruction, and it could be, White himself was intrigued by the speculation, that if his father had lived beyond the boy's early teens, William Allen White would have been a Democrat in Kansas like his father before him. His father had him breathing politics almost as soon as he was breathing air—by the time he was eight, he was attending political meetings—and the politics was Democratic. Allen White was apparently more trustful of parties than he was of men. He had few heroes, his son wrote. "Even Tilden, whom he considered a martyr, he accepted only at a liberal commercial discount."[28] Some of that same skepticism might have helped the younger White, who panted after one hero after another all his life. Otherwise, however, father and son were very much alike. They were both observers and commentators while at the same time managing to be participants. William Allen White, as a matter of fact, developed the faculty of standing off and observing himself in action, with many a resulting giggle and "Oh, pshaw!"

It was Allen White, moreover, who introduced his son to the newspaper business, though the fact that Willie's first job was in a newspaper print shop was incidental. What mattered to Dr. White was the fact that his boy was eleven years old and that it was time he learned the value of work. It was an easy matter to put young Will to work. "We did not need the money . . . but, alas for me," White wrote in his autobiography, "he was a Democratic politician and naturally had money invested in the poor little starved-to-death Democratic weekly. . . . In order to secure me employment, he had only to take me by the hand . . . and present me to the Editor."[29]

It would make a fine story if we could say that William Allen White was thus launched on his newspaper career at such an early age, but the facts, at least as White remembered them, are different. The boy discovered early that the paper itself was practically insolvent and that his father was paying his salary, slipping the money to "the Editor" so that young Will would not know about it. When the boy discovered the ruse, both Whites were humiliated, and the career in journalism had to wait another five years for its beginning.

Although William Allen White was to base much of his social thinking on the idea that Kansas was the last stronghold of New England Puritanism, and though he was to tie that belief to his own New England ancestry, his memory of his parents would belie any such connection. Dr. White, indeed, was a skeptic. Mary Ann Hatten White, on the other hand, was an

Irish immigrant Catholic, an orphan who had been reared in a Congregationalist home and who had attended Congregationalist Knox College.[30] While Dr. White "set great store by the Bible as literature and as a code of morals [he] had very little use for its theological implications. I gathered from their arguments," White added, "that my mother was still afraid of hell-fire and still hoped for wings."[31]

Religion was only one of the many things the Whites disagreed about. It is easier to list the things they argued about than to find something on which they were in agreement. Seldom had two people been more temperamentally mismatched than were Allen White and Mary Ann Hatten, if we are to believe their son's memory. The doctor was a man of large extravagances and small economies. He fancied himself the local Boniface, and he would not serve his paying guests anything but the best cuts of meat and the freshest of vegetables. He took young Will shopping with him and thus began the boy's life-long and knowledgeable interest in good food. But if it was Dr. White who selected the steaks and chops and roasts, it was Mrs. White who prepared them, and who wore herself out in the kitchen of the inn called the White House, trying to make a business out of what her husband considered pure pleasure.[32]

Where he was prodigal, she was frugal; where he was gay, she was dour; where he was romantic and sentimental, she was exceedingly practical. And if he was a skeptical Jacksonian Democrat, she was a passionate Republican, a veritable disciple of Abraham Lincoln. It was rather easy for William Allen White to lay his own cat-on-the-fence attitude to this blending of the ideas of his father and mother. It was no wonder, he said, "when election time came around, this black abolition Republican, who was my mother, and this Stephen Douglas Copperhead Democrat who was my father . . . had their purple moments. No wonder I grew up full of complexes, with a certain lack of conviction which comes from seeing both sides well presented by those you love and knowing full well there are two sides to everything, and that what seems black or white is generally gray."[33]

Generally gray, perhaps, but the fact remains that strong-willed, dour, determined Mary Ann White was the stronger influence on the life and career of William Allen White than was his father. His father taught him many things about people, about politics, about the woods and fields and streams around him,[34] but his mother put him to reading, encouraged his interest in music, and inculcated in him the virtues of her patron saint, Abraham Lincoln.[35] From his father William Allen White got his love of politics and his gentle skepticism. From his mother he got his Republicanism as a sort of lay religion.

"A captain of a woman,"[36] he called her in his obituary editorial about her, and she was that. In a time when college education for women was the exception far more often than it was the rule, she had set her sights on a college education and teaching career. With time out to earn money, and with time out to help her sister care for a growing family, she got what she went after. In the process she became imbued with her strong political views, for it was while she was attending Knox College in Galesburg, Illinois, that she heard the last of the Lincoln-Douglas debates. "There," as her son put it, "she fell madly, platonically, but eternally in love with Abraham Lincoln."[37]

It was this same determined woman who had insisted on an integrated classroom in her first school at Council Grove, Kansas. It was from his mother as much at least as from anybody else that William Allen White got his abiding faith in education as the answer to most of the problems in a democracy. The dependency between the two was mutual. So much was this apparently so that when young Will entered the University of Kansas, Mary Ann White packed her traps and moved to Lawrence to set up a home for him.[38]

Thus, though there was room to believe White's theory about his growing up to know that black and white usually were gray because he had heard both the black and white sides well presented in his own home, the influence was probably not so evenly divided between his father and his mother as he liked to believe. While Allen White was the prominent member of the marriage, Mary Ann White was the stronger of the two. It might well be true, as White surmised, that had his father lived, the Democratic party would have had another member, but there is room for doubt. True, he was a schoolboy Democrat and was almost choked to death with his campaign scarf for his trouble, but he had accepted his father's political faith as other children accepted their parents' religious faith, and as unthinkingly. And he fought on the school ground for that faith. "It never occurred to me to fight for my mother's faith,"[39] he wrote.

It was not so much his political training that interested White's mother as his cultural training. By the time he was ten he was reading, or having read to him, Dickens, Anthony Trollope, Tennyson, Wilkie Collins, and Charles Reade, "after Dickens had played out."[40] Something of his own indiscriminate reading was foreshadowed, too, in the fact that he also was to remember Felicia Hemans ("The boy stood on the burning deck. . . .") and the Seaside Library, which White later remembered as "pirated reprints of English novels whose vogue has now passed, and whose titles mean nothing."[41]

But just as he went to all the Sunday Schools in rotation, more for the society they provided than for the instruction, he also discovered the town library alone and "went stark mad over Mark Twain at a dozen years."[42] By the time he was in high school, he was buying pirated editions of English authors and devouring the humor papers of the time: *Texas Siftings, The Spoopendyke Papers, The Arkansaw Traveler, The Detroit Free Press,* and the writings of Opie Read, Bill Nye, M. Quad, and Bob Burdette.[43] This reading, containing the artistic use of exaggeration, the straight-faced tall-tale-telling that the American newspapers had inherited from the frontier humorists, was to have a marked effect on William Allen White's mature style. Add to this his careful study of the King James version of the Bible, and the Biblical sonorities sometimes became inverted and came out like this injunction to dieters: "Look not upon the gravy in the boat when it is brown."

If, then, his father's largest bequest was a love of politics and a faith in its efficiency for ameliorating social ills, his mother's largest bequest was a love of reading and a belief in the necessity of an educated electorate. This was one of the strong underpinnings of the stage which White was building even before he had decided what part to play on that stage.

2

"Multitudes in Me"

Bent Murdock was the first political boss William Allen White ever knew. "Uncle Bent" entered his life shortly after the death of the elder White, and became a sort of foster-father to the boy. Thomas Benton Murdock was editor of the *Walnut Valley Times* in Eldorado and later edited the *Eldorado Republican.* He was also a state senator, the political boss of Butler County, and, as White remembered much later, the "vice-regent" of the railroads, the packing houses, and the banks of Kansas. A director of a small branch of the Santa Fe Railroad, he often rode in a private car. He had railroad passes, not only for himself and his family, but for the political delegates whom he picked to go to state conventions.[1] Here was the epitome of the rural American political boss before the turn of the century, and the memory of Bent Murdock's little kingdom stayed with White so well that he could detail it some sixty years later:

> He was the representative in Eldorado, and in Butler County, of the . . . reasonably benevolent plutocracy that was governing our land. It was his job to see that the county convention was packed with Republicans who would nominate for the legislature Mr. Murdock's friends, who in turn would vote as he suggested on . . . matters pertaining to railroad rates, corporation laws, the control of insurance and banks. Through the county convention he controlled the nomination of judges for our part of the state and, while we were function-

ing as a representative democracy, we functioned through Mr. Murdock largely. . . .[2]

White was soon working for Murdock on the *Republican,* and, as he goes on to say, "For all my wide reading, I saw no obliquity in this scheme of things, and I was happy to be—through Mr. Murdock—a humble servant in the great creative scheme of government. I was not quite so conscious of it then as I am now . . . but I knew definitely and with conscious and probably obvious pride that I belonged to the governing classes."[3]

In his description of Bent Murdock, White was describing the man he was destined to be, had not other influences prevailed. Indeed, White did become a boss of sorts for a time, though he denied it, and he looked upon the boss system at one time in his career as a necessity—a necessity as long as there was an uneducated electorate.

At first glance, and according to his own recollection, White's formal schooling was not one of those influences calculated to break him out of the Bent Murdock mold. Yet that schooling did help. He went to the College of Emporia for one unsatisfactory year, but if he had not spent that year in what was then a third-floor college in a downtown Emporia office building, he might never have met Vernon Kellogg. Kellogg, who was later to become director of Belgian Relief in World War I and secretary of the National Research Council, was already showing the interest that was to make him one of the nation's best-known biologists. He was, by White's account, a bookish boy, and this bookishness is what first drew the two together. From that time on, Kellogg whetted White's interest in biology, which until then had been anything but keen, and fed him books and guided his interest in the biological sciences until the friendship was broken by Kellogg's death.

Besides all this, Kellogg was at this time, and later when he and White both went to the University of Kansas, the hero White needed. His comment on his friendship with Kellogg points to a vital trait in White himself. "For I was always a blabby kid and never self contained," he wrote, "and always loved heroes."[4] He not only loved heroes, he needed them—first his father, then Bent Murdock, then Vernon Kellogg, then Theodore Roosevelt, then (though with mixed feelings) Woodrow Wilson. And there were princes as well as kings among the heroes: Senators Robert M. La Follette and William E. Borah; William Rockhill Nelson, of the *Kansas City Star*; and Major General Frederick Funston, hero of the

Philippine insurrection, among them. If we look ahead a bit, we see that White was happiest during the Progressive Era in American politics because there were many princes fighting the dragon of special privilege under the banner of Theodore Roosevelt, a seemingly invincible champion, and White himself was a lordly knight in the field. A good part of his education came from seeking out the hero and offering him the sword of a fighter in the cause.

At the University of Kansas, to which White transferred after his year at the College of Emporia, he became acquainted with a group of young men who were destined to become as important in their fields as he was to be in his. Among them were Henry Riggs, who became professor of civil engineering at the University of Michigan; Frank Craig, who was at one time president of the Oklahoma Bankers Association; Herbert S. Hadley, governor of Missouri in the days of the Progressive party; William S. Franklin, professor of physics at the Massachusetts Institute of Technology; Edward C. Franklin, professor of chemistry at Stanford University and president of the American Chemical Society; Frederick Funston; and Schuyler Brewster, who became attorney-general of Oklahoma. Add to these the staunch and life-long friendship which was formed on the University of Kansas campus between White and the future senator, William E. Borah.[5]

All of which is to indicate that most of William Allen White's education came from the people he met, the people he knew, lived with and worked with. For all that, however, he learned a great deal from some of his University professors. He learned more than his economics, sociology, history, and political science from Professor James Hulme Canfield, father of the future novelist, Dorothy Canfield. It was Canfield, White said, who advised him to go into the Republican party rather than to stand as an independent or as a hopelessly out-numbered Democrat in Kansas.[6] Canfield had waged the political wars as an independent. A brilliant and liberal thinker in his own right, he nevertheless thought that by remaining an independent he had wasted his political powers.[7] It may even have been from Canfield that White got the idea of an extension of the Puritan doctrine to politics. It was this idea, as much as anything else, which kept him in the Republican party long after he had ceased to believe in much of what the party was doing.

Besides Canfield among White's teachers at the University of Kansas, perhaps the most important was William Carruth. A teacher of German at the University, Carruth is perhaps best known for his poem, gently conciliatory between the forces of science and the forces of religion, which asserts that "Some call it evolution; others call it God." Carruth taught White a good deal more than the German he was being paid to teach. It was he who supplied White with what became almost the motto of his life: Make your private sentiment public opinion. To teach him literature and guide him into the world of literary criticism, there was Arthur Richmond Marsh. He introduced White to the criticism of Arthur Hugh Clough, Augustine Burrell, and Andrew Lang, and set him to reading *The Nation.*[8]

Thus White had a taste of the academic life. But mathematics was completely and forever beyond him, and after three tries at it, he gave it up and left the University of Kansas without having obtained a degree. Besides, according to his own recollection, he was too busy working for the *Lawrence Journal,* working on the campus literary magazine, stringing for St. Louis and Kansas City newspapers, and mixing vociferously in campus politics to let his class work interfere with his education. "I suppose," he wrote later of his university experience, ". . . that social and political leadership, plus the Unversity library, represented the organization interest which stimulated my intellectual growth more than the professors and the classrooms—vastly more!"[9]

Actually, White gathered his real education much as his friend and fellow Kansas editor, E. W. Howe, had gathered his; much as William Dean Howells, who was White's literary idol and later his friend, had gathered his; much indeed as William and Henry James had gathered theirs. He learned from the life around him, in the print shop, at home, at political meetings, through his own independent and omnivorous reading, and through travel. Though his university education was more extracurricular than academic, it suited him well, for it was at the University that he served his real apprenticeship in politics and mixed the relatively benign explosives provided in the laboratory of college journalism. White said:

> The Kansas State University of 1888 was an epitome of its environment. . . . There went the sons and daughters of the squires of the manor, of the gentry and nobility, and of the high lords of politics and business. In their blood was the struggle of the hour—the tremendous desire to make a material world out of raw material. . . . We had bred in politics, and we took university politics into the

> academic cloister. . . . There we conducted our business under a boss system, with all its chicane, with all its terrors and its spoils, after the manner and methods used by our fathers to rule their little satrapies and fiefs.[10]

This was the way White remembered it, but there is some doubt that the University of Kansas was so topheavy with the sons of the elite as he remembered. Granted that the quest for the bachelor's degree was not so nearly universal then as it is now, it is still true that White himself was working his way through college and had inherited neither great wealth nor great political power. The same thing could very probably be said of a good many of those who were going to the University in 1888. At any rate, it is safe to guess that the University was not blessed in White's time with a completely gold-plated population. Chances are, given White's predilection for politics and given the color of the politics of the time, that he gravitated toward the group he described. Chances are, too, that when he came to write his autobiography, he remembered the Borahs, the Kelloggs, the Funstons, and the rest as what they had become rather than what they had been when they were college mates.

Memory can sometimes be as good as fact, however, in the making of a man. The fact is that William Allen White learned at the University of Kansas political methods which he was alternately to employ and combat throughout a long life. Although he was to protest often and quite futilely that politics meant very little in the overall picture of his life, he was fooling nobody but himself with such protestations, and there is room to doubt that he was even fooling himself.

He was an observant student in the University of Kansas school of interfraternity politics, and what he learned he put to immediate use on the county level in Kansas. In preparation for a county Republican convention in 1899, after he had begun to establish himself in Emporia, White's faction gathered the night before the caucus to agree on a ticket. It was apparently a rump caucus before the fact, and Will White was the chairman of it. He assigned a different man to nominate each man the faction wanted in the delegation. He gave each of his nominators a number and memorized the names and the order in which they should be recognized. And he saw to it that he was to be chairman at the caucus meeting. The result was as smooth and professional a job of railroading as had been seen in those parts for a long time. "I opened the meeting on the tick of the clock. . . ." White remembered. "Then I shut my eyes and recognized Number One amid the clamor of voices."[11] And so on, be it added, through the entire slate and to the consternation of the old hands who had thought to have the convention in their pockets.

Thus, whether he knew it or not, the greater part of White's training was aiming him right at a career in politics. Any apprenticeship which begins at the age of eight, continues in the shops of politically dominated weekly newspapers, is refined in political jousts on the campus, and culminates in county caucuses is likely to produce a prize specimen of the political animal. And this was William Allen White. He was voting in county caucuses before he could legally vote in the general elections. He was reporting political news for daily newspapers by the time he was eighteen. He knew the inner workings of political machinery at an age at which a youth of another time would know the intricacies of four-barrel carburetion.

Under the circumstances, it is really not surprising that when William Allen White began his newspaper career in earnest, he chose to go to work for the now defunct *Kansas City Journal.* Young White had been building a reputation as a newspaperman for quite a while before he quit the campus for good and went looking for a city news job. The *Kansas City Star* had begun to reprint his stuff in 1890,[12] and Colonel William Rockhill Nelson of the *Star* offered him a job at the same time that the *Journal* made its bid.

White went with the *Journal* primarily because at that time it was his kind of newspaper. It was a sort of metropolitan daily edition of the *Eldorado Republican.* It was a safely conservative Republican paper controlled by Willis and Charles Gleed, who did for the railroads, the packing houses, and the other controlling interests in Kansas City what Bent Murdock did for them in Eldorado and Butler County.[13]

The *Kansas City Star,* on the other hand, the paper whose personality was that of its owner and publisher, Colonel William Rockhill Nelson—fiery, independent, aggressively non-partisan, boss-hating, interest deriding—was just a bit too skittishly independent for the young Kansas countryman.[14] He had spent twenty-five years growing up in a society which said that all was well with the world. He had worked on newspapers whose main source of income had been the county printing—the patronage plum by which the little papers were held in line—and whose principal reason for being had been to serve as a political mouthpiece.[15] He had gone to school with his peers. He had learned his grass-roots politics from the men who controlled politics at the grass-roots.

So Will White went to work on the *Journal* and there enhanced his reputation as a reporter and political observer through the stories he sent to Kansas City from the legislative halls in Topeka. The influence of the two Kansas City papers was felt in Kansas as much as in Missouri, as the circulation figures showed, and White's principal job on the *Journal* was to report the politics on the Kansas side of the Missouri River.

Meantime he had met Sallie Lindsay, a Kansas City school teacher, who was destined to be the love of his life and the co-chairman of his career. Like Mary Ann Hatten White, she was to be strength to William Allen White. He was writing poetry in imitation of James Whitcomb Riley at the time they met and reading it before meetings of the Kansas City Literary Society, to which they both belonged. They shared an interest in the drama and in music, and beyond that, she made his dreams her dreams.[16]

When Will White quit the *Journal* in a rage because the telegraph editor had buried what should have been a front-page story—a clear beat over the other reporters on a political coup in Kansas—Sallie Lindsay was the first to hear about it.[17] She also heard the happy ending of the story, of how White had gone across to the *Star* offices and had been hired on the spot as a writer of "minion" editorials, those light personality pieces, personal essays, drama and music reviews that were used to fill out the editorial columns. It was soon after this, in April 1893, that Sallie Lindsay and William Allen White were married, and she became a full partner in all his activities.

During the two years that followed, Will White worked for and with William Rockhill Nelson, the creator of one of the most important organs of news and opinion in the Midwest. The editor and publisher of the *Kansas City Star* was to have a great influence on White's aims and purposes as a newsman. He taught White his newspaper ethics and a sense of journalistic responsibility. He also made it clear to his young editorialist that a good editorial writer had to be first of all a good reporter. He had to know whereof he spoke.[18] For that reason as much as for any other, Nelson sent White out on a series of journalistic investigations of the Kansas City utilities, the stockyards, and the real estate interests in the city. White was working, for the first time in his life, on a newspaper whose policies were not dictated by a political party but by a strong individual personality.[19]

Yet, he could not foreswear the accumulated experience and training of the first twenty-five years of his life, so that, as far as he was concerned, the Colonel was often wrong, and the product of Kansas precinct and county caucuses still saw his major duty as a responsibility to the neatly ordered society around him. That is why much that he learned from Carruth and Canfield, from Marsh and Nelson, lay dormant in William Allen White, but it is also a good part of the reason that White had become known as an astute observer of Kansas-Missouri politics by the time he was twenty-seven years old. He reported the politics of his time as he knew the politics of his time, from the inside and sympathetically, and by 1895, he had built a newsman's reputation that would have opened the door of any editorial office in the country to him.

But Will and Sallie White had other ideas. It was stimulating to work for Colonel Nelson. If he had to work for somebody, Nelson would certainly do. But White had the itch to be on his own.[20] He wanted, as he said, to make his own mistakes and his own successes. And in 1895, with Sallie's full concurrence, he cut his anchor. With three thousand dollars of borrowed money, he bought the struggling Emporia, Kansas, *Gazette,* the second daily in a small farming community.[21] And his rival, the crusty old editor of the *Daily Republican,* greeted the arrival of the newcomer with a two-line item: "Will A. White, of Kansas City, has bought the *Gazette* from W. Y. Morgan. Next!"[22] What he could not have known was that, to use one of White's favorite expressions, the young bull had arrived to horn the old bull out of the herd.

In the beginning, as far as political philosophy was concerned, the arrival of the new editor made little difference. William Allen White, at the threshold of his long career as editor and publisher of *The Emporia Gazette,* was the product of the time and place in which he grew up, of family, friends, and working companions, and of the academic and professional training of those times. As such, he looked out upon his world through the eyes of a defender of the faith. That faith was in progress as exemplified by the railroads, the packing houses, the utilities, and other manifestations of a rapidly coalescing capitalistic industrial economy. It was a faith in the righteousness of the "best people." It was faith in the world as it stood. The virus of reform had not yet invaded the bloodstream of young Will White. At the age of twenty-seven, reform seemed to him the province of the malcontent. The new-minted editor saw in the new world coming a continuation of the old–and to him, that was as it should be.

3

The Emerging Image

"A good front is rather to be chosen than great riches."[1] This was White's comment about his arrival in Emporia in June 1895, to become publisher and editor of the *Gazette.* That arrival and his solution to the problem it presented were typical of the man. After a train trip across eastern Kansas that had given him time to build many dreams, he was confronted by the usual crowd that gathered at a small town station to watch the trains come in. Some of the men in the crowd knew him from his boyhood days in Emporia. Some remembered him as a student in high school and at the College of Emporia. And he had been seen around town for some days before as he was closing the deal to buy the paper. Besides that, he had become known in his own right for his reporting in Kansas City and, in 1893, had even published a book of verse with Albert Bigelow Paine, the future biographer of Mark Twain. White's contribution to *Rhymes by Two Friends* was mostly watered-down James Whitcomb Riley, rural dialect newspaper verse. But the vogue for Riley and for imitation Riley was high, and the book had sold out in sixty days.[2]

In other words, White knew he was being watched. He had come to town with exactly one dollar and twenty-five cents in his pocket. The problem, as he was to write about it in his autobiography, was whether he should carry his own luggage and walk to the boardinghouse or spend a fifth of his fortune and take a hack to the hotel. He took the hack. "I never regretted it," he said. "I was never one to make money by saving it."[3] The issue was probably in doubt for only a flicker of a second. The phrase "public image" was still mercifully in the future, but William Allen White, even at the age of twenty-seven, was beginning to create the public image by which he was to live. If White the young man was not conscious of this image-making, White the old man certainly was. Among other things, his autobiography consists of one rather startled discovery after another of the images that made up William Allen White.

Much of the autobiography, as Will White enters adolescence and goes on into his college career, is taken up with the single fact of his clothes consciousness. From the time he showed up at the University of Kansas wearing a broad-brimmed "gambler's Stetson" until we see him in a *Life* photograph shortly before his death, his hat pushed back on his head, his lips pursed on a Coke straw at the local drug store, William Allen White played his roles.[4]

Hence he took the hack. Hence he went down to the *Gazette* on Sunday afternoon, and there, scared and proud, William Allen White sat in the little office with the scuffed oilcloth on the floor, and wrote his salutatory editorial to the people of Emporia:

ENTIRELY PERSONAL

June 3, 1895

To the gentle reader who may, through the coming years during which we are spared to one another, follow the course of this paper, a word of personal address from the new editor of the GAZETTE is due. In the first place, the new editor hopes to live here until he is the old editor, until some of the visions which rise before him as he dreams shall have come true. He hopes to sign "from Emporia" after his name when he is abroad, and he trusts that he may so endear himself to the people that they will be as proud of the first words of the signature as he is of the last words. He expects to perform all the kind offices of the country editor in this community for a generation to come. It is likely that he will write the wedding notices of the boys and girls in the schools; that he will announce the birth of the children who will some day honor Emporia, and that he will say the final words over those of middle age who read these lines.

His relations with the people of this town and country are to be close and personal. He hopes they may be kindly and just. The new editor of the GAZETTE is a young man now, full of high purposes and high ideals. But he needs the close touch of older hands. His endeavor will be to make a paper for the best people of the city. But to do that he must have their help. They must counsel with him, be his friends, often show him what their sentiment is. On them rests the responsibility somewhat. The "other fellows" will be around. They will give advice. They will attempt to show what the public sentiment is. They will try to work their schemes, which might dishonor the town. If the best people stay away from the editor's office, if they neglect to stand by the editor, they must not blame him for mistakes. An editor is not all wise. He judges only by what he sees and hears. Public sentiment, so long as it does not assert itself, so long as it is a silent majority, is only private sentiment. If the good, honest, God-fearing, law-abiding people of any community desire to be reflected in the world, they must see that their private opinion is public opinion. They must stand by the editors who believe as they do.

It is a plain business proposition. The new editor of the GAZETTE desires to make a clean, honest local paper. He is a Republican and will support Republican nominees first, last, and all the time. There will be no bolting, no sulking, no "holier than thou" business about his politics–but politics is so little. Not one man in ten cares for politics for more than two weeks in a year. In this paper, while the politics will be straight, it will not be obtrusive. It will be confined to the editorial page–where the gentle reader may venture at his peril. The main thing is to have this paper represent the average thought of the best people of Emporia and Lyon County in all their varied interests. The editor will do his best. He has no axes to grind. He is not running the paper for a political pull. If he could get an office he wouldn't have it. He is in the newspaper business as he would be in the drygoods business–to make an honest living and to leave an honest name behind. If the good people care for a fair, honest home paper, that will stand for the best that is in the town–here it is.

In the meantime, I shall hustle advertising, job work and subscriptions, and write editorials and "telegraph" twelve hours a day in spite of my ideals. The path to glory is barred hog-tight for the man who does not labor while he waits.

WILLIAM A. WHITE[5]

The editorial did what good salutatory editorials are supposed to do: it set the tone of the *Gazette* as White intended to write the *Gazette.* It is rather amazing that "Entirely Personal" stood up through all the long years of William Allen White's editorship in all respects except White's avowed dependence on the "best people." And except for that single snobbish reference, the editorial would serve as a credo for anyone going into small-town community journalism today.

In his first editorial, White committed himself to a life of editorial service to Emporia, and he took a vow of political chastity. Politics, much as he might say "politics is so little," remained a primary interest in the life of the young editor until he was an old editor. Public political office, however, tempted him only once in his long career. Even that time he went reluctantly into office-seeking, not for the sake of office-seeking but because in 1924 he could find no one else in either party to stand and fight against the Ku Klux Klan.[6] National committeeman he would be, twice as a Republican and once as a Progressive. He would make speeches for candidates he wanted to support. He would run the campaigns of politicians of his persuasion and even turn the *Gazette* into a political propaganda sheet during heated campaigns. When his influence was high in the councils of the Republican party, and when it was so high in the Progressive party that the Republicans tried with all the blandishments at their command to persuade him back into the fold, William Allen White could have been governor of Kansas or United States senator from Kansas—simply by saying that he wanted to be governor or senator. But White knew from the beginning of his editorship something that he may have learned from William Rockhill Nelson. A newspaper's political influence declines when that influence is known to be for sale. White knew, too, that though he intended to edit a straight Republican paper, he did not want any political strings on him which would *force* him to run a straight Republican paper.[7]

Luckily for the person who wants to know what White thought about White, he was always doing such thinking in print. We can infer, as some have, for instance, that he already had in mind a wider influence than that encompassed by Emporia and Lyon County—or even by the state of Kansas. "He hopes to sign 'from Emporia' after his name when abroad. . . ." could only mean that, though his roots were to be in Emporia, he hoped his tendrils would wander far and wide. Certain of his detractors have attempted to make much of this, but there is really not much to be made of it. Surely the image that Will White saw in the mirror of his mind on that quiet Sunday afternoon was the hopeful image of a young man who believed in his power with words and who hoped that that power would help him make his private sentiment public opinion. Just as surely, if he had any of the yeastiness of youth about him at all, he would hope that his influence would not stop at the borders of his home county. What is remarkable about this is not that Will White should see visions and dream dreams, but that, in the end, he was able to make so many of the dreams come true.

There is in this first editorial a certain sententiousness, a certain pastoral concern for his people that never left White. He became, in fact, one of the best lay preachers ever to use the editorial page as a pulpit. White was eventually to lose his faith in "the best people." By 1924, when "Entirely Personal" was reprinted in *The Editor and His People,* White was to say in a footnote, "I have lost some faith in this lot; but I have gained some faith in just plain folks."[8] As if to make sure that he was not misunderstood, when he reprinted the editorial many years later in his autobiography, he also reprinted the footnote. But it was to take a dynamite blast to shake that original faith. This was the best of all possible worlds, and William Allen White, from his observation post in the middle of the nation, looked upon his domain and called it good.

Of course there were rumblings. There were always malcontents. These were the rabble-rousers who were always yelling for reform. White had heard the rumblings grow in volume. He had seen the court houses and the school houses lighted up across the prairie as the farmers met to protest the squeeze of the railroads and of eastern money, but this was not his fight. This was the fight of "the others," not of "the best people."[9] As a matter of fact, he had made his earliest fame in Kansas with his first piece of fiction, written for the *Eldorado Republican* in the midst of the Farmers' Alliance foment in 1891. As Bent Murdock's willing mouthpiece, he had been fighting the Alliance ever since he had begun to work on the *Republican.* Because he was who he was and what he was, he took great joy in the fact that he was hanged in effigy in an Alliance parade, chuckling even in later years over the "Silly Willie" emblazoned across the effigy's capacious bottom.[10]

Much as he enjoyed being caricatured in the Alliance parade, however, young Will White saw himself as a defender of the faith. All around him he saw and reported evidence of a growing discontent in the grass-roots where he learned his politics, but the cloud had not yet mushroomed to rebellion, and White failed to see the significance of the protest meetings that erupted across the Midwest in the 1890s. The platform of the People's party, drawn up in 1892, was to him, if it was anything, the ravings of the yet-to-be-named lunatic fringe. That platform called for government ownership and operation of public utilities, including railroads; flexible currency; free and unlimited coinage of silver at a ratio of sixteen to one; increase in circulating capital to not less than fifty dollars per capita; graduated income tax; direct election of United States senators; limited government revenue; establishment of a postal savings bank; and land reform.[11] Moreover, these demands did not spring full-grown, but were the culmination of the work of farmer and labor organizations going back to the St. Louis Demands of the Southern Alliance and the Knights of Labor.[12]

White could not have been oblivious to the foment. He was living in the middle of it. He reported the doings of Mary Ellen Lease, part harridan, part goddess, a great exhorter, "as sexless as a cyclone."[13] He wrote stories about her as she stormed over Kansas like an August tornado, admonishing the farmers in revival-like meetings to "raise less corn and more hell." He knew Sockless Jerry Simpson, who was starting his political rise on the strength of an opponent's jibe.[14] He was in a position to see that the whole Midwest was smouldering. But even in the midst of the fight, and White was vocal enough to be both heavy artillery for the Kansas Republicans and prime target for the Alliance and the Populists, he did not see that the slogans in the parade were slogans of a revolution. Instead, he went to the Kansas Republican convention and helped with the reorganization made necessary by Alliance victories in 1890. Then he came back to Eldorado, sat down in the *Republican* office and wrote "The Regeneration of Colonel Hucks," a story teaching the moral that the upright and just were at home in the bosom of the benevolent and forgiving Republican party and that true penitence lay in denouncing the Farmers' Alliance and all its works and ways.

White himself was to say of the story, "It was all emotion, all sentiment, and probably all nonsense."[15] It was. It rings like a lead quarter as far as believability is concerned, and the end of the story is a perfect example of uncontrolled sentimentality:

> As he drove into his front yard that night he noticed the old regimental flag waving over the door. Inside the house he observed that "mother" had brought out the pictures of Grant and Sherman and Lincoln, which she had put away the year before. They were hanging in the best room with little "Link's" faded blue soldier-cap in the center of the group.
>
> "Did you have a nice time at Topeky, William?"
>
> "Yes, Mother," and after a pause he added as he looked at the little cap and the old flag, which now and then floated in through the door, "and say, Mother, 'his soul goes marching on.'"
>
> For Colonel Hucks was never what you would call a "soft" man.[16]

Bad as it was, it was no worse than a good deal of the newspaper fiction of the time. "The Regeneration of Colonel Hucks" was important in the development of William Allen White for two reasons: it made him known throughout the state and the Midwest as a political spokesman, and it marked one of his major preoccupations as a writer of fiction. "The Regeneration of Colonel Hucks" was reprinted in both the *Kansas City Journal* and the *Kansas City Star.* Then Senator Preston B. Plumb, friend of White's father and a power in the Republican party in Kansas, saw a perfect propaganda instrument in the story of Colonel Hucks' return to the Republican fold after wandering for a season in the wickedness of the Farmers' Alliance. He had the story electroplated and sent, at the expense of the Kansas State Central Committee, to every Republican paper in the state.[17] It was White's first breakthrough into anything more than local prominence, and it was on the strength of "The Regeneration of Colonel Hucks" that the *Journal* and the *Star* sought him simultaneously to come to the big town and write editorials.[18]

This little story of less than three thousand words is important also in White's development as a writer of fiction. In it is the kernel of much that White was to say as an artist in the years to come, for in it White retells the story of the Prodigal Son. In this case the Prodigal Son was Colonel Hucks, a veteran of the Civil War, a staunch Republican of the type that equated the Grand Old Party with the Grand Army of the

Republic. But in the years of unrest when the revolt was beginning to swell, Colonel Hucks suffered an aberration. He wandered from the fold of true believers into the wickedness of bimetallism. His contrite return in the state convention at Topeka has all the elements of religious revival in it.

The story of the Prodigal Son was to haunt White for the rest of his days. This first appearance was to be followed by the feminine counterpart in "The Prodigal Daughter" and "The Record on the Blotter," both of which were to appear in White's first book of fiction, *The Real Issue.*[19] The Prodigal Son is most completely delineated in White's major novel, *A Certain Rich Man,* but he also appears as society itself in White's assessment of American society in the 1920s. Indeed his letters show that if he had written a Warren G. Harding biography, as Brand Whitlock, reform politician and novelist, was to urge him to do, Harding, too, would have been cast as the Prodigal Son.[20] There is much evidence in his autobiography that White saw even himself in this role, worshipping at the altar of Mammon during the Hanna-McKinley reign and returning to his father's house only after seeing the light of Progressive reform.

Thus "The Regeneration of Colonel Hucks" was of primary importance in the emerging image of William Allen White. In the years of White's apprenticeship on Republican newspapers in Eldorado, Lawrence, and Kansas City, belief in the Republican party became an act of faith. White protested that he went into the party with his eyes open, and that joining the Republican party was the only way to get ahead in Kansas politics. Of course there was truth in the protestations. Nevertheless, the connotation of a lay faith remained. It had to be so, for faith in the Republican party formed part of the background against which White saw himself, and to destroy the background would have been to distort the image. And if, in those first days when the image was taking shape, the Farmers' Alliance was a stench in the nostrils of the righteous, the Populist party, its rightful heir, was the devil of anarchy itself. The pillars of the temple were being shaken; the veil of the Ark of the Covenant was being rent by unclean hands.

To be sure, before he had finished his long career, White had supported every plank in the People's party platform except those dealing with currency. But in the midst of the fight and before he had had a long life in which to meditate the political changes he had seen, he literally equated Populism with anarchy. Populism was an attempt "to destroy American institutions, to deprive the honest, God-fearing, upright American citizen of the "right to enjoy the fruits of his endeavor."[21]

The young man who prayed the "best people" to hold his hand while he tried to give them a newspaper worthy of them came to his editorship at a time when the best people and all that they stood for seemed in danger of defeat. Naturally, he rushed immediately into the fight. That was what he was there for, to make his private sentiment public opinion. He summed up his private sentiment in an editorial called "The Sweep of It" in the heat of the first McKinley-Bryan campaign.

> "Every man for himself and the devil take the hindmost" is a fair statement of the American government as it exists today.
>
> But during recent years, there has grown up in the west the un-American doctrine of state paternalism. It is claimed . . . that when one man is weak, when he fails to get on in the world, when he finds himself at the bottom of the heap, the state should help him up. The believers in the new creed hold that it is the duty of the state to check the accumulation of one man's wealth and to end another man's poverty. They say that the man with the large fortune and the man who commits a crime are both subjects for state interference. They say that the man who is without means is the nation's ward, that he should be protected against the "oppression of wealth."
>
> These two theories are violently antagonistic—one is American, Democratic, Saxon; the other is European, Socialistic, Latin.[22]

If this was youthful arrogance, it grew not so much from an obeisance to wealth as from White's conception of respectability. The doctrines of the Farmers' Alliance and of the People's party were not respectable in White's eyes, either in the campaign of 1896 or in the campaign that preceded it, because they had not yet been accepted by the "best people."

Later, White wrote about Bryan's first nomination, "It was the first time in my life and in the life of a generation in which any man large enough to lead a national party had boldly and unashamedly made his cause that of the poor and the oppressed. . . . It was the emergence into middle-class respectability of the revolution that had been smoldering for a quarter of a century in American politics."[23] There were the keys to the kingdom: "respectability" and "middle-class." On these two terms

White based his whole political philosophy. On them he based both his reason for fighting the Populists and his reason for joining the Progressives. In fact, it was on these two terms that he founded an entire theory of political evolution.

Neither Bryan himself at that time nor the doctrine he espoused was respectable to White or to White's patrons. But then William Jennings Bryan was admittedly a peculiar phenomenon in American politics. Twice a member of Congress from Nebraska, three times Democratic candidate for President, secretary of state in the early years of the Woodrow Wilson regime, and prosecuting attorney in the famous Scopes trial which tested the right to teach evolution in Tennessee schools, Bryan was the evangelical voice of the radical Midwest. His memoirs reveal a deeply religious man whose religion was literal and fundamental.[24] They also reveal a man whose belief in the power of oratory was astounding. His own oratory, which was for the most part florid, orotund, and filled with the standard classical allusions, must have needed his voice and stage presence to make it effective. In print his speeches read like rather bad high school declamations.[25] It was with his voice that Bryan became the prophet, the preacher. Others were to reap where he had sown, this man whose equipment was more of the heart than of the head. Nevertheless, he continued to be a strong force in the Democratic party through 1916.

It is little wonder, given White's background and political training, that he looked with fear upon "the boy orator of the Platte." It is no wonder at all that he was to look back on that momentous first campaign and write, "It seemed to me that rude hands were trying to tear down our national life, to taint our currency with fiat."[26] He scoffed at the claims of the Populists, and the voice of the *Gazette* rose in hysteria throughout the summer of 1896. On July 31, for example, White wrote:

> The question before the voter of this country—of Kansas, of Emporia—is shall American institutions prevail; shall every man have the right to enjoy the fruits of his own endeavor, or shall political and financial anarchy prevail?
>
> The man who supports the Populists in this election . . . is lending his voice and influence to the cause of anarchy.[27]

Believing that, William Allen White had to deride the claims of the Populists and support William McKinley for President, even without his avowal of a straight Republican ticket.[28] But he did not like McKinley. He would have much preferred "Czar" Tom Reed as the Republican candidate. Reed, who was Speaker of the House and as much a dictator in that chamber as the more famous Joe Cannon was ever to be, was even more conservative than was McKinley. Moreover, in the 1896 campaign, when the currency issue was made paramount, Reed stood squarely for the gold standard. McKinley, throwing a wider net for votes in the general election, took no firm stand.[29] And White was always to insist that he accepted the high tariff policy of the Republican party, which he disliked, in order to have the hard-money, gold-standard monetary policy, which he considered the kingpin of the nation's economy.

Besides, as White saw it, William McKinley was always on stage, always acting the part he thought the President of the United States should act, "destined," White said, "for a statue in a park, and . . . practicing a pose for it."[30] The young Kansas editor had formed his first impression of McKinley as he rode across Kansas on a campaign train with him in 1896. He had watched the candidate play the role of the consummate politician, doling out the exact amount of time and friendliness necessary to each visitor, holding court, making sure that no man got more nor less of the royal audience than the political amenities required. This was not White's kind of man. Whatever his politics, the man White liked had to be open and emotionally free. White could recognize the fact that everyone plays a role, or a collection of roles. He could even stand aside on occasion and giggle at his own performance. But he was uncomfortable when the naked mechanics of the staging showed through, as they seem to have done with McKinley. Nevertheless, White was convinced that not to support the Republican ticket was to invite anarchy. Besides, he admired Mark Hanna, the boss who had made a candidate out of McKinley.

It was at least partly because he was the open, emotional man that he was, ruthless yet honest in his ruthlessness, that Mark Hanna the man remained a hero to White long after White had learned to despise Hanna's political aims. He was a symbol to the Kansan of the power of the best people. Hanna was, in fact, the epitome of the political boss, primarily because he was the first national boss. There had been other bosses—Thomas Collier Platt and Matthew S. Quay and Richard Croker, to name three—but they were city or state bosses, limited in their objectives. Marcus Alonzo Hanna, though he began as the boss of Ohio and could have been one of the crowd of state bosses, became unique in American history to that time. He represented a culmination of the growth of business in politics. The growth began soon after the Civil War, following the rise of the economic power of the railroads. Hanna became the symbol of that power, the symbol of business in politics, honestly, explicitly, ruthlessly so. To White he represented the defense of the citadel of things-as-they-were.[31]

White was disturbed by the imputation that Hanna bought the 1896 election for McKinley. He admitted that Hanna had raised more money among banking and manufacturing interests than had ever been raised for a political campaign in the history of the United States. He insisted, however, that the Democratic party also had adequate funds with which to win if the election could have been won with money. Hanna was admittedly a kingmaker, said White. He picked McKinley, sold him to the Republican party, and made him President. But, White said, the principal weapon McKinley used was not money, but fear. He played on the fears of White's own agrarian, small-town middle class. He used fear as a unifying force with the plutocracy. That plutocracy, if one is to believe the picture that White painted in his books, looked upon the Populist-Democratic uprising in the South and West somewhat as the Romans must have viewed the approach of the barbarians from the north. Hanna also used fear, amounting to coercion, to control the labor vote: fear that the destruction of the gold standard would prolong the depression. But this begs the question. Hanna collected the money and used it, and if he used it only to buy propaganda to complement the fear, he still used it.

The other bosses were little men in White's eyes. Thomas Collier Platt he called an earthworm, burrowing his way through the subterranean passages of New York State politics.[32] It was not the fact that Platt was a boss that disturbed White; it was the kind of a boss Platt was. The fact that Richard Croker was the boss of New York City did not bother White nearly so much as the fact that he was at the same time the boss of Tammany, the symbol of everything in the Democratic party that White disliked.

As might be expected, Will White was himself an eminently practical politician. In the days of the 1896 campaign and for some time afterwards the boss system seemed to him useful and right. "The organization usually succeeded," he wrote. "That is why I was in the organization. . . ."[33] He was on intimate terms with Cyrus Leland, the Kansas Republican boss of the time, and with the Gleeds, one of Wichita and one of Kansas City, who controlled the railroad patronage. He exchanged favors with the bosses of the Midwest and dealt with them knowing that they were the men who could get him what he wanted in politics. Indeed, the time was to come when White himself was to be considered a boss in Kansas politics, though by that time he would have relinquished the idea of the necessity of bosses—at least in rural, agrarian, middle-class America—and would deny rather vehemently that he was a boss at all.[34]

Heated as the 1896 campaign was, however, and as deeply involved in it as White was, he had time to make a collection of short stories that he had begun to write when he began to write for newspapers. Some of the stories, like "The Regeneration of Colonel Hucks," had appeared in the *Eldorado Republican,* others in the Sunday supplement of the *Kansas City Star,* and still others not at all, since they were rewritten from *Star* rejections.[35] He worked over these stories on the kitchen table after putting in a full day on the *Gazette.* When he and Sallie had edited them to their satisfaction, they sent them to Way & Williams, a young Chicago publishing house.[36]

Sallie had in the meantime become ill, and the doctor had discovered a spot on one of her lungs. That was the reason that on July 13, 1896, William Allen White was in a hurry. He had sent Sallie to Colorado for a rest, and he was to go to her that evening by train. He had also just been to the post office, and among the exchange newspapers under his arm was a package from Way & Williams, the proofs of his first book, *The Real Issue.* At this time too, White had been lambasting the Populists with more and more vigor, and he could not walk down the street without getting into a discussion with the Populist farmers. Any other day, he would have parried their thrusts, danced nimbly away from their verbal bludgeons, and continued on his way. But today they surrounded him. They bullied him. "I was froggy in the middle, and I couldn't get out," he recalled. Finally, he bulled his way through the circle of hecklers and hurried angrily to the *Gazette* office. There, in the heat of his anger and of his impatience to be in Colorado, he wrote the editorial which was to put him on the national stage as "The Regeneration of Colonel Hucks" had introduced him to the Midwest.[37]

The editorial, one of four key pieces which marked White's advance from local to national prominence was "What's the Matter with Kansas?" White wrote it at top pitch, slammed it on the copy hook, and headed for Colorado. Some of the facts and many of the figures of speech in the editorial had simmered in White's mind for a long while. He told the story of its genesis in the preface he wrote for *The Rhymes of Ironquill,* Eugene Ware's collected poems. He was sitting in Ware's Topeka law office about a month before the editorial appeared. Deeply disturbed by the Populist ferment, Ware was characteristically pouring acid on it.[38] White warned him that, with Ware's permission, he was going to use some of the older man's ideas and figures. Ware told him to go to it, and White did. As he noted in his autobiography, "I remembered what Eugene Ware said and added frill for frill to his ironic diatribe, and it came out pure vitriol":

> WHAT'S THE MATTER WITH KANSAS?
>
> Today the Kansas Department of Agriculture sent out a statement which indicated that Kansas had gained less than two thousand people in the past year. There are about two hundred and twenty-five families in this state, and there were ten thousand babies born in Kansas, and yet so many people have left the state that the natural increase is cut down to less than two thousand net.
>
> This has been going on for eight years.
>
> If there had been a high brick wall around the state eight years ago, and not a soul had been admitted or permitted to leave, Kansas would be half million souls better off than she is today. And yet the nation has increased in population. In five years ten million people have been added to the nation's population, yet instead of gaining a share of this—say, half a million—Kansas has apparently been a plague spot, and, in the very garden of the world, has lost population by ten thousands every year.
>
> Not only has she lost population; but she has lost money. Every moneyed man in the state who could get out without loss has gone. Every month in every community sees someone who has a little money pack up and leave the state. This has been going on for eight years. Money has been drained out all the time. In towns where ten years ago there were three or four or half a dozen money-lending concerns, stimulating industry by furnishing capital, there is now none, or two or three that are looking after the interest and principal already outstanding.

No one brings any money into Kansas any more. What community knows over one or two men who have moved in with more than $5,000 in the past three years? And what community cannot count half a a score of men in that time who have left, taking all the money they could scrape together?

Yet the nation has grown rich; other states have increased in population and wealth—other neighboring states. Missouri has gained over two million, while Kansas has been losing half a million. Nebraska has gained in wealth and population while Kansas has gone downhill. Colorado has gained every way, while Kansas has lost every way since 1888.

What's the matter with Kansas?

There is no substantial city in the state. Every big town save one has lost in population. Yet Kansas City, Omaha, Lincoln, St. Louis, Denver, Colorado Springs, Sedalia, the cities of the Dakotas, St. Paul and Minneapolis and Des Moines—all cities and towns in the West—have steadily grown.

Take up the government blue book and you will find that Kansas is virtually off the map. Two or three little scrubby consular places in yellow-fever-stricken communities that do not aggregate ten thousand dollars a year is all the recognition that Kansas has. Nebraska draws about one hundred thousand dollars; little old North Dakota draws about fifty thousand dollars; Oklahoma doubles Kansas; Missouri leaves her a thousand miles behind; Colorado is almost seven times greater than Kansas—the whole west is ahead of Kansas.

Take it by any standard you please, Kansas is not in it.

Go east and you hear them laugh at Kansas; go west and they sneer at her; go south and they "cuss" her; go north and they have forgotten her. Go into any crowd of intelligent people gathered anywhere on the globe, and you will find the Kansas man on the defensive. The newspaper columns and magazines once devoted praise to her, to boastful facts and startling figures concerning her resources, are now filled with cartoons, jibes, and Pefferian speeches. Kansas just naturally isn't in it. She has traded places with Arkansas and Timbuctoo.

What's the matter with Kansas?

We all know; yet here we are at it again. We have an old mossback Jacksonian who snorts and howls because there is a bathtub in the State House; we are running that old jay for governor. We have another shabby, wild-eyed, rattle-brained fanatic who has said openly in a dozen speeches that "the rights of the user are paramount to the rights of the owner;" we are running him for Chief Justice, so that capital will come tumbling over itself to get into the state. We have raked the old ash heap of failure in the state and found an old human hoop skirt who has failed as a businessman, who has failed as an editor, who has failed as a preacher, and we are going to run him for Congressman-at-Large. He will help the looks of the Kansas delegation in Washington. Then we have discovered a kid without a law practice and have decided to run him for Attorney General. Then, for fear some hint that the state has become respectable might percolate through the civilized portions of the nation, we have decided to send three or four harpies out lecturing, telling the people that Kansas is raising hell and letting the corn go to weed.

Oh, this is a state to be proud of! We are a people who can hold up our heads! What we need is not more money, but less capital, fewer white shirts and brains, fewer men with business judgment, and more of those fellows who boast that they are "just ordinary clodhoppers, but they know more in a minute about finance than John Sherman;" we need more men who are "posted," who can bellow about the crime of '73, who hate prosperity, and who think, because a man believes in national honor, he is a tool of Wall Street. We have had a few of them—some hundred fifty thousand—but we need more.

We need several thousand gibbering idiots to scream about the "Great Red Dragon" of Lombard Street. We don't need population, we don't need wealth, we don't need well-dressed men on the streets, we don't need cities on the fertile plains; you bet we don't! What we are after is the money power. Because we have become poorer and ornerier and meaner than a spavined, distempered mule, we, the people of Kansas, propose to kick; we don't care to build up, we wish to tear down.

"There are two ideas of government," said our noble Bryan at Chicago. "There are those who believe that if you legislate to make the well-to-do prosperous, this prosperity will leak through on those below. The

Democratic idea has been that if you legislate to make the masses prosperous their prosperity will find its way up and through every class and rest upon them."

That's the stuff! Give the prosperous man the dickens! Legislate the thriftless man into ease, whack the stuffing out of the creditors and tell the debtors who borrowed the money five years ago when "per capita" was greater than it is now, that the contraction of currency gives him the right to repudiate.

Whoop it up for the ragged trousers; put the lazy, greasy fizzle, who can't pay his debts, on the altar, and bow down and worship him. Let the state ideal be high. What we need is not the respect of our fellow men, but the chance to get something for nothing.

Oh, yes, Kansas is a great state. Here are people fleeing from it by the score every day, capital going out of the state by the hundreds of dollars; and every industry but farming paralyzed, and that crippled, because its products have to go across the ocean before they can find a laboring man at work who can afford to buy them. Let's don't stop this year. Let's drive all the decent, self-respecting men out of the state. Let's keep the old clodhoppers who know it all. Let's encourage the man who is "posted." He can talk, and what we need is not mill hands to eat our meat, nor factory hands to eat our wheat, nor cities to oppress the farmer by consuming his butter and eggs and chickens and produce. What Kansas needs is men who can talk, who have large leisure to argue the currency question while their wives wait at home for that nickel's worth of bluing.

What's the matter with Kansas?

Nothing under the shining sun. She is losing her wealth, population and standing. She has got her statesmen, and the money power is afraid of her. Kansas is all right. She has started to raise hell, as Mrs. Lease advised, and she seems to have an over-production. But that doesn't matter. Kansas never did believe in diversified crops. Kansas is all right. There is absolutely nothing wrong with Kansas. "Every prospect pleases and only man is vile."[39]

Some of White's—or Ware's—facts were out of joint. The reports of the U.S. Bureau of the Census show that the population of Kansas increased rather steadily until about 1935, for example. But White stuck to his guns. The trouble with Populism was not Populism itself. The trouble with Populism was the fact that it did not grow out of the small-town, agrarian middle-class, the bankers, the independent businessmen, the well-to-do farmers. This was the class, as far as White was concerned, then and always, which made up the backbone of America. The people in Populism were the rag-tag and bobtail of the population, the malcontents, the talkers-on-street-corners, the radicals, the have-nots; and to William Allen White in 1896 a have-not was a have-not simply because he was thriftless or lazy or both.

One thing must be kept in mind about "What's the Matter with Kansas?" It was written at white heat. It said all the things that White had been prepared to say through all his heritage and training up to that August day in 1896. White wrote it not as reportage but as polemic, and as polemic it had far greater effect than its young writer could have imagined.

It was printed on the following Monday, and by Tuesday, the office in Emporia was beginning to get mail about this piece of ball-bat irony. When Sallie and Will got back to Emporia, they discovered that the mail had grown into a young mountain and that they had come back to fame. "What's the Matter with Kansas?" literally picked William Allen White up out of the ruck of Kansas country journalism and put him on the national stage as editorialist, politician, political and social commentator, and writer. Nearly every Republican newspaper in the United States reprinted "What's the Matter with Kansas?" and Mark Hanna told White that the Republican National Committee, of which Hanna was chairman, used the editorial more than any other single document in the 1896 campaign.[40]

More substantial rewards came in the form of assignments from *McClure's*, *Scribner's*, *The Saturday Evening Post*, and *Collier's*.[41] To top off this heady mixture, the publication of "What's the Matter with Kansas?" coincided with the publication of *The Real Issue*. White welcomed the additional publicity, but he must have been almost immediately ashamed of the violence of "What's the Matter with Kansas?" He threatened to withdraw *The Real Issue* if the publishers included the editorial in the book, as they wanted to do.[42] Regardless of his eventual feelings about it, White was a long time living down the diatribe, and long after his own views had completely changed, the *Gazette* was getting requests for reprints of the editorial.[43]

Nevertheless, that editorial represented White's thinking at the time, as it represented the thinking of the "best people" with whom he had allied himself. This was not so much making his private sentiment public opinion as it was crystallizing the opinion that already existed among those who believed in the sanctity of things-as-they-were. For the second time—and not for the last time—William Allen White had said the right thing at the right time. His career moved forward. Eastern editorial doors opened to him. He went to Chicago to help push his book, and there he met for the first time the members of Chicago's growing literary circle.[44] He went to Ohio and attended Mark Hanna's victory dinner.[45] He had become, finally and importantly, Mark Hanna's political creditor.[46]

The publication of *The Real Issue* helped too. As White himself said, the book was unfortunately titled, a misfortune that probably cut into into its sales. But it contained, rather incongruously, in a collection that was concerned primarily with small-town politicians on one hand and the defeat of the farmer in the short-grass lands of western Kansas on the other, "The King of Boyville." This story brought a letter from *McClure's* asking permission to reprint "The King" and calling for six more "Boyville" stories at $500 each.[47] White wrote the stories, and after they had appeared in *McClure's,* gathered them together and published them collectively as *The Court of Boyville* in 1899. In retrospect, "The King of Boyville," Piggy Pennington, modeled, as Christopher Morley implied, on the boy Willie White,[48] ranks with Booth Tarkington's Penrod and Little Orvie and with Clarence Buddington Kelland's Mark Tidd. Still there is in the diction of the story itself a mist of sentimentality that would have gagged Tom Sawyer or Huck Finn.

The rest of the fifteen stories in *The Real Issue,* save for the irretrievably bad "Regeneration of Colonel Hucks," fared better. White knew Kansas, all of Kansas, as perhaps no other writing man knew it, and he knew the people of Kansas. He could write as cleanly and powerfully in the short story as he could in the editorial. Writing about the state he loved, he said:

> Crossing the Missouri into Kansas, the west-bound traveler begins a steady, upward climb, until he reaches the summit of the Rockies. . . .
>
> The hills and bluffs that roll away from the river are covered with scrub oaks, elms, walnuts, and sycamores. As the wayfarer pushes westward, the oak drops back, then the sycamore follows the walnut,

> and finally the elm disappears, until three hundred miles to the westward the horizon of the "gently rolling" prairie is serrated by the scraggy cottonwood, that rises awkwardly beside some sandbarred stream oozing over the moundy land. . . .
>
> The even line of the horizon is seldom marred. The silence of such a scene gnaws the glamor from the heart. Men become harsh and hard; women grow withered and sodden under its blighting power. The song of the wood birds is not heard; even the mournful plaint of the meadowlark loses its sentiment, where the dreary clanking drone of the windmill is the one song which really brings good tidings with it. Long and fiercely sounds this unrhythmic monody in the night, when the traveler lies down to rest in the little sunburned, pine-boarded town.[49]

"A Story of the Highlands," from which this is taken, is the tale of the gradual attrition of the Burkholders. This gently bred and cultured couple from the East face the promise of spring in western Kansas and the frustration wrought by drought and dust, terrible loneliness, and never-ending toil. Western Kansas breaks them. That is the story. It is true, real, and uncompromising.

The same judgment applies in varying degrees to such stories as "The Reading of the Riddle," which, in a way, curiously anticipates Sherwood Anderson, and "The Story of Aqua Pura."[50] "The Reading of the Riddle" is the story of lonely Flora McCray and her father's young partner, John Howard. It is the story of the decay of what passed for high society in the skeptical, laughing town of Willow Creek. The story pivots around Flora's date with John to a taffy-pull, and of the long buggy ride home and of the "fancied transgression."[51]

"In Willow Creek," the story ends, "where they scoff and giggle at sordid things, in Willow Creek the hard, the arid, the barren, they say—no matter what—but in and out of the narrow ways, turning the sharp corners with the rest, with tired feet, and timid, unsure hands, there goes a woman whose womanhood came to her as a dream—in the night."[52]

"The Story of Aqua Pura" tells the hopes, pretensions, and failure of a boom town in western Kansas, and the stubborn clinging to the dream by the town's last inhabitant. In it, White analyzes Kansas for his readers. "People who write about Kansas," he says, "as a rule, write ignorantly, and speak of the state as a finished product. Kansas, like Gaul of old, is divided into three parts, differing as widely, each from the other, as any three countries in the same lattitude on the globe. . . . Eastern Kansas is a finished community like New York or Pennsylvania. Central Kansas is finished, but not quite paid for; and Western Kansas, the only place where there is any suffering from drouth or crop failures, is a new country—old only in a pluck that is conquering the desert."[53]

In these stories, White restrained his tendency to editorialize, to gossip. He let his people talk for themselves. In most of the stories in *The Real Issue,* there is an objective irony like that of E. W. Howe in *The Story of a Country Town* or of Edgar Lee Masters in *Spoon River Anthology,* without their inverse sentimentality. The stories in *The Real Issue* are calmly drawn, low-key pictures of the rather primitive social life on the Kansas prairie when that life was beginning to feel the pressure of the boom and the blight of drought and grasshoppers and economic collapse. If, in some of the stories, White pointed rather obviously to already obvious morals, that was his method. He was from the beginning of his career a moralist and a preacher. It mattered very little whether his pulpit was his editorial page or his book.

How much of the success of *The Real Issue* can be attributed to White's notoriety as the author of "What's the Matter with Kansas?" is impossible to assess. The fact stands, however, that the year 1896 marked not only a watershed in American politics and economics, but a watershed in the life of William Allen White. Using as a springboard one editorial about a newspaper-column long and one slim volume of short stories, he leaped from obscurity to fame. The image White had begun to build when he was writing editorials for the *Eldorado Republican,* a good part of the image he foresaw when he wrote "Entirely Personal," had now come into focus. Now he could sign his name, "W. A. White, *from Emporia,*" with the knowledge that he was bringing some fame to his hometown by so signing. Now he was a maker of opinion, not only in Emporia, Lyon County, Kansas, but everywhere good, stalwart, God-fearing, respectable, middle-class Republicans read their newspapers. To use a favorite White figure, Archimedes had used the little lever of his daily newspaper, and with it he had moved his world. He was making his private sentiment public opinion.

"What's the Matter with Kansas?" gave Will White an extension on his Archimedean lever as far as his national importance was concerned, but he was still William Allen White from Emporia, and in 1899 he strengthened that lever at home. He ran a street fair.[54] It was not an original idea. As he acknowledged in his autobiography, Ed Howe had been doing the same thing in Atchison for two years. But if it was not Will White's idea, it was Will White's fair, and it put him in more solidly with the home folks than anything he had done before. What he had learned about the uses of a newspaper as an instrument of propaganda White practiced in the promotion of his fair. So assiduously did he beat the drums that the *Kansas City Times* was moved to remark, "If you don't want to read about Will White's street fair in Emporia, read the *Emporia Republican.*"[55]

Though he had the help of two Emporia merchants in rounding up the capital for the fair, the promotion was a one-man show. White collected and disbursed the funds, hired the acts, arranged transportation for six visiting bands and for representatives of Indian tribes, and even ordered the tents and arranged booth space.[56] Through his railroad connections and through a friend of a friend of a friend in Chicago, he was also able to exhibit the *pièce de resistance* of the fair: the first automobile ever to be seen west of the Mississippi.[57]

It was a full life, with Sallie and Will working together on the paper by day and reading and writing together in the evenings. And when young Bill was born, and four years later their daughter Mary, the family was complete, the picture was complete, and their happiness was complete.

Two things that White brought with him when he stepped onto the national stage remained with him for the rest of his life: belief in the middle class as he defined the middle class,[58] and belief in respectability as a prerequisite for the success of any social or political idea.[59] For the rest, it is remarkable how soon the convinced conservative was to see himself as a rampaging radical. The image had just come clear, although it had been forming from the time White had begun to think. It was the image of a young maker of public opinion for whom his world was the best of all possible worlds. It was the image of a young man who believed that change in the present order of the world was tantamount to destruction. It was the image of a young man to whom Mark Hanna and all that Mark Hanna stood for were the ultimate in righteousness, as regards politics and business.

No sooner had the image come clear, however, than it was to be shattered and reshaped. No sooner had William Allen White rocketed to national prominence as the champion of things-as-they-were than he met the man he took to be the prophet of things-as-they-ought-to-be. No sooner had Mark Hanna been enthroned as the hero to whom White gave his sword and his hand in battle than he was deposed by a younger, shinier hero. For the world turned upside down for William Allen White when he met Theodore Roosevelt.

4

The Road to Damascus

If "What's the matter with Kansas?" put William Allen White on the national stage and gave him wider scope for his talents than the confines of the Midwest, meeting Theodore Roosevelt gave him a new vision and showed him new uses for those talents.[1] White's record of that meeting is ecstatic. In later years, he warned his readers about the ecstacy,[2] but to the end of his days, White's hero remained the dramatic, dynamic Theodore Roosevelt.

According to White, Roosevelt changed him almost instantaneously from a somewhat smug conservative into a fighting liberal. Even if one takes "liberal" in the context of White's conception of middle-class respectability, his enthusiasm seems to have been premature, not to say misplaced. When they first met in 1897, Theodore Roosevelt was as much a conservative as was William Allen White. Roosevelt was several years away from donning the mantle of respectable liberalism that he would eventually assume.[3]

In White's memory of it, however, Roosevelt acted on him as a shock treatment. The young undersecretary of the Navy opened for the young Kansas editor a new heaven and a new earth. When he came to write his autobiography in his 70s, White remembered Roosevelt as savagely opposed to Mark Hanna and to the plutocracy for which he stood.[4] "That was the order I had upheld," White wrote, "to which I was committed, to which I had given my soul. . . ."[5]

White seems to have misread Roosevelt completely. Roosevelt may have been, as Henry F. Pringle pointed out, "faintly nauseated" by Hanna's program of advertising McKinley.[6] Nevertheless, he overcame his nausea sufficiently to become one of McKinley's frontline campaign speakers.[7] Actually, up to this point in their careers, White and Roosevelt had been amazingly alike in their social and political thinking. Roosevelt had instituted some reform in the Civil Service Commission and had been a vigorous reformer as Police Commissioner of New York City.[8] But he had also seen the Haymarket riot and the Homestead strike–industrial parallels of agrarian unrest–as White had viewed the farmers' uprisings.

Roosevelt's campaign speeches in 1896 were fully as emotional and as conservative as White's editorials in the same period. There was no intellectual objectivity, no limited liberalism, for instance, in a speech equating Eugene V. Debs, William Jennings Bryan, and John Peter Altgeld with French revolutionaries Marat, Barrere, and Robespierre.[9] It was no embryonic liberal who supported the ultra-conservative, Speaker Thomas B. Reed, for the Republican presidential nomination in 1891,[10] and who went to Mark Hanna to offer his services in the 1896 campaign.[11] Finally, no man who said in a newspaper interview that "the sentiment now animating a large portion of our people can only be suppressed . . . by taking ten or a dozen of their leaders out . . . and shooting them dead"[12] could be the prophet of a new age that William Allen White saw in him.

Yet White was to write of his friend as if he were the heir apparent to the mantle of liberalism. Bryan obviously could not wear the mantle with the grace of Roosevelt. In the first place, Bryan was an advocate of the supreme heresy of bimetallism. Second, he was a Democrat, and finally, he was an agrarian radical, not a sane, middle-class liberal.

To the career of William Allen White, however, it makes no real difference that he saw Roosevelt as he wanted him to be much more than as he was. Theodore Roosevelt was, perhaps unwittingly, the catalyst that made a respectable rebel out of William Allen White. But in the beginning they were nearly twins in their thinking. Both men had been born into upper-middle-class respectability, with the purple on Roosevelt's toga perhaps a little darker than the purple on White's. White came to consider that accident of birth with ironic detachment. Roosevelt never did. He must always be riding, literally or figuratively, at the head of his regiment. Though he probably would have deprecated the idea, White became the real rebel of the two, became an honest liberal within his definition of liberalism. Roosevelt was a reformer, and his reforms toward "distributive justice" were liberal reforms. But the reforms came from the top. Roosevelt was not a democratic reformer; he was patriarchal.[13]

Even so, Roosevelt was good for White, simply because of what White thought Roosevelt was. On that basis, perhaps no two men in the history of American politics were better suited to work together in turbulent times. Moreover, they had the good fortune to appear on the national political scene at exactly the right time to be remembered as prime movers in the reform wave that broke over America at the turn of the century. Besides, they went together like a pair of gloves. They were as one in their sentimentality, in their enormous zest for life, and in the fact that they functioned best when involved in a "cause" or faced sufficient opposition to test their mettle.

So it was that when, a few months after that first meeting, Roosevelt sent White his *American Ideals and Other Essays,* he completely vanquished his Kansas squire. "I read it with mingled astonishment and trepidation," White wrote later. "It shook my foundations, for it questioned things as they are. . . . As a defender of the faith, I had met my first heretic."[14]

William Allen White had, in fact, been meeting heretics since he and Bent Murdock had noticed the rumps of the seedy farmers sticking out of the windows of the Butler County courthouse during the Farmers' Alliance uprising.[15] Those were surely heretics who hanged White in effigy in Eldorado,[16] and surely he must have met heretics every working day since he became editor of the *Gazette.* The difference, of course, was obvious. Theodore Roosevelt was not only a rebel and a heretic. He was a heretic who was also a rich young ruler. The combination was odd and disquieting.

Still, it is difficult to imagine Roosevelt's little book overturning White as completely as he remembered being overturned. It is about as incendiary as a wet firecracker. The Rooseveltian wrath comes down upon the "mere money-getting American,"[17] but for the most part, the essays plead for political morality, for "fervid Americanism,"[18] for action as opposed to criticism, for a fuller participation of college graduates in politics,[19] and against free trade.[20] The last essay in the book, "The Vice-Presidency and the Campaign of 1896," was a curious bit of foreshadowing, considering Roosevelt's subsequent career. It called for the delegation of more power to the vice-president.[21] But that could hardly be called a revolutionary idea.

If Theodore Roosevelt was not a heretic, at least he was the first reformer White could look up to. Perhaps he was indeed the first one that White had really seen. The heretics of White's early experience had been merely zealots, fanatics, demagogues—people who really did not fit into the picture as White saw it. As such, they could be safely discounted. Theodore Roosevelt, on the contrary, was a part of the picture and could not be ignored. Theodore Roosevelt was, after all, respectable. Thereafter what had been European, Socialistic, Latin, and un-American in White's eyes became the righteous, one hundred percent American struggle for "distributive justice." As White himself interpreted the event, he had traveled his Damascus Road. He that had been Saul persecuting the Populists had seen a great light and become Paul, forever thereafter lamenting his past sins and preaching unto righteousness.

Ironically, while White was prepared to accept Roosevelt as the prophet of the world to be, Roosevelt was equally joyous in hailing White as the defender of the faith that was. He wrote to Attorney General Philander C. Knox in 1901: "There are few men in the United States whom I more cordially respect than I do Mr. White. In the worst days of the Populist excitement he fought the battle for decency, sanity, and honesty against very great odds, way out on the picket line."[22]

In at least one respect, the two men were in complete agreement from the beginning—reform was a matter of righteousness and of moral regeneration. The evil lay not in the political machinery but in the uses to which the machinery was put. William Allen White and Theodore Roosevelt, therefore, took the weapons of the old guard with them into the new camp. Both of them had climbed the political ladder from the precinct, and both were practical politicians above all else. White was sometimes unhappy with Roosevelt's willingness to take half a loaf, and he admired the fighting, uncompromising Robert M. La Follette. Still, his own tendency to look at both sides of any question and his long established habit of abiding by political necessity kept White himself from being an uncompromising battler.

White recognized this characteristic in himself and in other politicians. It may have been for that reason that he was always more than tolerant of the politician as politician. In 1901, for instance, he published a book of political short stories called *Stratagems and Spoils,* the first fruits of his Damascan encounter. In the preface to that book, he defended politicians as being "about as honest in their business as storekeepers are in their business, or lawyers . . . or bankers or preachers, or day-laborers, or farmers, or college professors. . . ."[23] The average county convention, he added, ran on "a moral plane about as high as the faculty politics of the average University, or that of the church politics of the various religious organizations."[24]

White and Roosevelt worked in politics with the machinery that was available to them, and that included the machines. White got Cyrus Leland's pledge for Roosevelt long before the 1904 campaign opened.[25] Leland was the boss of the Kansas Republicans. Roosevelt went to New York boss Thomas Platt to assure himself of the New York delegation.[26] By August 15, 1901, White was writing to Leland that the machine forces of New York, Kansas, Illinois, Massachusetts, and Colorado had been pledged to the Roosevelt candidacy in 1904.[27]

"The machine in politics," White wrote, "is the thing which a defeated candidate uses as an alibi for his own shortcomings."[28] At the same time, he made a distinction between a machine and a "real machine," the real machine being that group which binds itself together "to repeat its victories and consolidate its gains." The distinction, in White's mind, between "a machine" and a "real machine" was apparently one of means and ends. When the machine became a self-perpetuating end in itself, it became a "real machine." When the machine was organized and perpetuated to carry out a political program, it was a legitimate instrument of political action. Given this distinction, there was reason to run with the machine, and White ran with the machine of some sort all his political life. In the 1890s, he said, "We controlled our state senators and our members of the house of representatives at Topeka. We named United States Senators. We gave color to the legislation. I was making my private opinion public sentiment. . . . I did not stand aloof and sniff. If, as Senator Ingalls had said, 'the purification of politics is an iridescent dream,' I had some control over the nightmare."[29]

Politics was never an end in itself to William Allen White. Not even making his private opinion public sentiment was an end in itself, though he gloried in it. Politics and publication were means. Before White's conversion to the gospel according to Roosevelt, they were means of keeping this best of all possible worlds from being overturned. Afterwards, they were means to a better world.

Yet for all his pleading "a vague, wistful idealism,"[30] White was a hard-nosed pragmatist in his means. He thought he saw the better world coming through Theodore Roosevelt. Therefore, with all the deliberation of a seasoned organizer, he began to do what he could to help that new world to birth. He was not over-eager. Though he became Roosevelt's man with their first meeting, he knew that 1900 was not his hero's year.

"I do not think there is any sentiment," he wrote to a Roosevelt boomer in 1899, "nor any possibility of manufacturing sentiment that will defeat McKinley for the Republican nomination in 1900, and to do so in naming Roosevelt would only gather enemies about him that would hurt his campaign in 1904. No man can out-do me in loyalty to the hero of San Juan; but I think that practical sense demands that his friends shall bide their time."[31]

Here was the practical politican analyzing possibilities, and here was the romantic follower of the hero of San Juan. The Spanish-American War had stirred him, as it had stirred the rest of the nation. In regard to Roosevelt's part in the war, Roosevelt, White, and—for the most part—the rest of the nation were in complete agreement. They all thought Teddy Roosevelt was a handsome, dashing, romantic hero. In his treatment of the war itself, White followed a pattern he was to retrace in World War I and World War II. In the beginning, he opposed the war utterly, speaking of the Cuban revolt as "a crate of tommyrot."[32] He praised McKinley's message of April 12, 1898, for its manliness and its lack of jingosim and demagoguery.[33] In the end, however, he was even writing editorials in praise of war as war.[34]

Though he deplored those war-heated editorials on reconsidering them, he was to follow the same pattern in 1914-1917 and again in 1941-1944. In going from opposition to reluctant acceptance to full participation, William Allen White not only interpreted his midwestern readership correctly, he typified it. The editorials he wrote during this time indicate that he had learned well not only the philosophy of Theodore Roosevelt, inspired by Admiral Alfred Thayer Mahan, but that he also knew by heart Kipling's song of the white man's burden.

"Only Anglo-Saxons can govern themselves," he editorialized on February 16, 1899. "The Cubans will need a despotic government for many years to restrain anarchy until Cuba is filled with Yankees. . . . It is the Anglo-Saxon's manifest destiny to go forth as a world conqueror. He will exterminate the people he cannot subjugate. This is what fate holds for the chosen people. . . ."[35] This was no Archimedes moving his world. This was, to use another figure White used about himself, a bubble on the stream of history. Even when he thought he was moving his world through his political activity, he quite often simply went along for the ride. He did not become an insurgent until the Republican party in Kansas was predominantly insurgent. That insurgency was born in the Midwest in the hard times of the 1870s. It had its first political expression in the Greenbacker campaign of 1872.[36] And White gained national prominence fighting a rearguard action against that insurgency. He did not become an insurgent until insurgency became a force, a respectable force, in national politics. Seen from this angle, White was no maker of public opinion. He was a funnel through which respectable public opinion could be poured without fear that it would be diluted or adulterated.

The same can be said for White's celebration of Theodore Roosevelt. He was reporting at least as much as he was creating public opinion, and he was publicizing the character Roosevelt had finished creating with his dash up San Juan Hill. That character was the Man of Action. Roosevelt had created it as New York assemblyman, Civil Service commissioner, Police commissioner, rancher, hunter, undersecretary of the Navy, soldier, and governor. It was a part with which the adolescent nation could joyously identify itself. It was also a part requiring many costume changes, though the part itself was always basically the same. Romantic, active, chivalrous, morally upright, and strenuous, it was the part of an overgrown Boy Scout.

It is best, however, not to be too hard on romantics. If Theodore Roosevelt was above all a romantic figure, if William Allen White—for all his hard-headed sense of business and of political reality—was a romantic, the revolt in which they both participated was also, and necessarily, romantic. Reform is by its very nature romantic, carrying with it as it does a necessary idealism, a belief in progress, and an impatience with the *status quo*. The very concept of democracy is romantic. The supremacy of the individual citizen, with his concomitant rights and duties, is a romantic notion. So is the idea of the government as an agency of human welfare. And so, finally, is revolution to bring about those democratic ideals.

The peculiar thing about the respectable revolution of the late nineteenth and early twentieth centuries in the United States was that, though it was fought with all the acrimony of moral absolutism, the weapons of the war were political and economic. These included federal conservation of lands, the Federal Trade Commission, the direct primary, the initiative and referendum, the Postal Savings Bank, the Pure Food and Drug Act, federal arbitration of labor disputes, and the graduated federal income tax. The insurgents and the standpatters fought for and against these issues as expressions of righteousness or as engines of iniquity. It was a war of moral issues, but the combatants fought out this war in the political arena.

William Allen White and Theodore Roosevelt became symbols of that respectable revolution in its latter stages. Each believed in social progress through the ameliorative power of government. Since each had come to that belief from a background of emotionally articulated conservatism, each man brought to the new belief an emotional reaction to that conservatism. Moreover, the respectability they both demanded of their politics severly limited the liberalism they espoused.

The men were too much alike to be adequate foils for each other, but there was a major difference between them–White looked at both sides of a political question as a man in a moral universe, and Roosevelt looked at both sides of a question to discover the politically expedient thing to do. To White, political expedience was a means; to Roosevelt it appears to have been occasionally an end in itself. Each man, however, could convince himself of whatever he wanted to believe.

Meantime, here stand two young men about to embark on a journey during which they will be closely yoked until the older one dies. Even after death has separated them, the Kansas editor will continue to feel the influence of the New York gentleman in politics. They will journey together toward "distributive justice." They will see before them the vision of a new America, an America in which the predatory plutocrat will suffer restraint and the man who works with his hands will get a fair share of the wealth he produces. All this will come about, according to the vision, not through a revolution of the working classes, but through the concern of the professional men, the small businessmen, and the independent farmers–the middle-class respectable citizens–for their downtrodden brothers.

Each man saw in the other rather more of himself than was actually there, but such misinterpretation made little difference in the relationship between them. White saw Roosevelt as much more the champion of

White's middle-class respectable liberalism than Roosevelt was ever to be. Roosevelt, on the other hand, saw White only gradually as a man who would go much further along the liberal road than Roosevelt ever imagined.

While Roosevelt actually brought White from Hanna-McKinley conservatism to Progressive liberalism, he was truly a catalyst and remained unchanged himself. In other words, William Allen White's experience on the Road to Damascus was based on an illusion of what might have been. Still, since the illusion was as effective as the actuality would have been, the resulting conviction and repentance were also more or less permanent and equally effective.

5

A Case of Galloping Insurgency

Whether or not Theodore Roosevelt was the shining knight of liberalism that William Allen White saw, White himself grew rapidly from the reactionary young provincial who wrote "What's the Matter with Kansas?" to the national spokesman for midwestern middle-class liberalism. Ironically, that same anti-Populist blast that put him in Mark Hanna's debt also opened editorial doors through which White would pour ardently Progressive articles in years to come.[1]

Though "What's the Matter with Kansas?" and *The Real Issue* made possible Will and Sallie White's first trip east of the Mississippi,[2] Will White was not quite a boy out of the Kansas sticks when he went to Chicago for the first time. He had covered the 1896 Republican convention for the *Gazette* and for the *St. Louis World.*[3] At that convention, he witnessed what he was later to regard as the first great split between the East and the West in the Republican party, between the creditor, who stood for a strong gold standard plank, and the debtor, who opposed such a plank.[4]

White's first experience in writing about national politics set a pattern he was to use for the next forty years. He learned to look behind the scenes for the story. He was to cover most of the conventions of both major parties for the rest of his life, and his reports of those conventions were to be mostly feature pieces and interpretive essays.[5] What newspapermen call "hard" news, on anything but the local level, interested White very little. He couched the behind-the-scenes stories he wrote for a variety of syndicates, not in the language of a reporter only, but in the language of authority.[6]

In 1896 White was just beginning to get that authority, and in 1896 he began his career as a Roman rider. On that trip to Chicago he met writers who were to become increasingly important in the literature and journalism of the early twentieth century. Among them were George Ade, Finley Peter Dunne, Hamlin Garland, and Henry B. Fuller, writers for two of the most important publishing houses of the time, Way & Williams; Stone and Kimball.[7]

From this point on, William Allen White was to ride, not two horses, but the three horses of politics, journalism, and literature. Politics remained the lead horse, with journalism and literature serving it. This is not to say, however, that White neglected his newspaper for politicking. *The Emporia Gazette* was in the best tradition of good midwestern country journalism. It reported the local and state news and subscribed to a once-a-day news summary service from the Associated Press. It covered international news more or less incidentally at that time. Its editor was interested in Emporia and Kansas, and in the national scene as it impinged on Emporia and Kansas.[8] When it came time to sum up, White wrote, "People choose their paper not because of its politics but because of its integrity, its enterprise, and its intelligence."[9]

Yet, one of the things that gave White's life a kaleidoscopic quality was that he trained in the era of subsidized journalism and grew up with the *Gazette* into the era of advertising. He learned his propaganda techniques working for partisan, subsidized papers, and after he could count on advertising for revenue, he still used those techniques to make his private opinion public sentiment.[10]

He used the *Gazette* unmercifully to propagandize his projects, not only that street fair that made him a "somebody" in his own town, and a variety of fund-raising drives, but the Theodore Roosevelt campaigns, all the reforms of the Progressive Era, and finally, in the early days of World War II, the Committee to Defend America by Aiding the Allies. From the beginning, William Allen White *was* the *Emporia Gazette.* He handled or oversaw everything from reporting to makeup, from selling advertising to following up on delinquent accounts. His natural style was one of freewheeling hyperbole, like this cry out of the depths of a Kansas August that he wrote to the National Advertising Company in 1899:

Some two weeks ago you wrote me that the check for the balance

> due the GAZETTE on Paine's Celery, and the Diamond dyes business would be forwarded as soon as your treasurer got back, in a few days.
>
> Kindly give my compliments to your treasurer, and tell him I trust he is enjoying a felicitous summer but that his delay in getting back and signing my check is causing a poor country editor to sweat on the plains of Kansas, with his tongue dragging out three yards, when he might be sitting in the dusky dells of Colorado.[11]

White's identification with the *Gazette* was one of the reasons he could never be lured away. Among other reasons was the fact, largely unspoken, that it is better to be a big frog in a little pond than a small frog in a big pond. It is also true that by the turn of the century, White was looking for a bigger body of water and was becoming a state and national political power. He himself dated his political emergence with the 1908 campaign,[12] but he also said, ". . . In those five years from 1898 to 1903 I stepped out into the big wide world. . . . Politically, I met two living Presidents and two ex-Presidents, and had become a member of the executive committee of the Republican state central committee of my state. And I had definitely become a member of the governing, if not the ruling, class of my state."[13]

About this time also, the McClure group came into White's life. S. S. McClure and his managing editor, John S. Phillips, had more to do with making William Allen White a liberal than did Theodore Roosevelt, and Roosevelt may simply have brought to flower the kind of liberal White was to be. The distinction is not as obscure as it might appear. White was immensely stimulated by the people he met in the office of *McClure's Magazine.* McClure himself was a bundle of energy who knew what kind of copy sold magazines. Phillips encouraged White almost too much, sending him home with more assignments than he could possibly handle. Ida M. Tarbell was there, too. She was working on her Lincoln biography at the time.[14]

From then on, White's letter files bulge with correspondence with these and with other writing reformers. He wrote to Lincoln Steffens, to Ray Stannard Baker, to Hamlin Garland, to Oswald Garrison Villard.[15] Not all of this vital and exciting group was associated with *McClure's,* but they all had the *McClure's* point of view. They were people with whom White could try ideas. He was broadening his base, lengthening his Archimedean lever.

By 1899, he had his base and his lever. His street fair at home and his contacts in the state and the nation had prepared the way for him to make his private sentiment public opinion. Small wonder, then, that when he wrote to midwestern political leaders about Roosevelt or to Roosevelt about them, he wrote as an authority. The vice-presidential candidate made a midwestern campaign swing in the spring of 1899. When he got home, he found from White a collection of clippings from Kansas and Missouri newspapers. White advised him that a note to each editor would do him much good, not only in the current election, but in 1904.[16]

Among the papers and men White mentioned in his letter to Roosevelt were the *Kansas City Journal,* W. Y. Morgan of the *Hutchinson News,* and Harold Chase of the *Topeka Capital.* He had worked on the *Journal* and knew its railroad connections. He had bought the *Gazette* from W. Y. Morgan and he had known Harold Chase, "a Harvard man and a bully fellow,"[17] from the days when White had been a political reporter in Topeka. These were men and papers White did not "train with," but they represented an important segment of the Republican party in Kansas, and White was not one to overlook any bets. The advice itself was something like irrigating the ocean, for Theodore Roosevelt was also a man to use any influence that came to hand, but the knowledge of the Midwest that White gave Roosevelt was undoubtedly of great value to the candidate.

At this time, White was in correspondence with most of the political leaders of the Midwest, with members of both the conservative and liberal wings of his own party and with the progressive Democrats as well. He was a go-between and an errand-boy, but he was also an arbiter. He figured largely in Roosevelt's plans from the beginning, for he was a principal pipeline of political information. In his attempts to get Kansas boss Cyrus Leland together with Roosevelt, White wrote that Roosevelt wanted to meet Leland, wanted "the friendship of our fellows," and told Leland that Roosevelt was a square man and that "if he wins, he will show his appreciation of that friendship in a substantial and manly way." He went on to tell Leland that he thought Roosevelt was at that time the strongest man in Kansas. Admitting that three years might make a great deal of difference, White added, "Yet I think, if the sentiment is kept (very gently and without too much show of design) organized and agitated, the situation can be held as it is until 1904."[18]

In the meantime, he was writing this appraisal of Leland to Roosevelt:

". . . All I know about Leland," he said, "is that I have known him very intimately for six years and have known his reputation for ten years. He is a blunt man with primitive passions," wrote White, "who is a good hater and a loyal friend. I have never heard any scandal connected with his name. I have never heard that he offered a man a bribe or that he took a bribe in all his forty years in Kansas politics. I know that his influence is for clean men in public office. . . . His ideas on the fine points of honor are not so keen as those of Mr. Carl Schurz and Mr. Godkin, but I absolutely know of places where he had the opportunity to do nasty little things and make money and he has turned them down. . . ."[19]

This, in essence, is White's picture of an honest professional politician. Politics had its rules the same as any other profession, and as long as a man lived up to those rules, White could work with him amicably.

In this same period, he was writing to E. Montgomery Reily, Kansas City, Missouri, broker and early Roosevelt supporter, against centralizing the organization of Roosevelt clubs in Missouri: "Kansas people are peculiar people," he warned. "They are willing to lead, but never to follow. The moment they get an idea a man is leading them they proceed to knock on him and knock hard. The trouble with you and Anderson [the Kansas organizer of Roosevelt clubs] is this," White said. "Anderson thinks he can get Roosevelt clubs just as easy as you can and regards any offer of aid as unnecessary and extraneous. The Kansas papers have been gently guying Roosevelt club No. 1, because of the 'No. 1.' That is the Kansas nature," White seemed to grin, "and they can't help it any more than they can fly."[20]

During this same period he wrote to Leland that Roosevelt "does not encourage the Roosevelt clubs and thinks they are a mistake."[21] He was speaking for Kansas and the Midwest to Roosevelt, and for Roosevelt to the Midwest. As for himself, he wrote a rather strange thing, considering that he was in the midst of the most concentrated political activity. ". . . I hate Topeka and I hate politics," he wrote to a correspondent in St. Mary's, Kansas. "There is no office in this bright, beautiful world that I would take from a cabinet position down to the Emporia Post Office."[22] It is true that he never wanted political office, but if William Allen White hated politics, he was the champion masochist of the Midwest.

Meanwhile, he continued to send political analyses to Roosevelt. He had a scheme to get Missouri into the Republican camp. "Missouri has been treated by Hanna as a southern state. . . .," he wrote. "Yet I believe, if some sort of system of local control of federal patronage could be established to put the selection of local federal officers in the hands of business Republicans rather than the Kern's machine Republicans only it would be wiser."[23]

White made a trip west in 1902 and came home to write Roosevelt that California, Oregon, Wyoming, Washington, and Colorado were so enthusiastically in favor of Roosevelt that "no power on earth" could defeat him in those states.[24] Utah, however, was a different story. Utah, said White, "is a rotten borough. . . . They are bound and gagged by crass, brutal ignorant money and the politicians there are liable to do more or less as they please." There was a bright side to the picture, however. "I would judge from looking at them and sizing them up," White wrote, "that they are not the kind that would be pleased with your administration; but they are bandwagon statesmen and there will probably be no trouble from them."[25]

Apparently, White succeeded in getting Roosevelt and Leland together, because in the same letter he wrote, "In Kansas as you know, the Leland fellows organized the convention, wrote the platform, and I suppose you will know where to find them when you want them."[26] This was the pragmatic politician talking, the party man who knew that no reform was possible without election. In fact, White was not quick to abandon his conservative friends at all. "My best friend on the Kansas delegation," he wrote to Congressman D. B. Henderson of Iowa in 1899, "is Chester I. Long, who has been in congress off and on . . . since 1894 . . . Chester wants a place on the ways and means committee . . . and I want him to have it. If you can help him you will greatly oblige him and place me in your debt, so that I cannot easily repay you."[27]

This was the same Chester I. Long who, as a spokesman for the railroad interests in Kansas and as candidate for United States senator, was to become a victim of White's vigorous campaigning. Even in 1900, White wrote Charles F. Scott, conservative editor of the Iola, Kansas, *Register,* that he was going to support Morton Albaugh, an old-line Kansas machine Republican, but that "there is a small coterie of men who do not work with the party."[28] This was a considerable time after the momentous meeting with Roosevelt, in fact, after White had begun planning and working for Roosevelt's presidential nomination in 1904. It is possible that White was working with the materials at hand to produce the kind of world he foresaw; it is more likely that he did not immediately become a reformer and a member of the insurgent wing of the Republican party.

By 1900, however, White's mildly muckraking biographical pieces about Presidents, bosses, and other political figures had begun to appear in *McClure's Magazine* and *Cosmopolitan.*[29] At the same time, White was writing for *Scribner's* a series of novelettes which expressed better than his political reporting his growing concern for morality in politics. These stories he gathered into a book which he called *Stratagems and Spoils.*[30] Dedicated "TO THE KANSAS CITY STAR, an honest newspaper . . .," *Stratagems and Spoils* is a series of portraits of men and their women in contemporary politics. "The Man on Horseback," for instance, is the story of Joab T. Barton, financier and overlord of Brookdale Park, and of the use he makes of the social ambition of the wife of his chief opponent. In Joab Barton, the young insurgent Republican portrayed his first plutocrat, a man who, "for all practical purposes . . . owned the soul of Brookdale Park. . . ."[31] He also used the story to contrast the old world of Joab Barton with the new world that was to come under the leadership of men like Kelsey. But Barton beats Kelsey in "The Man on Horseback," and he does it by playing on the social ambitions of Kelsey's wife.

The behind-the-scenes influence of women in politics runs as a second major theme through these stories of the fight between the new insurgency and the old conservatism. In "A Victory for the People," as in "The Man on Horseback," the public, represented by the newspapers, does not recognize the power behind public men. When the governor appoints an anti-railroad man to fill the unexpired term of a man who has been in the pay of the Cornbelt Railroad,[32] the liberal press raises its voice in jubilation. The press does not know that only the intervention of the governor's wife has prevented a railroad-approved appointment.

These first two stories in the collection present a clear view of White's ambivalent attitude toward women and their influence on men in politics. The wife of the governor in "A Victory for the People" is a bluff, hearty, almost masculine countrywoman, in direct contrast to the feminine, feline wives of Barton and Kelsey in "A Man on Horseback." White carries the contrasting aspects of feminine influence through all of *Strategems and Spoils.* "'A Triumph's Evidence'" tells a kind of Adam and Eve story for the Railroad Age. White's Eve first regenerates the soul of a garden-variety politician through her love, then she seduces him into selling his soul to the railroad. White's shifting attitudes toward the women in his stories is surprising, given the apparent adulation he accorded his mother and his constant reiteration of the importance of his partnership with Sallie Lindsay White.

The best story in the collection illustrates best White's belief in the personal equation in politics. When the story first appeared in *Scribner's* in 1900, Theodore Roosevelt called "The Mercy of Death" White's best work to that time.[33] Perhaps the qualification is unnecessary. In its grim intensity and inevitability, the story reminds one of Frank Norris's *McTeague.* In fact, it is an inevitability which White was unable to achieve either before or after "The Mercy of Death."

Tom Wharton, the protagonist of "The Mercy of Death," had appeared before in White's fiction. He was the same Tom Wharton of the title story of *The Real Issue.* In that story, Tom Wharton had come home from Congress ready to retire, realizing finally that the real issue was honor. He had succumbed again to the lure of politics, however, when he learned that he could buy convention delegates for twenty-three hundred dollars. The descent he began then, Tom Wharton completed in "The Mercy of Death." In this story, White analyzed greed as a master passion. Here, the woman was Wharton's mistress, and his wife was a nonentity. Wharton's woman was a partner in his greed and a partner in his degradation. "The Mercy of Death" is a powerful piece of writing and a powerful, if somewhat melodramatic, preachment for honesty in politics.

White drew the other side of the shield in "'A Most Lamentable Comedy.'" In it he told the story of the rise and fall of Dan Gregg, Farmers' Alliance governor. If Joab Barton is White's caricature of a plutocrat and Tom Wharton his picture of a kept politician, Dan Gregg is his honest radical reformer corrupted by the taste of power. The woman in this story is a socialite reformer who, with the help of a college professor, gives Dan Gregg delusions of grandeur. Gregg succumbs to the love of power, to the need to be elected, and the voters defeat him and send him back to the street corner.

It is eminently just that White dedicated the book to the *Kansas City Star.* It was on the *Star* that he learned to look inside the whited sepulchers of respectability, and the stories in *Stratagems and Spoils* take the reader behind the facade of country-state politics into the passions that control those politics. Reviews of the book were generally favorable.[34] They should have been, for here White was at his best as a writer of fiction.

It was not fiction, but the portrait of an active politician, which nearly involved White in a libel suit. In the December 1901 issue of *McClure's,* White published a biographical sketch of Thomas Collier Platt, New York political boss and enemy of Theodore Roosevelt.[35] Naturally, the portrait was anything but flattering. (White called Platt, among other things, an "earthworm.") Platt threatened to bring suit. Scribner's had just published *Strategems and Spoils,* and recognizing the value of the publicity, White appeared to welcome the suit.[36] Certainly Sam McClure knew a good thing when he saw it, and word got around that he had engaged Thomas B. Reed, the old "czar" of the House of Representatives, to defend White.[37] McClure denied it, but for whatever reason, the suit never came to trial. It was perhaps a good thing for White that it did not. As it was, he suffered a nervous breakdown, partly from overwork and partly as a result of the threatened suit.[38]

At the time, White denied that he had gotten any of his information about Platt from Roosevelt, but on March 20, 1901, Roosevelt had written to White from Oyster Bay, inviting him to "be sure to come out and stay with me. I will tell you all about Platt and how to get a letter to him."[39] White did back up the Roosevelt information through an interview with Platt himself. He also continued to deny any Roosevelt influence, and he got a bit waspish about it. Writing to "Dear Charles" (it might have been Charles Gleed of the *Kansas City Journal*) White said, ". . . I do think . . . that the 'Journal's' Washington correspondent is mighty nasty to me . . . insinuating first I got my stuff about Platt from Roosevelt; and second that I got what a tenderfoot would get in a bar room. . . . I didn't get any of my Platt stuff from Roosevelt and I didn't get any of it in a bar room."[40]

That is all very well, but by 1939, speaking at the annual Roosevelt Memorial Association dinner, White was telling the story this way: ". . . I had written a very mean piece in the *McClure's Magazine* about Tom Platt, I had got most of my material from Theodore Roosevelt, and Platt had been bombarding the White House and Roosevelt and demanding that I be barred. . . ."[41]

In any event, the article was written and published, *Strategems and Spoils* got reams of free if indirect publicity, and Will and Sallie White went to California for six months while he recovered from a nervous breakdown.[42] The incident reveals a couple of things about White. He was then and he would always be sensitive about his ability as a reporter. He was not quite so sensitive, in the heat of battle, about the truth when anyone called that ability into question. It may be, however, that he was like Roosevelt in being able to convince himself that he had done what he said he did, after the fact. It may also be that he was simply protecting the source of his information in the best reportorial tradition. Roosevelt apparently played the game of know-nothing to the hilt. He wrote White to reassure him, saying, "Now, old man, don't talk nonsense. If Senator Platt comes in again I shall show him your note, and tell him that of course I never inspired any attacks on him, but that equally of course I must continue to have as my friends whomever I wish."[43]

Whatever the truth of the matter, the Platt incident did nothing to diminish White's reputation as an interpreter of the American political scene. He was soon selling articles to *Collier's* and to *The Saturday Evening Post,* as well as to his regular markets. The political portraits kept coming. Roosevelt, Cleveland, Harrison and Croker all got the White treatment. White's sketches were much more balanced than might be expected from the new-fledged fighting liberal.[44] If the portrait of Roosevelt was only this side of idolatrous, that of Richard Croker, head of the hated Tammany Hall, was a nicely balanced job, settling somewhere between denunciation and appreciation.[45]

Roosevelt, incidentally, was delighted with the Croker article. "Here you are living in a small town out in Kansas," he wrote White, "not accustomed to the conditions of life in a seething great city, pay a somewhat hurried visit to New York; and yet you sketch Croker as no one in New York, so far as I know, could sketch him. . . ."[46]

White had correctly analyzed Roosevelt's chances for the presidential nomination in 1900: they were nonexistent. Moreover, Senator Platt's New York machine was determined to bury Roosevelt in the vice-presidency. The Colonel of the Rough Riders had come back to New York to win election as governor, and the young upstart had not come to heel as Boss Platt thought he should. Therefore, over the protest of Mark Hanna, who did not want Roosevelt within one life of the presidency,[47] Platt maneuvered Roosevelt's nomination.

Roosevelt, of course, did not like being kicked upstairs. He wrote to White, " . . . The whole point is that when I accepted the Vice-Presidential nomination I had to make up my mind to see my factional foes triumph in New York State, and I accepted the nomination knowing perfectly well that New York State would be against me thereafter."[48]

Despite the fact that he and White were busy lining up the state bosses for Roosevelt's nomination in 1904, the future President added, "I know that none of us will ever lose sight of the prime fact . . . that the only thing that can make me a candidate will be a genuine popular feeling that I should be the candidate."[49]

The 1900 campaign was practically a rerun of the 1896 campaign, except that McKinley compiled a greater electoral majority over Bryan than he had the first time.[50] The McKinley conservatives could have seen an ominous sign in the popular results, however. While McKinley polled 7,200,000 votes. Bryan was totaling nearly 6,400,000 and Eugene V. Debs, the Socialist candidate, counted nearly 100,000 votes.[51] In 1896 McKinley had polled 7,035,638 against Bryan's 6,467,946. It was an indication to the advocates of things-as-they-were that they had not yet come to the darkest part of the woods. Rebellion was as much in the air then as it had been in the days of the Populists. The major difference, said William Allen White, was that now Populism had been Democratized, washed, shaved, dressed respectably, and put on the national stage.[52]

He could just as well have argued that William Jennings Bryan and Adlai E. Stevenson lost to William McKinley and Theodore Roosevelt because Bryan insisted on beating a dead horse. He insisted on restating the bimetallism issue in almost exactly the same terms as those of the 1896 Democratic platform. This despite protests from his friends that gold discoveries in the Klondike and in South Africa had killed the free coinage of silver as a political issue.[53] Yet White himself said, "How could we know that the Klondike gold mines and those in South Africa would solve the problem that Bryan had set, and make the issue of free silver at sixteen to one a dead cock in the pit?"[54]

Nevertheless, the gold strikes did eliminate bimetallism as an issue, and they also eliminated the pressures that made inflation a vital issue. As for anti-imperialism, the third leg on which Bryan's platform was supposed to stand, insisting on that was like playing King Canute with the sea. The capture of Manila had made America's subsequent foreign policy inevitable. The destruction of the Spanish fleet had created a power vacuum into which the United States had had to move. To have done otherwise would have been to invite Germany or Japan to conquest by default.[55] Besides, America had just won a "bully little war," and she was much more ready to listen to Roosevelt and Mahan and other preachers of Manifest Destiny than she was to hear Bryan's sermons on moral isolationism. Even the traditionally isolationist Midwest was not wholly behind Bryan. White himself was then insisting on the right—nay, the duty—of the chosen Anglo-Saxons to rule the world, and White was fairly representative of the Midwest.[56]

It was as if William Jennings Bryan had gone into the 1900 campaign wearing blinkers and ear-plugs. If it had not been so, he might have been President. But it was so, and McKinley won, and the conservative business community, ignoring the shrinking plurality of the vote, congratulated itself again.

Then McKinley was assassinated, and what Mark Hanna had feared came to pass. Theodore Roosevelt became President of the United States.

White was with Roosevelt in the White House on the first night of Roosevelt's administration.[57] He was to remain with the new President from that time until Roosevelt died, with him in spirit when he could not be with him in the flesh. Their voluminous correspondence indicates that Roosevelt relied on White heavily for political assessments of the Midwest and particularly of Kansas. In preparation for the 1904 presidential bid, they began to take on each other's coloration. It might as well have been White as Roosevelt, for instance, who wrote that he wanted it understood that "the prime movers in forcing my nomination are men like you and Major Hood . . . like the farmers, small businessmen and upper-class mechanics who are my natural allies. . . ."[58] The irony here is that Major Hood was a particularly reactionary individualist, the banker who had staked White in the early days of the *Gazette.*[59]

Still, Roosevelt and White did start at approximately the same place, and White was to call the farmers, small businessmen, and upper-class mechanics the backbone of democracy throughout his career. By 1902, also, Roosevelt had made his reputation as a trust-buster, attacking the Northern Securities Company. He won that case in 1904,[60] and by 1905 he was to tackle the Beef Trust. He was more and more to come to the position, however, that bigness simply as bigness was not an evil, and that regulation rather than dismemberment was the answer.

White agreed with this stand, but only in part. Both men were concerned with honesty and morality in government, but White's theorizing was to take him much further to the left than Roosevelt would ever go. Though he supported such orthodox insurgent measures as the headless ballot, initiative and referendum, direct election of United States senators, and the graduated income tax, White would also advocate state ownership of railroads and grain elevators.[61] It is understandable, then, that by 1910 at least one correspondent was to accuse this one-time page in Mark Hanna's train of being a Socialist.[62]

Primarily, though, White considered all these measures as means to honesty and morality in government by way of removing temptation from corruptible men. He was on the lookout for such temptation all the time, and he wrote Roosevelt in December 1904 that he approved of everything Roosevelt had done except "giving the fourth-class postmasters to the congressmen to be devoured."[63] To give congressmen the right to remove the rural postmasters at will was to pave the way for machine politics and corruption in farm states like Kansas, he pointed out, because "in close counties, the fourth-class postmasters can control any rural county."[64] If the postmasters controlled the counties, and the congressmen controlled the postmasters, corruption was inevitable.

It was not the tariff, he wrote to another correspondent, nor the currency nor new laws that were the political issues of the time. It was rather "the honest enforcement of existing laws, so that a crook cannot defraud the people, while he is drawing their taxes as his salary."[65] This letter indicates that White was not quite ready to jump, but it was not long before he was advocating Progressive legislative reforms as a means of making sure that a crook could not defraud the people while they were paying his salary.

While he was thus theorizing, he was also offering to Roosevelt the propaganda techniques that he had learned early and had honed by use ever since he learned them. As 1904 opened and the stretch drive for the Roosevelt nomination began, White wrote to Roosevelt that the *Chicago Tribune* had offered him eight thousand dollars a year for a series of weekly articles. "It might be that I could help direct public sentiment in a helpful way," he wrote. "Of course," he added, "there must not be the slightest hint of the source of my inspiration, or it would be flat and worse."[66] This, as far as White was concerned, was simply another opportunity to make his private sentiment public opinion. The William Allen White of "What's the Matter with Kansas?" had all but disappeared. He who had used his connections with the Santa Fe railroad to get an automobile to Emporia for his street fair now wrote to the Missouri Pacific declining that road's offer of passes for White, his family, and his staff. He could not accept the passes, he wrote, feeling as he felt about the railroads and their power in politics.[67]

He was interested in two things in politics, in good government and in winning—and he was now willing to jump party fences to get what he was interested in. By 1908, the year in which, in his own estimation, William Allen White finally came to power, he could write to Mark Sullivan, ". . . I am like the grafter, in that I play Republican and Democrat alike, I want to win. . . ."[68] But he did not want to win simply for the sake of winning. As he went on to say, "It seems to me, that the fellows who are playing for good government can learn tricks from the fellows who are playing for bad government. They cross party lines for their ends, and we cross party lines for ours."[69]

In much the same vein as his letter to Mark Sullivan was another in which White justified working with men of all shades of opinion within the party itself. If a man stays in politics for ten years, he said, the kaleidoscope of events will pair him at some time with every other ten-year man in the party. "I am shuddering at the time," White wrote ruefully, "when I shall line up with [Charles] Curtis, but it will come, and probably if Curtis had the amount of philosophy that I have he would commit suicide in contemplating the day: but it is bound to arrive."[70]

Though White was slow to recognize it, by that time there was growing up in both the Republican and Democratic parties the nucleus of what was to become the Progressive party by 1912. The people with whom White worked from about 1904—Roosevelt and La Follette on the national scene, and Joseph Bristow and W. Roscoe Stubbs, for example, on the state level—were insurgents.

True, insurgency had been growing in the Midwest since about 1873. Now, however, it began to coalesce and to produce leaders of strength, stature, and staying power. The two leading insurgents in terms of staying power were Theodore Roosevelt and Robert M. La Follette. William Allen White was in the middle. He was confidant and friend of both men, and neither man liked or trusted the other.

Theodore Roosevelt acted on most insurgents as he had acted on White, as a catalyst and a promise. He acted on La Follette and his followers as an abrasive. And La Follette, strangely enough, was the only national leader, according to White, who was fighting Roosevelt's enemies. In White's recollection, it was all a matter of temperament. Roosevelt, he said, loved a compromise. "If he seemed to seek martyrdom, it was a delusion." La Follette, on the other hand, would take all or nothing at all. White said that La Follette actually wanted failure, because failure would dramatize his cause, "so that it might revive in triumph in another day."[71]

And there was Will White again, standing in the middle, looking at both sides. This time, though, there was no doubt about which way he would jump. He was, after all, much more like Roosevelt than he was like La Follette. He may not have loved a compromise, as he said Roosevelt did, but he knew how to use one when it was necessary. And he wanted to win. He and Roosevelt were right, too. If politics is the art of the possible, compromise is the brush and palette of that art.

Being Roosevelt's man, White accepted William Howard Taft as Roosevelt's heir apparent; and in April 1907 he wrote to La Follette, asking him to stand aside in favor of Taft. But he did not do it baldly. First he offered La Follette the Kansas delegation, then, almost as if he were doing the man a favor, he took it away from him, and finally, in as skillful a disarming maneuver as he ever employed, he invited La Follette to address a mass meeting.[72]

He insisted that what he had written were his own views, "not inspired by any one, not even remotely suggested by any one else. . . ."[73] In view of the Platt affair and the *Chicago Tribune* offer, it is possible that White did protest too much. It is particularly possible since the long letter to La Follette went out after White had received a rather querulous letter from Roosevelt accusing White of being for La Follette. Some of the sting is taken out of the letter by a parenthesis in which Roosevelt wrote: "(At this moment, Loeb, who is taking the dictation, interrupts me to say that you are for La Follette just as he is for him. In other words, as I am, that is, we are for La Follette when he stands against certain big corporation evils, and against him when he goes to a foolish extreme, or throws away the possible by demanding the impossible.)"[74]

Whatever one's suspicions may be, La Follette did go to Kansas during the 1908 campaign. He went at the behest of White, and he helped to defeat Chester I. Long, the railroad candidate for United States senator. He also helped secure the nomination of Joseph L. Bristow, *Salina Journal* editor and insurgent candidate for Senator.[75]

Roosevelt's parenthesis just about summed up White's feelings regarding La Follette, but at the moment, he had little time for such nice distinctions. He was throwing all his political acumen and energies into the campaign to nominate Bristow. On June 9, 1908, for instance, he sent identical letters to Bent Murdock of the *Eldorado Republican,* Gomer Davies of the

Concordia Kansan, Henry J. Allen of the *Wichita Beacon,* George W. Marble of the *Fort Scott Tribune,* A. L. Sponsler of the *Hutchinson Times,* and Harry L. Woods of the *Wellington News.*[76] In these letters, White asked for editorial endorsement of Bristow, and when the endorsements were forthcoming, White incorporated them into news stories which he sent to the *Kansas City Star* and other regional newspapers.[77] That way he blanketed the entire state with Bristow stories. He not only managed Bristow's campaign. He arranged a series of debates between Bristow and Long, and he all but put words in his candidate's mouth.[78]

At the same time, White kept an eye on Taft's chances in Kansas and wrote that Kansas was safe for Taft at the moment. He also wrote, however, that Long's campaign "gave the people the idea that Taft is with Long—that he is a conservative of the Aldrich type when it comes to actual votes and deeds." White wrote to Roosevelt that Long had said "in terms and specifically" that he had kept such things as declarations for physical valuation of railroads, direct election of United States Senators, and publicity on campaign expenditures out of the platform at Taft's request.[79] The chances are fairly good, given Taft's later performance with Aldrich and Joe Cannon, that Long was telling the truth. Nevertheless, Roosevelt had chosen Taft as his successor, and White could not or would not go behind that fact. Taft must be cast as nearly as possible in the mold of Roosevelt.

Although the Rooseveltian ideal obscured White's vision, it had also changed his vision. In ten years he had come to the place where he could say, "I no longer believed that whatever is, is right; but I did believe that it could be right. . . ."[80] By 1908 he was beginning to do his part to see that things were made right, at least from the insurgent point of view. Besides running the campaigns of Bristow and of Victor Murdock, who had captured a congressional nomination, White found time to help Governor Joseph Folk of Missouri and A. B. Cummins of Iowa.[81] He had become, in one campaign, a political power, not only in Kansas, but in the whole Midwest.[82] When Henry Allen congratulated him on being the new boss in Kansas politics, White of course, minimized his own importance and denied that the results of the campaign would lead him into a political career.[83]

It would never lead him into office seeking, but his was already a political career. By this time, he was a politician to his fingertips. In the 1908 campaign, he was out to defeat the railroad candidates, for the railroads were the black beasts of the midwestern insurgents. White himself said that he discovered reform when he "got licked in a railroad fight,"[84] and he used his fight against the railroads to concentrate and build his power. He ran Bristow against the railroads. Chester Long was merely the symbol of those railroads. So White arranged speaking tours for his candidates and persuaded national figures like La Follette to come out to Kansas and help slay the dragon. Not only that, but he prevailed on La Follette to put his office staff to work assembling Long's pro-railroad voting record. Then he wrote three articles around that record, had them electroplated, and sent them to friendly papers throughout the state.[85]

White did not deny that the people owed a debt to the railroads for what the railroads had done for the country. "But," he wrote to a railroad apologist, "the railroads should not try to boss our politics. They gave us Charley Curtis for United States Senator—a pin-headed, polly-foxing moral idiot. They did it as baldly and as brazenly as larceny was ever committed in a daylight holdup."[86]

The fact that the railroads controlled the legislatures, and through them the nomination of United States senators, was but one reason that, in White's eyes, the people were not running their own government, but it was a big reason. He wanted the people to cut loose from guiding-strings. That was why he had strongly opposed any suggestion that Theodore Roosevelt run for a third term. "In short," he wrote to Mark Sullivan in August of 1908, "I believe it is better . . . for the people to boss the senate in the interest of good government than for Roosevelt to boss the senate in the interest of good government."[87]

He had accepted Taft because Roosevelt had chosen Taft, but even in 1907 he must have had misgivings. Whatever they were, they had elicited from Roosevelt a passionate statement of his right to have a choice in the man who was to succeed him. "I am well aware," he had written, "that nothing would more certainly ruin Taft's chances than to have it supposed that I was trying to dictate his nomination. On the other hand, he pointed out, "it is preposterously absurd to say that I have not the right to have my choice as regards the candidates for the Presidency, and that it is not my duty to exercise that choice in favor of the man who will carry out the governmental principles in which I believe with all my heart and soul."[88]

Nevertheless, White, like a good many other insurgents, supported

Taft only because Roosevelt wanted him, and when the disillusionment came, it came with a thump. Victor Murdock was deep in the fight to unseat "Uncle Joe" Cannon, until then the undisputed dictator of the House of Representatives.[89] In the Senate, Joe Bristow was fighting the Payne-Aldrich Tariff.[90] In Kansas, Governor Roscoe Stubbs was pushing through a reform program that was to make Kansas a sort of laboratory, testing the workability of reform measures.[91] As for the President, Murdock was complaining to White, "No one knows for certain Taft's attitude toward Cannon."[92]

White was in the middle of the Cannon fight. He telegraphed the President, telling him that the insurgents were unhappy over the treatment they had been getting. Taft's letter in reply pretty much put White in his place. It could not have made him more friendly toward Roosevelt's successor. "I have your telegram," Taft wrote, "that sentiment in Kansas is with the insurgents. I know it is, and I expect it is generally so. But I have got a good deal more responsibility . . . than the public who are sympathizing with the insurgents."[93] Taft pointed out that he had a legislative program to push through, and he needed the backing of the Republican party to get it through. The ratio of regular Republicans was 190 to 30, he said, and to side with the insurgents at those odds would be to sacrifice his program. "Very early in the campaign," he wrote, "I thought of encouraging a movement to beat Cannon, but I found that he was so strongly intrenched with the membership of the House that that was impossible."[94]

If the practical politician had been uppermost at the time, White might have agreed with Taft. By this time, however, he was joyously "insurging" with all his might, and what he would have considered practical in another day he now considered overcautious. After all, the insurgents of the Midwest had won a number of important victories in the 1908 elections, and the winning insurgents had accepted Taft largely on Roosevelt's recommendation. They expected him to act, not like Roosevelt's successor, but like Roosevelt.

Assuming the voice of spokesman for the insurgents, White wrote to Hamilton Wright Mabie, of *Outlook Magazine.* Referring to Taft, White wrote vehemently, "We feel that his party solidarity proposition means Cannon and Aldrich solidarity. We feel that if the President expects to promote the new federalism as he promoted the new tariff bill, going only so far as he can go with Cannon and Aldrich, he will not go far."[95]

But White was just getting warmed up. "On the other hand," he wrote, "we feel and feel strongly, that the President has turned his back upon that strong element of conscientious independent open-minded Americanism, voiced by the insurgent Senators—a sentiment that always Mr. Roosevelt found behind him in his struggles."[96]

Not only that, but Taft was playing games with the machines. "The President in all his important utterances in the West has given strength to every state machine, however corrupt, and to every local boss however discredited."[97] To John Phillips of *McClure's*, White wrote, "Taft is getting a mighty hard drubbing from Republican papers out this way. I have never known a more serious revolt in this part of the country against any President."[98]

Kansas itself, White reported to Ray Stannard Baker, was going ahead with the program of Progressive legislation under the vigorous leadership of Roscoe Stubbs.[99] According to Stubbs, that program had already saved Kansas producers and shippers more than three million dollars through the introduction of the two-cent railroad fares and the reduction of freight charges on grains, coal, and other merchandise to the seaboard. The state printer reported to Stubbs that the new state printing law had removed a principal source of graft and would save the people of Kansas $50,000 a year, and by 1909, banks had paid to the state of Kansas $25,000 in interest on public funds which, said Stubbs, "under the old political regime went to the state treasurer."[100]

White attributed the success of the legislative program to the enactment of the direct primary law in Kansas. His letter files in this period are full of correspondence about this major weapon of reform. He still believed strongly in party responsibility, but he also believed that the voter was duty-bound, under the convention system, if his party's candidate was weak and corrupt and the candidate of the other party was clean and strong, to vote with the opposition.[101]

The direct primary provided the voter a solution to the problem of standing by his principles and making sure that the man who represented his party also represented those standards. Besides, the direct primary was the only way to smash "real" political machines.[102] It was a way for every man to make his private sentiment public opinion, and it so fascinated White that he wrote to state officials throughout the United States seeking information about it.[103] Much of this information went into a series of articles which ran in the *American Magazine* intermittently from January 1909 through February 1910, and which Macmillan published in 1910 as *The Old Order Changeth: A View of American Democracy.*[104]

In the midst of this most intensive political activity, and of a truly amazing lot of letter-writing, White still got out a newspaper six days a week, wrote a series of short stories for *The Saturday Evening Post* and the *Century*, produced the pieces that resulted in *The Old Order Changeth*, and worked on a novel. He gathered the short stories together and published them as *In Our Town* in 1906.[105]

In Our Town was White's second really successful book of fiction. It was artistically successful for the same reason that *Stratagems and Spoils* had been successful. In it White wrote about something he knew intimately, the people of a small town and their foibles as seen through the eyes of the town's newspaper editor—less stories, really, than character sketches of the people and the town.[106] White saw his town with a clear eye, and though he allowed his editor, Archimedes, to philosophize considerably, he kept him in character. He never stopped the stories to do his editorializing for him. These stories gave White a chance to poke fun at small-town types, the eastern dude, the small-town society matron, the boomer, the old-fashioned country editor. They also allowed him to castigate small-town bigotry. They were fictional essays, in fact, unpretentious and delightful.

In the meantime, and for ten years during his spare moments and his summer vacations in Colorado, White had been working on *A Certain Rich Man.* He saw this as his major work, and he lavished much care and many revisions on it. In a sense, it was his major work. It was a final summing up of the story of the Prodigal Son, a story White began to cast in the language of his own times with "The Regeneration of Colonel Hucks" and which he was to tell several more times. His son, W. L. White, believed, in fact, that *A Certain Rich Man* is the book for which his father will be remembered.[107]

It could be so. It reminds one of the business novels of the late nineteenth century, and it is in the mainstream of the fiction of its time, companion to Robert Herrick's *Memoirs of an American Citizen* and William Dean Howells' *The Rise of Silas Lapham.* It was a great popular success, going through four printings almost immediately and eventually selling, in various editions, a quarter of a million copies. It was later made into a motion picture.[108] The American reviews of the book were generally highly favorable; the British reviews ranged from high praise to bewilderment. The *London Daily Chronicle* perhaps put it best when its reviewer wrote, "Mr. White lacks only one thing to be a genius–unconventionality."[109]

It should have been a good novel. White knew his people and his locale, and he certainly knew his hero. He had been building and tinkering with John Barclay practically since his first short story. Nevertheless, despite the great popular success, despite the strong praise of people like William Lyon Phelps,[110] *A Certain Rich Man* is a failure. In the first place, White did not know when to stop writing. This is a strange failing, considering White's terse newspaper style and the fact that he had revised *A Certain Rich Man* time after time in the ten years he had been working on it. The book fails in the second place because what should have been tragic or heroic becomes soddenly sentimental. Finally, White became entangled in the machinery of his story. He kept reminding the reader that this was a piece of fiction arranged as a gigantic stage play, with chapter titles and headnotes which constantly pulled the reader out of his "willing suspension of disbelief."

Besides, the redemption of John Barclay is utterly unbelievable. Barclay had lied and cheated, bought congressmen and judges, sold his best friend's sweetheart for a bank loan and then caused the death of that friend, killed off competition ruthlessly, adulterated food for the mass market, and had seen his wife die of typhoid rather than interfere with the owner of the city waterworks, whose political power Barclay needed. The redemption and absolution that White devised for such a man was altogether too sudden and too lachrymose to be believed. The sentimental realist had succumbed to the sentimentalist.

A Certain Rich Man was indeed the story of the Prodigal Son, a prodigal son who returned, not to the home of his father, but to the home of his widowed mother, a woman strikingly like the author's portrait of Mary Ann Hatton White. One can easily read the book as the story of William Allen White's pilgrimage from the fleshpots and evils of reaction to his home in the bosom of the Republican insurgents. Perhaps that is why the reviewer on *The Nation* saw White's hope for ameliorative justice shining through the book.[111]

Vernon Louis Parrington, friend of White's young manhood in Emporia,[112] was to call the theme of *A Certain Rich Man* "fear of the economic city that draws the villager into its web."[113] It is a true statement, but only partly true. The theme of the book is exactly what White said it was–the return of the prodigal son to himself. White did fear economic centralization, but more than he feared centralization, he believed in the redemption of society through the regeneration of the individual.

A major part of his scheme for that redemption depended on the election of good men to political office, and the instrument that was to make possible such election was the direct primary. In fact, in this early period of his insurgency, White went even further in his campaign to involve the people directly in politics without interference from special interests or the convention system. He had always advocated party regularity, and he was to use party regularity in the future to help keep the Progressive party alive. Now, however, he was writing to Stubbs and to Ralph Stout of the *Kansas City Star,* advocating a mass ballot to eliminate party voting.[114] Not only that, but he called for a constitutional amendment providing that "when any act of the legislature had been resubmitted to the people and passed by two-thirds majority of the votes cast, that legislative act should become a law not subject to invalidation by any state court."[115]

It took the jolt of Roosevelt, perhaps, to get White to think in terms of the people, and maybe it took his association with the *McClure's* crowd to get his conservative feet off the ground. But once aloft, William Allen White flew fairly high. The year 1908 marked not only his emergence as a strong political figure in Kansas. It also marked White's takeoff into the wild blue yonder of reform—almost any reform.

He wrote to his university classmate William E. Borah to set about getting a direct nomination primary for United States senator as soon as he could. "It is the only safe-guard for an honest Senate," he assured Borah.[116] He wrote to Judge Ben Lindsey in Denver, and told the originator of the juvenile court how to get the direct primary in Colorado.[117] He put Stubbs in touch with Kate Bernard, a pioneer penologist in the Oklahoma Territory, to get Stubbs started on prison reform.[118] He rode the reform horse like a hungry jockey. At the same time, he kept his tongue securely in his cheek. "How would this do," he asked John Phillips of *McClure's,* "for my September contribution to Government by Magazine?"[119]

Witness also the following editorial, which appeared in the *Gazette* for December 10, 1909:

INSURGENTS

O come, my love, insurge with me, adown the bosky dell; we'll chase

> the nimble octopus across the barren fell; the moon is high, the tariff, too, is rising every hour; so come, my love, insurge with me, here in my sylvan bower. Yes, come, my love, and trip with me the light fantastic toe; and as we slip along let's trip our agile Uncle Joe. The differentials are in bloom, the ad valorem beams; the rules are moaning at the bar, while dimpled freedom screams. Then come, my love, let us insurge; Ah, let us rage and snort; O let us paw the soft lush grass, while our two souls cavort. The time is ripe, the hour is here, our song will be no dirge; O let us whoop and fly the coop—come on, O let's insurge.[120]

White was obviously having the time of his life, and he was also obviously moving further and further away from the position that he had taken as a young man. Rather suddenly, considering the years that had gone before, he had come to believe in direct democracy, at least as direct as geography and population permitted. The feeling persists, as one reads White's letters, that while he was in earnest about reform, he felt deliciously that he was playing the devil with the established order. Reform was fun!

The basic reform was honesty in government not only for William Allen White but also for most of the respectable middle-class reformers in Kansas and the other midwestern states. Honesty in business and politics—regeneration of the body politic—that was the answer to the woes of the nation.

Plunged as he was in reform, White was increasingly unhappy with the Taft administration. He was not alone. Ida M. Tarbell wrote him, "Taft is done for, I fully believe. I have failed yet to meet a single person in whom he has aroused the least respect. Not a man of discernment, but what shakes his head over him."[121]

For all his "insurging," though, White still found himself in the middle. People were writing him from all over the country saying, in effect, "See, the Populists were right after all," and a Presbyterian minister in Idaho added, "You still abuse them, but we all know where you get your ideas. It shows on the outside."[122] White did still abuse the old Populists. The revolution he was involved in was middle class and respectable; the Populist revolt had not been. White wrote to Roosevelt, "I do not know how much good the extremist does. There must be pioneers in every army and advanced thinkers in every cause. They sow where others reap and it is probably necessary, and we probably need John Browns, but I am a little skeptical about the ultimate good that they do."[123] On the other hand, White was writing insurgent editorials which embodied Populist ideas, and when he was accused of socialism, he wrote that he did not care whether or not the Socialists endorsed his ideas. The question was, he said, were the ideas true?[124]

By 1910 White was a wheelhorse among midwestern insurgents. In his estimation, he was more responsible for the insurgent campaign in Kansas than was any other man.[125] He received calls for help from Kansas insurgents and from others such as Albert J. Beveridge of Indiana and Robert M. La Follette of Wisconsin.[126] He arranged Victor Murdock's speaking itinerary, kept in constant touch with insurgent leaders in Topeka, and got credit for the success of their campaigns from at least two state candidates.[127] It was during this period that he was moved to protest that he was not a Warwick, not a kingmaker, but that he was just a "poor, fumbling dub" who was doing everybody's business because it had become nobody's business.[128]

At about this time, too, the twin ideas of a third party and of Roosevelt's being a candidate in 1912 began to bedevil White. At first he was completely against Roosevelt's candidacy. He could not conceive, he said, of Roosevelt's being a candidate unless Taft was definitely out of the picture.[129] Yet, White could stomach Taft for only so long. He had tried to tell Taft that the insurgents would behave themselves if Taft would stop supporting Aldrich and Connon.[130] He had tried to work with Taft as he had worked with McKinley and Roosevelt, but the two men could not communicate with each other. If it came to it, then, Roosevelt would have to run and White would have to support him.

White did not want a third party, either. He wanted to work inside the Republican party, but Taft seemed to him a real stumbling block. "What a genius for fumbling Taft is!" White wrote in exasperation to Mark Sullivan.[131] Besides, White was testing the political winds, and it began to look to him as if Roosevelt was the only person who could save the Republican party in 1912.[132] White had gone into Colorado and some other western states to line up insurgent candidates for governor and congressman in 1910, and on the basis of the tour, he wrote to Bristow, to Nelson, and to Dante Barton of the *Kansas City Star* that Taft was a dead issue.[133]

As for a successor to Taft, White was willing to support La Follette as long as he was a candidate. He wrote to Senator Bristow, however, that Roosevelt had enough strength to win in the Midwest, and that if it came to a showdown, La Follette would be a lost cause.[134] In the same letter, he admitted and reiterated Roosevelt's weakness for compromise and then performed an interesting trick in mental gymnastics. Roosevelt believes that compromise is his strength, said White, "but men like you and I believe it is his weakness. But it is just that weakness that makes him strong in this crisis. We can and will nominate Roosevelt."[135]

However odd that sounds, White was at least correct in a prediction he made in the same letter, that Kansas would be for Roosevelt overwhelmingly against either Taft or La Follette. In typical White fashion, he followed that prediction with a projection of it. "I think you will find," he wrote, "that the sentiment of Kansas is the sentiment of the nation."[136]

From this distance, it would appear that both Ida M. Tarbell and William Allen White were victims of too-limited sampling. The states White toured and the people Tarbell talked with were already insurgent states and insurgent people. And the states which were to hold preferential primaries, either legitimately or by legislative subterfuge, were strong Roosevelt states or they would not have fought so hard for the primaries in the first place.

William Allen White saw himself as a professional observer of men. Unless one can blame his performance at this time on the fever of insurgency, it is strange, then, that he did not read William Howard Taft any more clearly than he did. If Taft was more conservative than Roosevelt, only his performance in the Paine-Aldrich Tariff fight and the insurgents' fight to unseat Speaker Joseph Cannon indicate it – those and his performance in the Ballinger-Pinchot controversy over conservation. Actually, Taft's Congress passed more reform legislation and his attorney general prosecuted and won more anti-trust suits than did Roosevelt's Congress or his attorney general.[137]

But the Progressives regarded the passage of the Paine-Aldrich Tariff bill as a sell-out—as indeed it was—and they looked upon Taft's support of Cannon as traitorous, and White, taking his cue from Bristow and Murdock in Congress, believed it, too. Strangely, White did not become involved in the Ballinger-Pinchot affair at all, though it was at least as dramatic and as much a Progressive rallying as were the other two fights.

From Taft's point of view, he did not make a wrong move. He had called Congress together in special session to redeem a campaign pledge to revise the tariff schedules. It was to be a hard fight, and he knew it.

To get any kind of revision, he would have to work with the Republican majority, and in the Senate, Nelson Aldrich, the ultra-conservative senator from Rhode Island, controlled that majority absolutely.[138] The bill that came out of the House contained a number of downward revisions, but what with objections from special sectional interests and the pressure from Aldrich, the bill as it was finally passed was amended 847 times.[139] In the end it was very little different from the Dingley Tariff, which had been passed in 1897, and which the Paine-Aldrich Bill had been designed to supplant.

The insurgents were furious, but they might have swallowed the tariff—or at least the furor might have died down—if Taft had not set out to defend the revision as the best tariff bill that had ever been written, and if he had not pointed out that the Republican promise had been to revise the tariff, not necessarily to revise it downward.[140]

For Taft, it was a matter of working with the party whose ticket he headed, and that party was the Republican party, not the insurgent splinter nor "the broken reed of the Democracy" nor a coalition of the two. It does not appear that Taft ever had any intention of supporting a tariff bill of which Aldrich would have disapproved. For one thing, he and Aldrich were closer in their political philosophies than had been apparent to the insurgents when they accepted Taft in 1908. For another, Taft thoroughly approved of legislative action originating entirely in Congress. He opposed the introduction or guiding of legislation by the executive on constitutional grounds.

Again it was a matter of party solidarity in the fight around Joseph Cannon. The Speaker of the House was the absolute dictator of that body. He controlled the Rules Committee and made committee appointments. It was to him that a congressman had to go—to the old man's private office—if he wanted to get a bill reported out of committee.[141] He was as conservative, at least, as Nelson Aldrich. Making sure that the mouth of the goal was small in the first place, he himself acted as goalkeeper and made sure that none of the Progressive shots got through. The Progressives, in coalition with the Democrats, finally succeeded in democratizing the House by making the job of the Speaker elective, but not without opposition from the White House.[142]

The Progressives lost the Paine-Aldrich fight, but they fought bitterly and vocally and gained much publicity, a great deal of voter sympathy in the middle of the nation, and a prime campaign issue. They won the fight to democratize the House—and helped keep Uncle Joe Cannon in the Speaker's chair because they liked him as a man—and gained a campaign issue.[143] Ostensibly, they lost the Ballinger-Pinchot battle. After an exhaustive investigation, the investigating committee found Ballinger innocent of wrong-doing and upheld the dismissal of Chief Forester Gifford Pinchot for insubordination. The case revolved around turning the Cunningham Claim, a large coal and timber area in Alaska, back to private exploitation. Louis R. Glavis, Ballinger's own young chief of the Field Division of the Department of the Interior, discovered the Cunningham deal and told Pinchot. Pinchot sent him to Taft with the report and Taft concurred in Ballinger's firing Glavis for insubordination. When Pinchot, a crusader for conservation, would not let go of the case, he too was fired.[144]

If the majority report exonerated Ballinger, the minority reports, written from evidence assembled by Louis Brandeis, then a young lawyer, gave the Progressives additional ammunition.[145] So it was that William Howard Taft, though his administration brought into being much of the reform legislation that the insurgents had been clamoring for since 1900, could do no right. He had been impolitic regarding three incendiary issues, and those issues had made anything else he did inconsequential in the eyes of the insurgents.

William Allen White said it rightly when he said, "What a genius for bungling Taft is!" Yet it was bungling, not with program, but with people. Taft had never before held an elective office. He was not adept at working with people as a politician must work with people, kindly, genial, jovial though he was. He was a big, lethargic man, given to hastily written speeches and fierce defense of his actions after the fact. It was not a matter of program or policy. It was a matter of personality. He was not Theodore Roosevelt.

Neither was he Robert M. La Follette, for that matter, and in the early stages of the insurgents' disenchantment with Taft, it was to La Follette that those insurgents looked for leadership. Beetle-browed, shaggy-maned "Battling Bob" La Follette was the perfect symbol for the insurgent cause. He had had to take two runs at it, but he had defeated a lumber industry-sponsored opponent and had made a national reputation as a reform governor in Wisconsin. He had put in a comprehensive reform program in his state that became known as the "Wisconsin Idea," and he had battled the conservative forces to a stand-still.[146] If Taft should falter, he had a good chance to be the Republican presidential nominee in 1912. But that was before Theodore Roosevelt came home from Africa.

6

Bull Moose Resistant

White resisted the idea that Roosevelt run for President in 1912, and he resisted mightily. After all, in 1910 many of the states already had the direct primary, and there was hope for recall and referendum, and insurgency was making great gains against the old guard conservatives in state governments and in congressional delegations. True, he said, the people might go further faster with Roosevelt in the White House, but they would get where they were going then in the security of Roosevelt's leadership and not under their own power.[1]

Roosevelt, in the meantime, wrote repeatedly to White that he would not be a candidate in 1912. "One word about politics," he wrote on October 12, 1911.

> I suppose that what I say will have no weight with you; but I do emphatically feel that I have a right to expect every friend of mine to do everything in his power to prevent any movement looking toward my nomination, no matter what the circumstances may be. However it came about, you would find that people would believe that somehow or other I had instigated it, or had been a party to it, and I believe it would be a weak and not a strong nomination. If there were a necessity to sacrifice me for the greater good, I should not feel at liberty to protest; but I do feel at liberty to protest against being sacrificed when the sacrifice will merely do harm to the cause we have at heart.[2]

As late as January 16, 1912, Roosevelt was writing to Frank Munsey, the millionaire publisher who was to become one of the financial backers of the Progressive party bolt:

> I am not and shall not be a candidate. I shall not seek the nomination, nor would I accept it if it came to me as the result of an intrigue. But I will not tie my hands by a statement that would make it difficult or impossible for me to serve the people by undertaking a great task if the people as a whole seemed definitely to come to the conclusion that I ought to do that task.[3]

Roosevelt sent White a copy of that letter on January 26. It shut the door, then it immediately opened the door again—just a crack.

There seems to have been little reason for this backing and filling as far as White was concerned, if he, like many of the Progressives in the Midwest, was committed to La Follette, as he was.[4] But many of the Progressives, White included, were committed to La Follette only because they could not have Roosevelt. If they could find a way out, most of them would take it.

For things were not going well at all for La Follette, even in a Progressive stronghold like Kansas. White reported trying to line up La Follette support in 1911. He himself was campaigning vigorously for the job of Republican national committeeman. He went after the job, he reported, "like a wolfhound." "While I did not want the job," he said, "I also did not want to be defeated."[5] In three county conventions in Kansas that winter, the La Follette forces were defeated. "It was jarring," White reported.[6]

The way out came suddenly on the night of February 2 in Philadelphia. La Follette had been campaigning hard, to the limit of his strength. He came to Philadelphia to speak at the annual meeting of the Periodical Publishers Association of America, and whether he was heartsick at the illness of his daughter and the fickleness of some of his supporters, or whether, as White reported, he was "dead tired, dog-tired after a terrible day in the Senate," this fighting, biting, incisive speaker made a speech that was a fiasco. Beginning by lambasting the great corporations and their control over government, he ended by nearly accusing the publications his audience represented of being the mouthpieces for those corporations.[7]

"Remember," says White, "that these Publishers were conducting magazines that were anywhere from liberal to radical." In that audience, too, were all the Progressive leaders in Congress and on the eastern seaboard.

Let White tell what happened.

> It was after ten at night when the toastmaster came to him. Just before he rose to speak, his secretary told me, he took a great gobletfull of whiskey and swallowed it neat, as a stimulant. He was not a drinking man. But, his secretary said, sometimes, to stoke up his machine, he used any stimulant that might be at hand and had no bad consequences, contracted no bad habits, but kept his machine going when his normal strength was gone. He had his manuscript that night at the dinner, and for ten minutes or so, perhaps twenty, he read along fluently and well. Then he put his manuscript down for a moment to emphasize a point . . . he wandered a bit, repeated himself . . . he had lost his place and read for five minutes or so paragraphs that he had already read . . . the second time he departed from his manuscript he began to lose control of his temper. He came out of his fury maudlin. . . . For nearly two hours . . . he raged on and on, saying the same things over and over at the top of his voice. It was a terrible spectable.[8]

And it was enough. The next day, La Follette's office announced that he was canceling some speeches because of fatigue, but the rumor spread that he was withdrawing from the race. By the time the rumor had been squelched, the damage had been done. Even Senator Joseph Bristow, who, White said, had no use for Roosevelt, came over to the Roosevelt camp. The loss of three counties and Bristow's switch convinced the Kansas insurgents. "What we did," said White, "was simple enough. We stopped insisting on La Follette delegates to the national convention and let nature take its course."[9]

For all the apparent vacillation that his correspondence shows, Roosevelt was a good enough politician to know that his chances for nomination and election would be better in 1916 than in 1912. As his letter to White indicated, Roosevelt had an idea that whoever the Republican candidate was in 1912, especially with Woodrow Wilson making a reputation as the reform governor of New Jersey and looking more and more like a possibility for the Democratic nomination, that Republican nominee would be a sacrifice. If anybody was going to be sacrificed, Roosevelt preferred that it be William Howard Taft.

Then why did he finally consent to become a candidate—nay, maneuver so that it looked as if he had a mandate to run from six Progressive governors?[10] In the first place, he was becoming more and more disillusioned with Taft. From the Payne-Aldrich tariff fight, through Taft's lining up with Joe Cannon, to Taft's trust-busting activities, to the reciprocity treaties which Taft's administration negotiated with a number of nations, Roosevelt was convinced that his erstwhile crown prince was wrong.[11]

More and more he had come to think—and to say so in speeches and in articles for *Outlook Magazine,* of which he became one of the editors, that bigness simply as bigness was no crime, and that some concentration of industrial wealth was necessary for progress. Rather regulation than dismemberment, he said.[12] As to reciprocity, that was all right *vis à vis* the British Empire. The idea of tariff reciprocity with any other countries roused Roosevelt's nationalism, never too far submerged, anyway.[13]

As a matter of fact, Theodore Roosevelt had been bitten by Herbert Croly much as White had reported earlier that "Roosevelt bit me and I went mad."[14] Croly's bite was in his book, *The Promise of American Life,* an anti-Jeffersonian blueprint for the American future based on big industrial combinations, big labor unions, and a strong, executive-directed government charged with regulating both giants in the interests of the nation as a whole.[15] It was the "New Natonalism," and on August 31, 1910, at Osawatamie, Kansas, Theodore Roosevelt took that "New Nationalism" as his slogan and *The Promise of American Life* as his creed.[16] He took them mostly because they agreed pretty much with what he was thinking anyway. He fitted Croly's picture of the New Natonalist executive as if he had sat for it. If you did not believe it, all you had to do was ask him. Besides, from the not unreasonable conclusion that not all trusts are bad and not all labor unions good he hadcome to believe with Croly—and perhaps before he read Croly—that one should use discrimination in prosecuting the trusts, that combination did not necessarily equate with criminality.

Two other apostles of the New Nationalism became intimates of Theodore Roosevelt. They were George W. Perkins of U.S. Steel, International Harvester, and the Morgan interests, and Frank Munsey, millionaire publisher and admirer of the German system of social control, who told Roosevelt, "It is the work of the state to think for the people and plan for the people—to teach them how to do, what to do, and sustain them in the doing.[17]

This was the intellectual baggage that Theodore Roosevelt brought with him to Osawatamie, Kansas, that day in August 1910, ostensibly to commemorate the bloody stand that John Brown had made there. John Brown got short shrift, however. Roosevelt launched almost immediately into his espousal of the New Nationalism.

At first glance, it seems incongruous that Roosevelt's farm-grown, Populist-engendered, trust-hating audience would have accepted the New Nationalism. But this was Theodore Roosevelt talking, the trumpet of the new reform. In the eyes of many in that audience, he was the saner heir of the mantle of William Jennings Bryan. He was still the Trust-Buster, and even in the New Nationalism, he proposed to keep those trusts, including the hated railroad combinations, in strict control. Besides, as his great friend and Kansas spokesman, William Allen White, said, he stood squarely on the Kansas Republican platform of 1910.[18]

White had written that platform, and he was proud of it. He remained proud enough of it that he was to quote from it at length in his autobiography.[19] Among other things, it called for the Kansas congressional delegation to vote for a revision of the Payne-Aldrich Tariff Act, based on the difference between production costs at home and abroad "with a reasonable profit for American manufacture." It pledged that the Kansas delegation would vote for a tariff commissioner, demand a vote on one tariff schedule at a time, and vote to make membership on important House committees elective. It provided jail sentences for willful violators of the anti-trust law, gave the Interstate Commerce Commission the power and money to determine the physical valuation of railroads, and promised to regulate capitalization of corporations and give the Interstate Commerce Commission authority over the issuing of stocks and bonds of common carriers. The Kansas Republican congressional candidates also pledged themselves to support the principle of conservation and to push for a constitutional amendment which would make possible the direct election of United States senators.

At the state level, the platform called for placing all public utilities, railways, telegraph, telephone, power companies, street railways, and gas distributors under a state board. That board would have authority over the issuing of stocks and bonds. It would also value the property for taxation on the basis of rate-making valuation. The state candidates would also support a law compelling firms doing business in Kansas to begin any litigation in the Kansas court, so that they could not "take refuge" in the federal courts until the Kansas Supreme Court had passed on their case. Other pledges included support for state constitutional amendments providing for the initiative, referendum and recall, a campaign fund publicity law, a presidential primary, ratification of the income tax amendment, examination of a state workmen's compensation law, and a state bank guarantee law.

Some of those pledges were twenty years in the fulfilling, but after more than fifty years, it is hard to think of them as revolutionary. Given the economic and political structure of the time, however, they were indeed revolutionary, and they worried the badgered financial and industrial establishment quite as much as Colonel Roosevelt's New Nationalism began to mollify it.

The Osawatamie speech could have done little to repair the estrangement between Roosevelt and Taft. It was an estrangement that was to grow more fixed and more bitter as the time approached for the Republicans to make a choice for the 1912 campaign.[20] The choice had narrowed to these erstwhile friends, now bitter enemies despite at least one attempt by the friends of both men to achieve a reconciliation.[21] Since the Philadelphia debacle, La Follette had been out of it, but he could not or would not see it. Though the desertion was almost complete by the time of the convention, he was to cling to his votes to the end.[22]

Meanwhile, Roosevelt had been wrestling with himself. He knew, or he suspected, that whoever became the Republican nominee would be defeated in the general election. He also knew that if he stayed out of the 1912 race and let Taft become the sacrificial goat, he would have a very good chance at the presidency in 1916. One writer suggests that Roosevelt was bored with inactivity, at any rate, with political inactivity.[23] White maintained that the clamor of the people was deafening, and that it turned Roosevelt's head.[24] Another possibility is that, feeling as he now felt, Roosevelt could not stand to see Taft where Roosevelt was sure he ought to be.

Whatever the reason, the clamor of the people must not have been quite as loud as White remembered it. For when Roosevelt decided to seek the nomination, still wanting to make it appear that the nomination sought him, he arranged for seven Progressive governors to sign a letter asking him to run. Without mentioning Roosevelt's part in the preparation of the plan or the letter, White said that William Rockhill Nelson, White's old mentor on the *Kansas City Star,* was among those instrumental in getting the governors to sign. Those governors were J. M. Carey of

Wyoming, Herbert S. Hadley of Missouri, Chase S. Osborn of Michigan, Robert P. Bass of New Hampshire, Chester H. Aldrich of Nebraska, W. E. Glasscock of West Virginia, and the radically Progressive governor of Kansas, Walter Roscoe Stubbs.[25]

With the "mandate" of the governors in hand, Theodore Roosevelt was ready to announce his candidacy for the Republican nomination for President. White had a speech to make at the Progressive Club in Boston in February 1912. He wrote Roosevelt about it, and Roosevelt invited him to dinner after the speech, at the home of Judge Robert Grant. Grant wrote, too, inviting White.[26]

That night, Roosevelt gave White a prepared statement for him to edit. It was Roosevelt's announcement. White says he knew what was in the wind and that he opposed the announcement to the end, agreeing to it against his better judgment. He thought Roosevelt was four years away from the presidency.[27] His friend Victor Murdock, congressman from Kansas, thought the Rough Rider was at least eight years away. "This rebellion," White quotes him as saying, "has a long, long way to go before it wins."[28] Murdock had been in the Cannon fight. He knew something about the strength of the opposition.

A few nights later, in Washington, White got hit with something that shook him up a good deal more than did Roosevelt's announcement. Once the die was cast, a group of Roosevelt supporters, including several members of the National Progressive Republican League, met in a Washington hotel room to make plans for the Roosevelt primary campaign. The National Progressive Republican League, of which White was a charter member, had been organized January 10, 1911, in the home of Senator Robert Marion La Follette,[29] primarily to beat Taft and secondarily to advance the presidential candidacy of Senator Robert Marion La Follette.

Now, about a year later, at least two of this same group—White and Senator Jonathan Bourne of Oregon—along with Senators George H. Moses of New Hampshire, Moses E. Clapp of Minnesota, Joseph L. Bristow and Victor Murdock of Kansas, Hiram Johnson of California, Albert Beveridge of Indiana, Joseph Moore Dixon of Montana, Jonathan Prentiss Dolliver of Iowa, and William E. Borah of Idaho were meeting to plan the campaign to secure Roosevelt's nomination.[30] White also remembered that Nebraska's George W. Norris brought in half a dozen more from the House of Representatives.[31]

The group elected Senator Dixon its chairman, and then Bourne stood up and dropped a bomb in their midst. "Gentlemen," White quoted him years later, "the first thing we have got to decide is a matter of fundamental policy. If we lose, will we bolt? To get this thing before the house, I move that we agree, here and now, and not be too secretive about our agreement that if we lose, we bolt."[32]

White always felt thereafter that Bourne's motion, which he says was not voted on, was the strategic error that lost Roosevelt the Republican nomination in 1912. Though the group that had gathered that night to plan strategy did not vote on Bourne's motion, the consensus was in the air. They would bolt if Theodore Roosevelt was denied the nomination in Chicago. And the news of the threat apparently leaked. It was exactly, White thought, what the GOP Regulars needed. They had time on their side. Win, lose or draw in the 1912 elections, they could wait. They had the threat of a bolt to bind them together and make sure that they controlled the party so that they could win four years hence, or eight, or twenty.[33] Besides, the Taft forces had not been idle. Already, the head of the party had ordered that the county conventions be held earlier than usual, before the Roosevelt forces could get organized. The Regulars had the South, and they knew it. The South would never win the Republican party an election, but it could help those in control of the party remain in control.[34]

The states that had the preferential primary would go for Roosevelt. They were Progressive states, anyway. But, though some six or seven more, by true primaries or by subterfuge, would be able to express the people's preference for Roosevelt by convention time, there were at the moment only half a dozen states in the whole country which had the direct primary on the books. Those that did not were being organized early by the Taft forces.[35] From this distance it would seem that Roosevelt was at a major disadvantage from the outset of the campaign. He had more popular support than Taft had, but Taft had the organization; he was in and Roosevelt was out. It is always easier to stay in than to get in.

It is true that there was a good deal of money that wanted to go to Roosevelt. A number of industrialists could not see how the country could avoid a Progressive President after 1912, and on the basis of the New Nationalism doctrine of Osawatomie, they thought they saw hope in Theodore Roosevelt. The hope began to wane when Roosevelt published in the January 6, 1912, issue of *Outlook* an article calling for popular recall of judicial decisions.[36] That hope disappeared entirely when on February 22, 1912, Roosevelt brought his program for judicial recall out in a full-dress campaign speech.[37] The business world set up a howl of rage. The courts were its last bastion of protection against the Progressive heresy. And out in Emporia, Kansas, William Allen White found himself trying to explain away what his Colonel had said.[38] But Roosevelt stuck to the speech and defended it vigorously,[39] and as a matter of fact, after the campaign, White was to write a letter supporting judicial recall on the state level. That was all Roosevelt had asked for. His one concession to the business community, in that speech in Columbus, Ohio, was to limit judicial recall to the state judiciary. Robert M. La Follette opposed the Roosevelt position, too. He thought the right of judicial recall ought to go all the way to the Supreme Court.

Judicial recall was harder for the business community to swallow than New Nationalism should have been for the rural areas, and Roosevelt lost much eastern money support, as White knew he would,[40] by making judicial recall an issue. Roosevelt's Columbus speech disturbed White as much as had the motion to bolt. He could not believe that Roosevelt had meant what he said, and even when he came to write his autobiography, he was still making excuses for Roosevelt. "I tried to explain," White wrote, "that he meant by recall of judicial decisions only the legislative enactments needed to amend the statutes upon which the decisions were made. Probably he meant something like that."[41] Probably, from what Roosevelt said later in the campaign, he meant exactly what he said.

Like many another President before him and since, Theodore Roosevelt had had his troubles with the judiciary.[42] He had a point in his favor, too. One of the reasons for the plank in the Kansas platform which would force corporations to begin any legal action in the state courts was that the corporations had a habit of running to the federal courts for a ruling on any case in which they had an interest. They knew, from the record, that the ruling would almost always favor them. The way White explained it was that the corporations (in Kansas and other midwestern states, the railroads; in Massachusetts, the textile industry; in Montana, copper; in Nevada, silver; in the Northwest, lumber) controlled the legislatures. The legislatures elected and controlled the United States senators, and the senators controlled judicial appointments.[43]

In November 1908, while he was still in the White House, Roosevelt had written White, naming two judges explicitly and saying generally that, while he believed there were few really corrupt judges, there were many who were unfit to sit on the bench. Besides which, he said, there was "altogether too much power in the bench."[44]

Even a radically Progressive state like Kansas had not touched the judiciary, however, and by 1911, Kansas had enacted about as thoroughgoing a Progressive program as could be found in the country. White outlined it for a proposed article for *Outlook,* though he said someone else should write the piece because he was a part of the story.

"Seven years ago," said White, "Kansas was governed by a railroad despotism. . . . The State Treasurer's money was farmed out and the interest made a slush fund; our State Printer's fees were a source of grief and our state institutions were filled with politicians; delegates rode to State conventions on passes and voted at the dictates of railroad attorneys. It was no more self-government than Russia. In five years," White wrote proudly, "we fought and cleaned up the whole system." Then he listed the major reforms, financial and penal as well as political, that the Kansas Progressives had been able to effect. "This is not the story of one man," he said. "It is the story of a people and I believe we can show any competent investigator that our laws are enforced with considerable rigor and that our state is an excellent example of the people governing the people."[45]

But nowhere in that considerable catalogue of reforms did White mention the judiciary. It does not seem reasonable, in view of the nature of the political structure in the railroad states, that the state courts were any less in need of reform than the state legislatures, and certainly White knew of bought federal judges, bought with railroad money by pre-Progressive Kansas senators.[46]

It was too touchy to tamper with the ultimate authority of the courts. It was further to the left than William Allen White, who by this time saw himself as a rampaging radical, was prepared to go. White suspected, moreover, that having to defend his position on the courts once he had taken it pushed Roosevelt further to the left than he wanted to go. But defend it Roosevelt did. The necessity for judicial recall was one issue upon which Theodore Roosevelt, the lover of compromise, refused to compromise throughout the campaign that followed.[47]

In the end, it probably did not matter nearly as much as it seemed to matter at the time. The financial support that Roosevelt lost by backing judicial reform made no difference in his campaign. With Perkins and

Munsey and a few others behind him, Roosevelt spent more money on the 1912 presidential campaign than any other candidate in the race.[48] As for the votes that he lost, Taft strategy had locked up the South before Roosevelt was off and running, and that gave Taft one-third of the votes before the nominating convention was organized for business.[49]

In Kansas, William Allen White was one of the wheelhorses in organizing the state delegations for Roosevelt. He made speeches, he horse-traded, he banged away at the Progressive cause in county conventions and in caucuses. He and about a dozen others had to fight to get county primaries to make sure that the state's delegates were for Roosevelt.

"I have been spending the better part of three weeks in this Roosevelt fight," he wrote to Victor Murdock in April 1912, "most of the time in Topeka. . . . We had the devil's own time doing this job. It looks easy now," he admitted, "but two weeks ago it was mighty scarey. We had to go into every single precinct in thirty or forty counties where caucuses had been ordered by the Committee and persuade the Committeemen to hold the caucuses open for two hours and allow the men to vote by ballot, which meant the primary," White pointed out, "though saved the other fellows' faces. We had to have organizers all over the Fifth and Sixth and Third districts and a part of the Seventh."[50]

In the end, such scrambling paid off. The Progressives won all but two congressional districts and carried the state convention. White won his race for national committeeman, and his old friend Henry J. Allen headed the Kansas delegation.[51] The state convention not only pledged its delegates to Roosevelt, but also pledged the presidential electors to vote for Roosevelt. That last move, taken by a number of Progressive states, was to cause considerable confusion later.

What had happened in Kansas happened wherever there was a state primary, except in the Dakotas, where La Follette delegates won.[52] On the basis of the popular vote, it was no wonder that the Progressive strategists were optimistic. When they met with Roosevelt at his home at Oyster Bay for one last pre-convention war council, as White said, "it was plain that we had the Republican sentiment of the country, as it was uncovered by direct vote of Republicans in state primaries, rather overwhelmingly for Colonel Roosevelt."[53]

These were not political tyros, though. They knew how the game was played. They knew, also, that the Taft forces were contesting the results in some convention states, and that if they won those contests, the Taft forces, through the national committee, would seat Taft delegates and control the convention.[54]

On the other side, too, particularly in the South, the Progressives planned to contest some delegations. Some of these contests were genuine; some were later admitted to be spurious.[55] Either way, with the chances of the national committee controlling the convention, and thereby controlling the credentials committee, it seems a strange strategy for the Progressives to have adopted. It had a built-in backfire.

It has been said that one of the reasons for the failure of Roosevelt's campaign for the regular party nomination in 1912 was that amateurs, almost exclusively, ran the campaign. Too many of those amateurs, according to this explanation, spent more time jockeying for position in the Roosevelt power structure than they did in working for their candidate, and, in the end, Roosevelt himself had to take over almost all the publicity functions of that campaign.[56] It has also been said that Roosevelt campaign publicity was hard to come by, because only a handful of the country's newspapers supported Roosevelt.[57]

It is true that the reform group in the Republican party had very little cohesion. The one thing its members had in common was the idea of reform itself. There was not even any real agreement about the direction the reforms should take. Roosevelt himself, if his conversion to the New Nationalism was as deep as it appeared to be, favored, not a democracy, but a corporate state. With him were Munsey and Perkins and the other representatives of the industrial and financial establishment.

On the other hand, there were the essentially agrarian, Jeffersonian radicals, like Roscoe Stubbs and Victor Murdock in Kansas, Cummins in Iowa, and La Follette in Wisconsin. The line, in Kansas, for example, went back to Populists like Sockless Jerry Simpson and Mary Ellen Lease. Then there were those who had no overall plan of reform. They were interested in specific reforms: conservation, women's suffrage, prohibition, penal reform, and control of whatever big interest seemed to be throttling a particular reformer's segment of the population. The Progressives were never a cohesive party—not even, before the bolt, a party within a party. They were a coalition of shifting concurrences of opinion. Naturally, then, there were always more chiefs than there were Indians. The wonder is that, given such divergence, the group which was finally to call itself the Progressive party achieved so much solid, lasting reform using the American political machinery.[58]

While it is true that the chiefs seemed to outnumber the Indians in 1912, they were not all bungling amateurs by any means. Since 1900 there had grown up in both major parties a group of able, vote-getting, campaign-winning Progressive politicans, at both the national and state levels. William Allen White himself was by this time an example of a seasoned campaigner, amateur only in the sense that he had not run for elective office nor drawn a salary for holding such an office.

If Roosevelt handled his own publicity, it could only have been because he wanted to do it. The midwestern newspapers, aside from the La Follette group, were solidly behind him, including William Rockhill Nelson's influential *Kansas City Star.* The Munsey string of newspapers supported him. The Progressive magazines—again except for the La Follette group—supported him. William Allen White was a master space-grabber and indefatigable in the cause. Roosevelt's friend George W. Perkins was no mean publicist himself.[59]

The eastern conservative press, led by *The New York Times,* did not support Roosevelt, of course. In fact, the big-city press generally, as could be expected, supported President Taft.[60] It is nonetheless true that except for the indiscriminate contesting of southern delegates, this inept group of little chiefs did pretty well by their big chief. They got him the support of the people. There was nothing they could do about breaking Taft's control of the convention except howl in anguish and righteous indignation. This does not mean that Theodore Roosevelt did nothing in his own behalf. He campaigned harder, perhaps, than any candidate had ever campaigned up to that time, roaring up and down the land, trading verbal punches with his erstwhile friend William Howard Taft until he literally had to give his voice a rest. He wrote White, begging off from an extensive speaking tour of Kansas that White had laid out for him.[61] As it turned out, all the Roosevelt forces in Kansas could have used the impetus that speaking tour might have given them.

As White indicated, he and the other Roosevelt lieutenants in Kansas had "the devil's own time" getting the Republicans of the state a chance to vote on their choice of candidate, but they did it, and Roosevelt went to Chicago with the popular vote of Kansas in his pocket. He also had in that same pocket the popular vote of every state in the United States whose people had been permitted to express a choice.

Taft went to Chicago secure in the knowledge that he who controls the national committee controls the credentials committee, and that he who controls the credentials committee controls the convention. Both men knew that. Roosevelt himself had used the same tactics in 1908 when he had forced a reluctant convention to accept Taft as his own candidate.[62] The convention had then thumbed its nose at Roosevelt by nominating arch-conservative James S. Sherman of New York as its vice-presidential candidate.[63]

As the climax of the struggle approached, the battle to come took on a classic pattern. The Taft forces held the castle of power, secure in the efficacy of the intricate war-engines of convention. The Roosevelt forces, mostly foot-soldiers from the Midwest, were to attack the castle repeatedly, noisily, and with little effect.

7

The Battle

As if he did not have enough to do, William Allen White contracted to cover the 1912 Republican National Convention for the George Matthew Adams Newspaper Service, and so he split himself in two. He had been successful in his fight to be elected National Committeeman from Kansas, and he had come to Chicago a week early, not only to file two stories a day about the pre-convention activities, but also to participate vigorously in those activities.[1]

It was probably a good thing that he had two jobs, for their pressures balanced each other. As a delegate, he headquartered at the Congress Hotel, the GHQ of the Roosevelt forces. As a newspaperman, he had working space at the Stratford Hotel with the rest of what he called George Adams' trained seals, cartoonists, Harry Webster and J. N. Darling, novelist George Fitch, and a girl reporter still in her twenties named Edna Ferber.[2] At convention headquarters, White was all a-bustle, helping get the Roosevelt forces organized. At the Stratford, the Adams crew worked together telling their readers the story of the most violent power struggle within a major political party in the history of American politics. It was a confusing and emotion-laden story.

The way White remembered that convention presents in capsule the way he grew to see the world and what he persisted in calling the revolution in which he participated. The air was filled with tension all that week as the delegates arrived. There was about the midwestern Roosevelt contingent a belligerency carried over from bitterly fought state campaigns, particularly in Kansas, in Missouri, where baseball bats had been in evidence, and in Oklahoma, where six-shooters had been kept handy for persuasion.[3]

There was also in the Progressive contingent a revivalist fervor reminiscent of the hymn-singing militancy of the Populists. Just as Ignatius Donnelly had aroused the Populists in the Omaha Populist convention of 1892,[4] so in 1912 Theodore Roosevelt, in an unprecedented preconvention speech to his followers, "churned the crowd," to use White's words. For three-quarters of an hour, he pulled out every stop against the "malefactors of great wealth," the thieving Regulars of the Republican party, and all the black beasts that the Progressives had inherited from the Populists. Then, having wound them up to their highest pitch, he sent his troops out to do battle with a ready-made motto for their battle-flag: "We stand at Armageddon and we battle for the Lord!"[5]

White had a front seat for the Armageddon speech, and he also covered the daily oratorical marathon going on in the Florentine room of the Congress Hotel. There, speakers from all over the country harangued the steamy crowds, whipping them up, and at the same time letting off steam themselves. The newspapers of the day reported fisticuffs on the streets and brawls in the bar rooms.[6] It was an explosive time. White wrote that both he and his friend William E. Borah had been more than a little frightened by the Armageddon speech. They felt somewhat as if they were walking on top of a sleeping volcano.[7]

White tried to analyze Roosevelt's reasons for coming to Chicago that week and for making a speech—that speech—in the Auditorium that muggy Friday night. Hatred of Taft was part of the reason, White thought, and fear of losing, perhaps, but never ambition. "Ambition, I am satisfied," he wrote, "was not the governing passion. . . . He would have compromised at any stage in the game if he could have saved his face by compromising."[8] Yet Roosevelt was to have his chance to compromise, and White was to be there to see it. It was, from the point of view of preserving the Progressive movement and keeping it in Republican hands, the only thing to do. Roosevelt, for once, acted like La Follette and preferred no bread at all to half a loaf.

William Allen White had a habit, however, of casting his hero in his own image. The political philosophy of Theodore Roosevelt that White extracted in his autobiography from the Armageddon speech is actually

White's philosophy, reiterated not only in the autobiography, but also in White's editorials, and explicitly or implicitly in all of his books of nonfiction. It can be found in *The Old Order Changeth,* in *Masks in a Pageant,* and in *Politics: The Citizen's Business,* and it is the thesis of *Some Cycles of Cathay* and at least a secondary theme in *The Changing West.*

White based that philosophy on what he called the third revolution. It was not a class war, labor against capital and management. Rather, it was the revolt of a middle class made up of small businessmen and professional people against both the power structure of finance and industry and the power structure of big labor. It was a revolution whose main weapon was social legislation. That legislation would make it possible for the broad middle class to be masters of their own political and social destiny. It would also make it possible for capable members of the lower economic class to migrate to the middle class and prevent potential plutocrats from migrating out of that middle class. Carried to its logical conclusion, White's middle-class revolution would bring about a one-class society, or a classless society whose base was the middle class rather than the proletariat.[9]

White said that this was also Roosevelt's philosophy, yet unconsciously, in his analysis of Roosevelt's position, he illustrated the difference between that position and his own. "The point I am trying to make," White wrote,

> –and I am sure it was the point of his Armageddon speech–is that that Roosevelt movement of the second decade of this century was not a class movement. It was a middle-class revolt against the injustice of our society, our industrial organization, our economic establishment, our political institutions. In so far as it had a proletarian angle, it expressed a big brother's pity, and attempted to implement his mercy toward the lesser and weaker members of his tribe and clan.[10]

It surely was not a class revolution. In those terms, it was no revolution at all, but a matter of Big Brother's assuming his burden. If White saw his "revolution" in this light, he missed the irony of it entirely. It is unlikely, however, that any of Roosevelt's hearers that night analyzed the speech. For them, it was an exhortation to do battle. The gauntlet had been thrown down. It was not all as cut and dried as White made it sound in his two-sentence report on the behind-the-scenes action before the opening of the convention. "The credentials committee had done its work," he wrote. "It had seated enough contested delegates to nominate Taft."[11] That is what happened, and that is what the regular organization of the Republican party had set out to make happen, but the organization had had some uneasy moments.

The Taft forces had used patronage, or the threat of its withdrawal, as a weapon, and several of the state delegations pledged to Taft were held together by that pressure and by other pressures. Taft was not dramatic; he did not command the loyalty amounting to dedication that Roosevelt commanded, and there was some fear in the Taft camp that a voting force held together by external pressure might explode in the direction of Roosevelt before the convention had nominated a candidate. Besides, there were sixty-two Negro delegates whose votes were in doubt to the last minute.[12]

Even though the credentials committee had done its work well, as White said, the fight was not over. Immediately after Victor Rosewater, acting head of the National Committee, called the convention to order, Governor Herbert Hadley of Missouri moved to substitute seventy Roosevelt delegates for seventy Taft delegates among the contested seats at the convention. Rosewater ruled the motion out of order and proceeded to the election of a permanent chairman.[13]

Against the advice of some of his lieutenants, Roosevelt decided to make a contest of the election.[14] The Taft candidate was Elihu Root, who had been a more or less intimate member of the Roosevelt official family. Now, however, Roosevelt said, he was a "representative of reaction."[15] He could not be allowed to take the chairmanship of the convention unopposed. After Hadley had refused to be the Roosevelt candidate, Roosevelt attempted to heal the breach between himself and La Follette by naming Wisconsin Governor Francis McGovern his candidate. The move did Roosevelt little good. In fact, he was forced to name McGovern over the objection of La Follette, and when the vote came, White said, the Wisconsin delegates "heroically deserted."[16] The other La Follette delegates followed Wisconsin's lead, and Elihu Root became permanent chairman of the 1912 Republican National Convention by a vote of 558 to 502, with only 29 more votes than he needed for a bare majority.[17]

It had been a noisy convention before this, with Roosevelt men shouting "thief" and "liar" and accusing the Taft men of every kind of larceny on the statute books and the Taft men returning the compliment. Now there was pandemonium indeed. No single speaker could shout down the passionate roar of the delegates, and many a speaker retired to his seat defeated by sheer noise.[18]

Through it all, gray, patrician Elihu Root stood calm and imperturbable, letting the sound roll over him and off him, knowing he had the controls in his hand. He knew, for one thing, that there were nearly a thousand policemen in the hall. From his place in the press gallery, White saw "the cordon of police that ran like a blue smear around the buff upturned faces of the delegates."[19] White knew that Root, as chairman of the convention, was also commander of that cordon of police, and could have called them into action with a gesture.[20] What White did not know until after the convention was that the rostrum railing had been wound with barbed wire before it had been draped with bunting.[21]

If ever the phrase "impotent rage" was appropriate, it was now. Only two men at that convention, apparently, had the presence or the respect of the delegates to make themselves heard over the roar of that rage. One was Elihu Root. The other was Roosevelt's floor leader, Herbert Hadley. Root was in the chair. He had command, and the delegates listened to him. They listened to Hadley because they liked this boyish, quietly humorous man who went calmly about the business of doing their business while they roared.

Hadley's first business, as soon as Root was installed in the chair, was to move again to seat the seventy Roosevelt delegates to the contested places in the convention.[22] That started what passed for debate again, and when the roar had subsided, Root had referred the motion to the Committee on Credentials, thus assigning it to oblivion. Then Governor Charles S. Deneen of Illinois moved that no contested delegate be allowed to vote on any of the contests. Before the vote, Root pointed out that prohibiting contested delegates to vote on the contest would make it possible for any minority to control any group simply by contesting enough seats.[23] Nevertheless, when the motion came to a vote on the floor, it lost by only twenty-four votes, 564 to 540. It was closer than the organization would have liked. In fact, the organization came within thirteen votes of defeat.[24]

Still, the margin of victory makes no difference. It is the victory that counts—or the defeat—and that defeat just about put an end to Roosevelt's chances for the Republican presidential nomination. There was still the Resolutions Committee, where the actions of the pre-convention committees were to be made permanent, but the Taft forces had taken no chances there, either. They had not only stacked the committee, they also limited discussion on any contested case to ten minutes.[25]

White sat through the whole streamrolling process, and in the midst of all the anger and recrimination and bitterness, he remembered this: ". . . every time a motion was offered by the Taft people, a thousand toots and imitation whistles of the steamroller engine pierced the air sharply, to be greeted with laughter that swept the galleries. An American crowd," said White, "will have a terrible time behind barricades, or surging up Pennsylvania Avenue to overwhelm the White House. It will probably laugh itself to death on the way." [26]

Some were not laughing, though. Theodore Roosevelt was "becoming deadly as his defeat approached," said White.[27] White was writing his news stories, wriggling in and out of the Florentine Room to pick up this backstage tidbit and that, caucusing with the Kansas delegation—all but two districts of which was solidly for Roosevelt, he remembered—and talking with Roosevelt.[28]

After the report of the Resolutions Committee, there was nowhere for Roosevelt to go but out, if he wanted to stay in business. Given the acrimony of the pre-convention campaign and of the convention itself, given the fact that he felt robbed of the nomination—and some historians would give him as many as fifty of the contested delegates—[29] Roosevelt could not have supported Taft. He was convinced that he had a mandate from the rank-and-file of the Republican party to be the party candidate for President.

In a way, Roosevelt built his own box. White said that he did not think ambition was the ruling passion behind Roosevelt's Armageddon speech. Yet until Taft's nomination was official, even after the bolt, couriers on both sides of the fight had attempted to get the principals to settle on a compromise candidate. The Taft forces would have accepted Governor Hadley. Hadley had endeared himself to the convention to the point that it gave him a standing ovation at one point in the proceedings. Roosevelt professed to favor Hadley, but he would accept no compromise that was not based on the seating of all the disputed Roosevelt delegates.[30] Considering the temper of the Roosevelt delegates and the nature of Roosevelt himself, it does not take much political acuity to guess who the Republican candidate would have been if Roosevelt had gotten his delegates.

As intimate as he was with Roosevelt and the Roosevelt circle, White must have known of this not-too-subtle maneuver, yet he is strangely silent about it in his letters and his published writing. In this one instance, not only does he make no attempt to justify Roosevelt's actions, he does not even mention them.

With the Hadley compromise aborted and with Hadley's parliamentary wriggling finally stopped short by the report of the Resolutions Committee, the bolt became inevitable. White says he rejected the idea at first. He says also that he rejected the idea of a third party, at first.[31] But as he had done several times before, after advising Roosevelt against a course he must have known Roosevelt was set on taking, he followed him. "He knew I would follow," White added.[32]

And so, when the convention was called to order on Saturday morning, Henry J. Allen, White's long-time friend and the chairman of the Kansas delegation, stood up, and in a speech that dripped irony all over them, bade the Taft delegates farewell for the entire Roosevelt contingent. Then all the Roosevelt delegates rose and marched out of the building, with as much dignity, said White, "as men of wrath can assume in defeat."[33]

White had a big story to write, the biggest political story of his political career—almost. For while he was writing the story of the Roosevelt bolt, filing his story, and then eating a large and leisurely meal to supplement the hot dogs and soda pop on which he had sustained himself all day, the rest of the Roosevelt delegates had met at Orchestra Hall, organized the Progressive party, listened to a "ripsnorting" speech from Roosevelt, and were off and running. The biggest political story of William Allen White's newspaper career was only the second-biggest story of the day. And it was too late to file another story.[34]

White had resigned as national Republican committeeman with the walkout, for two good reasons, he said: "First, we wanted to hold the Kansas end of the Republican national committee, and I would not even pretend to support Taft under the wicked circumstances which surrounded his nomination; second, we elected a good smiling Republican, who would go through the motions of supporting Taft with some sincerity and who was nevertheless politically aligned to our faction in Kansas."[35]

White had nothing to lose by joining the Roosevelt bolt. Though he was in politics up to his eyebrows and was expert enough at it to be a professional, his living did not depend on his political success or failure. Such was not the case with many other Roosevelt backers, and they had protested mightily before the break finally came. Herbert Hadley parted political company with Roosevelt when Roosevelt bolted, but

Hadley had more than political livelihood to prompt him.[36] Some of Roosevelt's convention supporters drifted back to Taft, and some were eventually to support Wilson.[37]

Though he said little about it, and though he had little or nothing to lose by it, White must have had some deep misgivings when he bolted with his Colonel. The Republican party had been William Allen White's political faith, and it was to be again. White had built his throne-room political career on party loyalty. Now, for all of America to see, he was disowning the party. He was breaking with the organization that had given him power and influence far beyond his station. When he bolted, he lost most of that power. If he knew what he was doing, he had to be troubled, and he must have known. He was, "of course," as he said, made national committeeman of the new party.[38] He records in his autobiography that he wanted the new party, not so that Roosevelt could be a presidential candidate in 1912, but to "hold him as our ace. . . . I did not want Roosevelt to bolt nor to run independently without the new party."[39] He wanted the new party as a protection for Roosevelt, yet it was a long time before he could be persuaded to put the new party on the ticket in Kansas as the Progressive party rather than the Progressive-Republican party.[40]

Another thing bothered him there in Chicago as the bolters completed their business and headed home to plant some Progressive grass-roots. That was the presence of George Perkins, the partner of J. P. Morgan. "He was too close to the Colonel," White recorded, "and we . . . Beveridge, Bristow, Amos and Gifford Pinchot, Hiram Johnson, Dolliver, Cummins, Senator Clapp, Senator Bourne, Hadley, Harold Ickes, Governor Osborn of Michigan, the New England crowd, and the New Jersey Progressives following George Record and Everett Colby—were not so close to the Colonel as we should have been that day nor, to peek ahead a little, in that campaign."[41]

What White did not realize, or if he did realize it, he did not record it, was that before he made the final decision to bolt the Republican party, Theodore Roosevelt had gone to this same George Perkins and to Frank Munsey, and Perkins and Munsey had pledged financial support for the Progressive campaign.[42] If he had known it, it probably would not have made any difference. He must follow where his Colonel led. He was on an emotional binge with the rest of the Progressives, and they were off to do battle for the Lord and for "social and industrial justice."

8

Bull Moose Rampant

Somehow, in the midst of that hectic summer of 1912, White found two weeks to spend in the cabin which the White family had recently bought in Colorado, a cabin which was to become a summer house and a yearly place of refuge and rejuvenation. By now young Bill and Mary were like true extensions of their parents, he bookish but athletic, too, loving the fields and streams and mountains; she coming out of her babyhood frailness, lively, impish, voracious for life. White had to squeeze those two weeks in between helping lay the groundwork for the Progressive party in Kansas, running his own newspaper, joining the Adams syndicate crew again to cover the Democratic national convention in Baltimore in July, going back to Chicago in August to attend the national convention of the Progressive party as committeeman, and then getting back to Kansas to run the Progressive campaign there.[1] He was a bouncingly busy man, and he apparently loved every minute of it.

He saw the Democratic convention as a rerun of the Republican convention, with variations. All the conservatives in the party, including the southern delegates who represented two-fifths of the voting strength of the convention, supported Champ Clark. The liberal wing of the party—once Bryan had made a futile and foredoomed gesture toward a fourth nomination—supported Woodrow Wilson.[2]

White did not like Wilson personally. He found him cold and "highty-tighty."[3] There are also evidences, particularly in the biography of

Wilson that he wrote in 1924,[4] that he did not trust Wilson politically. After all, the man was a Democrat, and a Southern, Bourbon Democrat at that. At the Democratic convention, however, White could rejoice in the nomination of Wilson over Clark. For, though he was a Democrat, Wilson was a Progressive. White could even praise the losers for closing ranks behind Wilson after they had lost the long and bitter fight for the nomination.[5] It was something that neither he nor the other Progressives had done after the nomination of Taft, and one wonders if White's words would have been the same if Clark had won the nomination and the Wilson forces had closed ranks behind Clark.

In the midst of his remembering the Democratic convention of 1912, White provided a glimpse of the way he saw himself and his role in American politics–and it is a strange glimpse. "Having a rather sketchy Republican loyalty," he wrote, "I was naturally for a situation that would bring liberal victories in both parties."[6] From the time he met Theodore Roosevelt, it was ever thus with William Allen White. Through the nominations, he would support the liberal candidate of the Republican party, when there was one, and the liberal candidate of the Democratic party. Except in 1912, however, when he could persuade himself that Theodore Roosevelt was the real candidate of the rank and file of Republicans, White voted for the Republican ticket straight down the line. His first political tenet was always party responsibility and party loyalty. His real power in politics was at the state level, and Kansas was a Republican state. He would work with liberals and conservatives, with bosses and reformers, so long as they were Republicans. He believed, though it was not precisely true, that Kansas represented the end of the lava flow of New England puritanism; and he saw himself, once he had been converted to Roosevelt insurgency, as a puritan in politics, an agency of purification from within.[7]

That was why it was so hard for him to give up the last vestiges of the party machinery that he had worked with since he was eighteen, and that was why, when he did cut away, he insisted on the same kind of party loyalty among the newly calved Bull Moosers. In 1912, he did have "rather sketchy Republican loyalty." But that loyalty was not so weakened that White would ever support a Democratic candidate, however much he would prefer the Democrat's program, or even his candidacy, over a Republican program and candidate.

So he could safely write his Adams syndicate dispatches from Baltimore with a Progressive slant. In the battle between Clark and Wilson, he would rejoice in the nomination of Wilson. His choice here had nothing to do with party loyalty. As for his position in the Progressive party, White and a number of other old hands considered the Progressive wing of the Republican party the party itself, as long as it was still alive and functioning. In effect, it was not the Bull Moosers who had bolted. The party regulars had made the break, had turned their backs on the wishes of the great majority of voters in the Republican party.[8]

So White stood on a table in the press gallery and cheered himself hoarse as the vote for Wilson finally tipped over the necessary two-thirds majority. Then he went home to help Roosevelt defeat Wilson.

"It was no easy job," White wrote, "when I got back from Baltimore, to assume my part of the leadership which was organized in Kansas from the grass-roots of the Progressive party in the campaign that was looming ahead of us."[9] That is all he said about the difficulties, but they were apparent from the letters he received. Those letters represented a reprise of the arguments that had been going on in Kansas between the regulars and the insurgents since 1908. On the one hand, there were those who protested that, though the Progressives might be right in their desire for "social justice," they were "progressing too far and too fast."[10] There were others who had much stronger objections to the Progressive program, who called the Progressives "the party of the red bandana."[11] Then there were regulars who were simply bewildered by White's actions. "Why is it," wrote a St. Mary's, Kansas, lawyer to White, "that men of your caliber 'get off' in this fashion, or rather in this no fashion? No man can say that you have been insincere in the past, no man can say that you are not a thinker; then why on earth don't you 'stay put'? Politics," added Bryon C. Mitchner, "are as bad as the times require. . . ."[12]

On the other hand, there were those, of whom C. C. Isley of Cimarron, Kansas, was typical, who called for a real Progressive party rather than Progressive Republican so that "we could go ahead and appeal to Democrats to join in the deal as a brand new deal."[13]

In another letter, Isley said that he would like to vote for Wilson, but that "voting an old party ticket of any kind a person is handicapped by being loaded up with a lot of fellows who are not interested in the things which interest us." Isley was also a seer of sorts. He added, "Wilson's nomination will probably defeat some good Progressive Republican Congressman which it ought not to do."[14]

Then there were those like O. Elsizer of Elmsdale, Kansas, who had some specific questions he wanted answered about Roosevelt's actions and activities at the Chicago convention:

> 1. Why did not former President Roosevelt favor Sen. La Follette for President?. . .
>
> 2. I would like a better explanation of the reason he gives for seeking the nomination this time after having said he did not want it four years ago.
>
> 3. Why was he not in favor of Gov. Hadley as a compromise candidate when he saw that it would unite the party and at the same time have a progressive candidate?[15]

To add to the confusion these samples of White's correspondence indicate, White himself was writing letters opposing the formation of a third party as such as late as July 23, 1912.[16] Understandably, it was no easy job for him to go back to Kansas and begin to help organize a Progressive campaign.

But he did go back. He and the other Progressive leaders in Kansas held their county conventions and their caucuses and made Henry Allen, who had been chairman of the Republican delegation from Kansas, chairman of the Kansas delegation to the first national convention of the Progressive party.

But there was a great deal of work to be done before the convention gathered in Chicago in the middle of August. In the first place, the Progressives had to make sure that Roosevelt had a place on the ballot for the August 6 primaries. The Kansas delegation had been pledged to Roosevelt before the Republican convention, and through the votes of the county conventions, Kansas electors had been pledged to Roosevelt in the national election. The same thing had happened in a number of Progressive states where the Progressives, who controlled the state Republican organization, had gotten pledged electors through what amounted to preferential primaries before the national convention.[17]

The Taft Republicans used two weapons to fight the Progressive maneuver. They petitioned for a place on the ballot for the convention-nominated candidate, and in some instances, they sought injunctions to keep the Roosevelt electors off the ballot.[18]

It was a sticky business in Kansas, because if Roosevelt could not appear on the ballot under the Republican label, or at least under the label of the Progressive Republicans, he would have to run as an independent. Under Kansas election law, the Progressive party would have had to be in existence by May to have secured a place on the ballot.[19]

Even though Taft had won the nomination in Chicago, the Roosevelt supporters in Kansas maintained that they had squatters' rights on the November ballot. The Republican electors in Kansas had been pledged, not to the eventual convention nominee, but to Theodore Roosevelt. Therefore, in Kansas, and in the other states where quasi-primaries had been held before the convention, Taft supporters petitioned to replace the Roosevelt electors on the general election ballot with electors pledged to Taft, as the duly nominated candidate.[20]

To fight this maneuver, Kansas Congressman Victor Murdock drew up a resolution, which the Kansas Progressives adopted. The resolution contained a sharp but rather obvious fish hook. It called for the Kansas voters to decide between the Taft and Roosevelt electors in the August 6 Republican primary election.[21] White prepared a news release incorporating Murdock's resolution, adding his own interpretation of the rationale of that resolution. "The constitution of the United States," he wrote, "leaves to each state its own method of expressing its choice for presidential candidates. In Kansas, the legislature has prescribed that we shall express our choice through a primary election. . . . Electors were regularly named in the Republican state and district conventions . . . and were instructed . . . as Roosevelt men. They have neither the legal nor the moral right to withdraw from the race."[22] The Taft people raised the issue, White pointed out, when Mortimer Albaugh and Dave Mulvane, two old-line Kansas Republican powers, asked that the Taft electors be put on the ballot by petition. "When these gentlemen did this," White wrote, "they recognized the right of these conventions to nominate these Roosevelt electors."[23] Whichever side lost in the primary, White argued, would still get on the November ballot by petition.

White touched all the bases in his statement. "The fact that the Progressive party may nominate Mr. Roosevelt at Chicago," said he, "does not obliterate the fact in Kansas, that he is a Progressive Republican, as we recognize Progressive Republicanism. A majority of more than 2,000,000 Republican voters at the primaries made him the real choice of the nation, as a Progressive Republican candidate, and we continue in Kansas to recognize him as a Progressive Republican candidate."[24]

If White's statement represents the thinking of the Kansas Progressive Republicans, they were a gymnastic lot. While they were touching all bases, they were also trying to keep their cake and eat it at the same time. White pointed out that the Roosevelt supporters could not run their candidate on a third party ticket if they wanted to, not only because of the law about filing in May, but also because "he is now the choice of the Progressive Republicans of Kansas." Those two facts, he said, made "our situation perfectly clear and logical, and our duty plain."[25]

For all that, the Taft forces were not having any, thank you. The hook showed through the bait. Why should they enter into a contest to decide who should be the Republican nominee for President? They had already done that, in Chicago, and they had won. What the regular Republicans had to do now was to get on the November ballot themselves and to prevent the Progressive Republican candidates from being on the ballot in the Republican column. They obtained injunctions to keep the Progressives out of the Republican column, and one of White's jobs was to help raise money to defend against the injunctions and to work with a committee of Progressive lawyers to deal with the injunction suits.[26] Meantime, the Kansas press was supporting the Roosevelt candidacy almost unanimously,[27] and the office of *The Emporia Gazette* had become, to all intents and purposes, the publicity clearinghouse for the Kansas Progressive Republican campaign.[28]

The August 6 primary was a clear-cut victory for the Progressive Republicans. But the Regulars were not dead yet. Not only did they still have recourse to the courts, but before the battle was over, the Roosevelt electors had resigned.[29]

There were other weather signals, too. The day after the primary, White received a letter from George Matthew Adams. Adams said he could not get newspapers in his string to handle Progressive copy "because they felt there was not enough general interest in the Convention to spend any money on it outside of their own men. It made me sore," Adams continued, "because the papers that have been so loud for Roosevelt took so little interest in these stories. . . ." On the other hand, he said he finally got them all "but the *New York Mail, Cleveland Leader* and *Pittsburg Leader,"*[30] and he had picked up the *Pittsburg Post* to substitute for the *Leader.* White now attended his third national convention in one year, twice in the double role of reporter and delegate.

That White had any doubt about Roosevelt's being the Progressive party candidate, as indicated by his statement attached to the Murdock resolution, seems fairly unreasonable. He may not have wanted Roosevelt to run in 1912 as a Progressive, but there was no other Progressive candidate on the horizon. The chances are that if Roosevelt had not run, George Perkins and Frank Munsey would have withdrawn their financial support. Besides, the party was tailored to Roosevelt's candidacy from the beginning.

Also from the beginning, the party suffered from schizophrenia. There were the reformers of every stripe on one side, and those who wanted to control the reform, to make sure their particular ox was not gored, on the other. Unfortunately for the health of the party, Theodore Roosevelt was apparently using it chiefly to vent his wrath at Taft and at being outmaneuvered in the convention, and he began to have second thoughts about a third party almost as soon as he had officiated at its birth.[31] Unfortunately for the party, the reformers needed the controllers a good deal more than the controllers needed the reformers, and what the controllers wanted was bound to color the deliberations of the convention.[32]

Even White had his doubts. He knew of the influence of George W. Perkins, and he called the chapter on Perkins in his autobiography "Enter A Smiling Villain," but he did not at the time of the convention, nor when he came to write his autobiography, seem to realize how close Roosevelt and Perkins were on questions like the tariff and anti-trust legislation. He distrusted Perkins so much because of the Morgan influence that he would not use one sheet of the Perkins-inspired Progressive party propaganda;[33] but, to look ahead a bit, he would not support Gifford Pinchot's attempt to get Perkins fired.[34] As a matter of fact, he wrote to Roosevelt at the time of the Pinchot-Perkins feud:

> I have not changed my opinion of the wisdom of putting Mr. Perkins at the head of the executive committee since I favored it in Chicago in August, 1912. For I believed then and I believe now that it was infinitely better since he was going to give his time and money to us, that we take it publicly, giving him public status rather than to accept it secretly and as though we were ashamed of it. . . . I have not found myself in wide disagreement with the Perkins position on the trusts, [White added] except in matters of emphasis and phraseology. Neither am I worried because he is a Wall Street man; for it takes all kinds of men to make a party, and decent men from every walk of life are

needed. [Then White added, almost, it seems, as an afterthought,] His position on organized labor as stated by his enemies seems to be unfortunate, but the facts may modify it.[35]

According to that letter, written in June 1914, White had favored the appointment of Perkins as head of the executive committee of the Progressive party when it met in convention in Chicago in August 1912. In fact, in another communication, White says he nominated Perkins for the job.[36] Writing in his autobiography, White said of Perkins at that convention, "He and his satellites and sycophants from Wall Street and lower Broadway, who had known Roosevelt in Harvard, loved him and misunderstood him; but they had their influence. Sometimes I felt even then the weight of their influence bore too heavily on the scales of his decisions."[37]

As suspicious as he was of Perkins and of Perkins' motives, it was still William Allen White who nominated him for the executive position. It was a matter of party. White was to express the idea best in a letter written in December 1914: "I fancy there are just as many tax dodgers and skinflints and horse thieves in the Progressive party as there are in any other party," he said. "But the tax dodgers and skinflints and scoundrels in the Democratic party believe in the principles of the Democratic party; and the tax dodgers, and skinflints and horse thieves in the Republican party believe in the principles of the Republican party, and our stinkers believe in our principles. So I have no objection to working with a man who is not a lovely character, in my own party," White concluded, "provided he believes as I do. But I have objected to working with exactly the same type of man in another party, because he does not believe as I do."[38]

For the rest, the make-up of the convention suited White very well. It was his kind of crowd. He enjoyed being radical, but he enjoyed it most when he could be radical and be understood in the bosom of the middle class. He contrasted the delegates he remembered from the Populist conventions with the delegates at the Progressive convention, and the contrast made him feel good.

Populists had been "the misfits–farmers who had failed, lawyers and doctors who were not orthodox, teachers who could not make the grade, and neurotics full of hates and ebullient, evanescent enthusiams." The Progressives were a different matter altogether. "Here were the successful middle-class country-town citizens, the farmer whose barn was painted, the well paid railroad engineer, and the country editor. It was a well dressed crowd. . . . Looking over the crowd, judging the delegates by their clothes, I figured that there was not a man or woman on the floor who was making less than two thousand a year, and not one, on the other hand, who was topping ten thousand. Proletarian and plutocrat were absent—except George Perkins. . . .[39]

William Allen White's insistence on the middle-class respectability of his revolution was his anchor to windward. It was fun to be a radical, but it was also good to have something to come home to. This is not to say that White was insincere in his desire for social reform. He fought for every social reform that was in the air at a time when ideas for reform swarmed as thick as moths around a street light, and he continued to fight long after a world war had intervened and sapped the fervor from the reform movement. But as he developed the idea of reform, he further developed the idea that the only successful social and political revolutions developed out of the moral indignation of the middle class.

So he went to Chicago almost a week before the convening of the Progressive party, sat on the platform drafting committee, and was able to incorporate much of the 1910 Kansas Progressive platform into the national platform for the 1912 campaign. He also tried, and failed, to include a prohibition plank.[40] As a matter of fact, it would seem that nearly every member of the drafting committee had come to Chicago with a ready-made platform in his pocket. It also seems that Roosevelt approved each of those ready-made platforms as it was brought to him.[41]

The platform as it finally appeared was a reiteration of the Progressive ideas that had been bubbling in the country since 1896. "For that day," said White, "it was radical."[42] There was one new plank which, in 1912, seemed to peek into a dangerous future. It called for limitation of armament and a limit of two battleships a year while arms limitation negotiations went on.[43] As might have been expected, in view of the heterogeneous nature of the party, the two planks in the platform that caused trouble had to do with the tariff and with antitrust legislation. The tariff problem was finally resolved with a plank that looked forward to a tariff commission, but the antitrust plank almost cost the Progressive party its financial backing.

The plank White and others of those he called left-wing Progressives wanted called for a list of specific activities that would be subject to court action under the anti-trust provision. The plank George W. Perkins and his supporters wanted was what White called "a general definition of the kind of antisocial conduct that should be indictable." The plank went back for compromise, and White's group thought that the language had been made sufficiently ambiguous that it could be adopted. Nevertheless, when the chairman of the platform committee read the antitrust plank, George Perkins stalked out of the convention, "a one-man bolt," as White said. The afternoon papers carried the compromise plank, but the morning papers carried the Perkins plank; Perkins was mollified and brought his money back into the Progressive party.[44]

For all his high-wire balancing act, White seems to have assessed the Perkins wing of the Progressive party correctly. To them this new party was no new party at all, but a vehicle by which they could recapture the Republican party for their friend Theodore Roosevelt.

That was only the major crack in the structure of the newly cemented party. The party itself was made up of contingents whose major interests covered the whole field of reform legislation and social welfare. Each group had its own pet project, and some groups looked askance at the pet projects of others. There were some, of course, like William Allen White, who performed the prodigious feat of riding all the reform horses at once, but the nature of the performance itself made the performers a minority among minorities.

Even so, the platform was finally hammered out and approved. Because the hammering had taken so long, the convention had gone ahead and, to no one's surprise, had nominated Theodore Roosevelt for President and Hiram Johnson of California for Vice-President. The delegates showed that they had not lost the revivalist fervor of their cause as they went out to carry the word to the grass-roots singing "Onward Christian Soldiers."[45]

White says in his autobiography that when the time came after the adjournment of the convention to organize the national central committee, he opposed vigorously the election of George Perkins as chairman of the executive committee. He quotes O. K. Davis, Perkins' publicity agent, to that effect in Davis' *Released for Publication.*[46] He remembers a letter from Harold Ickes to that effect, a letter written thirty years after the event. But his letters from 1912 to 1914, alternately supporting and damning Perkins, indicate that White had supported Perkins, had even, according to a telegram he sent to Roosevelt in 1914, nominated Perkins himself.[47] No wonder White bewildered his contemporaries. No wonder Davis wrote of him that he "is so progressive that he never is long in any one place politically. . . ."[48] There can be no doubt, however, that much as White reconciled himself to working with Perkins, he still went out of the convention hall after the singing of the Doxology and went home to organize the Kansas Progressive campaign, determined to have as little to do with the chairman of the executive committee as possible.

Some time in late August or early September, the Kansas secretary of state ruled in favor of the Taft electors, and White wrote to the Roosevelt electors to ask them to resign and go into the Independent column.

In a letter to E. M. Blomberg of Benton, Kansas, in which he explained all this, White added, ". . . We cannot compromise now and we cannot dilly-dally any longer. Some decisive action had to be taken and from reports I have heard from all over the state, I feel satisfied that this is the best thing to do. . . . I have nothing personally to gain in this fight one way or the other. I am putting the best there is in me and giving all of my time to this and will not get a cent out of it, and I stand to lose a good many hundred dollars."[49] Though he was accused of ordering the electors to resign, the letters show that he merely suggested the resignations. Moreover, seven of the eight Roosevelt electors had already resigned by the time White got around to writing the letters.[50]

Nevertheless, White was the kingpin of the Progressives in Kansas and he began to get letters addressed to Boss White and carrying salutations like "Dear Old Benevolent Dictator."[51] There was considerable disappointment among some of the faithful that the Roosevelt electors had been asked to resign and had done so. White had to point out, in letter after letter, and in the midst of getting the Kansas campaign for Roosevelt underway, that there was nothing else he could have done under the circumstances. The strange thing was that he did not suggest that candidates at lower levels move over into the Independent column, too. Or maybe it was not so strange. Ever since the first faint rumblings about a third party began to be heard in the sky over Progressive country, there had been those whose political lives were at stake who were fearful of making a complete break with the Republican party. White pointed out to his questioners that the only other thing he could have done would have been to take the case of the electors into court, and he doubted if the Supreme Court would or could act on the case before October, by which time it would be too late to do the Progressive cause any good at the polls. Meantime, he said, any other candidate who wished to was at liberty to move into the Independent column. It was, for all practical purposes, he said, the Bull Moose column.[52]

Some of White's correspondents found his methods a bit high-handed, and congressional candidate John H. Crider circulated an open letter titled "The Political Boss Revived in Kansas." "Now I am from conviction a progressive Republican," wrote Crider, "and have supported progressive Republican candidates in the primary and Mr. Roosevelt in the late primary, but I am not going to declare for 'Roosevelt electors on a Republican ticket' . . . I am not going to do this because it is supposed to be popular or because I want to go to Congress or to get the favor of Boss White or any other boss."[53]

There was some justification for White's enemies, and even his jibing friends, to call him Boss White that summer and fall. He was highly visible in the political market place. One of the first things he did after returning from Chicago was to put out a campaign letter under a Progressive party letterhead, announcing that he was national committeeman for Kansas in that party, and asking for a ten- to fifteen-thousand-dollar campaign fund.[54] He was determined not to take a cent from the national committee, because he suspected that the national committee's money came out of the pocket of George Perkins. If he did not take any of Perkins' money, then he could without qualm refuse the bales of Perkins-inspired—sometimes Perkins-written—publicity handouts. And he did. He also wrote circular letters to farmers' groups, railroad labor unions, and church leaders, both white and negro. He checked with J. N. Dolley, chairman of the Republican State Committee about a list of "a dozen reliable colored men." Dolley assured White that he was already working on the idea, trying to set up organizations of negro Republicans in several counties.[55]

He wrote to Professor Ernest Hewins of Fort Scott, Kansas:

> I would like greatly to see a model Progressive colored organization in Ft. Scott. You are the man to put this through. . . . This fight of ours is the same great fight that started over nineteen hundred years ago. It is that great dark cry of the masses asking for that which is rightfully theirs. We believe that with our broad platform, with our specific

promises, with the record and standing of our leaders, that we are fitted to advance this cause more in the next ten years than it has advanced in the last century.[56]

White thanked a Union Army veteran for a list of Old Soldiers' Homes and asked the veteran to canvass the homes for him for workers and votes.[57] He handled the printing of nomination papers to get a Progressive ticket before the Kansas voters. Besides the daily and weekly outlets for his material, and besides the weekly column he wrote for the *Kansas City Star*, another weekly column for the *Chicago Tribune,* and material for Will Irwin's "highbrow Bull Moose syndicate,"[58] White got such papers as the *Christian Baptist Herald* in Topeka to run his campaign material.[59] He went after the Jewish vote in Leavenworth, Wichita, and Kansas City, tried to arrange for Jewish orators and for campaign literature in Hebrew.[60] He wrote to Arthur McNay of Galena, Kansas, asking about the possibility of French, German, Swedish, and Austrian speakers in the Galena mining district.[61] He was consulted about getting Pinchot and Roosevelt and Beveridge to speak in Kansas.[62] He himself spoke in the state.

He remembered the summer as a mad and happy time. The response to all this activity was generally enthusiastic, although there was some dissent. One voter wrote that if he thought Roosevelt had any real chance of election, he would vote for him. As it was, he said, he was going to vote for Wilson to get the Progressive program. He advised White to do so, too, and to persuade other Progressives to do the same thing because, he said, you will never get those stubborn Democrats to jump party lines and vote with the Progressives.[63] Most of the objections, however, came from people who, while they were not standpatters, did not want to take a chance on the destruction of the Republican party. W. H. Bell of Belleville, Kansas, was typical. He wrote, "I am also a Progressive—but am willing at this time to abide by results at Chicago rather than to take sides with a Third Party, thereby disrupting the Republican party for years to come."[64]

Even though things kept going wrong for him, White's buoyant optimism kept bubbling forth. He could not get Beveridge to Kansas to make a speaking tour.[65] Roosevelt had to turn down a midwestern tour that White had laid out for him.[66] Even his old friend Joe Bristow begged off because of the pressure of legislation in Washington.[67] And in the middle of September, Sallie became ill, and they went out to their Colorado hideaway for her to recover.[68]

The biggest difficulty with the Kansas campaign, however, was finances. As chairman of the Kansas Progressive Republican Committee, White had released a letter on July 23, in which he had set forth his plans for a grass roots campaign. This was before he had gone to Chicago, before he had had his decisive run-in with George Perkins. The letter was an ingenious appeal. It went like this:

> Under the old plan of campaigning, the big concerns that get the benefit of tariff and other legislation used to be asked to contribute to campaign funds. Then they got their money back with 30 per cent interest in high tariffs and unjust rates of various kinds, legalized by those whose campaign expenses they paid. *This was wrong–dead wrong.* But we were all to blame–I was just as bad as the next fellow, and the next fellow was just as bad as I was.
>
> But we've got to quit. We've got to take charge of this government ourselves–you and I and the folks. For the man who pays the campaign expenses owns the government. We propose to carry Kansas for Roosevelt at the primary and at the polls by subscriptions from the folks. We don't need large subscriptions. But we do need lots of them. We don't want the big fellows. But we do want the fellow who has a dollar, or five, or possibly ten, to feel that this movement is his movement. . . . It is as though we were organizing a great stock company for good government in which every voter was a holder of preferred stock. . . . I believe that this is the first time a presidential campaign has been financed by the man from the grass roots.[69]

White even proposed to give a certificate to each contributor, and invited contributors to send their names to the State Historical Society "so that the names of those who subscribed may always be upon the roll of honor in Kansas."[70]

As it turned out, White got his small contributions. Letters accompanying the money were full of enthusiasm for the Roosevelt cause and bitterness against the standpatters, and they contained one dollar, two dollars, sometimes, though rarely, five dollars.[71] White had written to ask about the possibility of some fifty and one hundred dollar contributions, and he received the obvious answer. Those who had that much money to give were standpatters who would not give a dime to see Roosevelt elected to anything.[72]

Out in western Kansas, where Roosevelt support was vocal, the weather and disease conspired to cut down contributions. White decided to concentrate on central and eastern Kansas since it would not be moral nor fair to ask money from farmers who were fighting both a drought, with its consequent crop failure, and the horse plague.[73]

By the end of September, the Progressive campaign in Kansas was in financial trouble. "I have run this campaign on faith and voluntary contributions," White wrote. "The voluntary contributions have been coming in mighty slowly."[74] He had already contributed fifteen hundred dollars,[75] and David Hinshaw, White's right-hand man, was trying to round up campaign fund collectors to work on a commission basis, ten per cent of ten dollars and under and five per cent of anything above ten dollars.[76]

That was not all. It began to look as if the strongest Progressive on the Kansas roster, fiery Roscoe Stubbs, was going to have the fight of his life. The Progressives had persuaded Stubbs not to run for governor again, but to run for the United States Senate. He had opposed White's old friend and enemy, the railroads' errand boy, Chester I. Long, in the primary, and he had beaten him. White got word, though, that a good many Democrats had jumped party lines in the primary, just to vote against Stubbs, and as the election neared, White wrote more than once, "I wish something could be done to save Stubbs."[77]

As it turned out, nothing could be done to save anybody. Although White wrote that Roosevelt ran a strong second to Wilson in Kansas,[78] as he did in the nation, White's letters indicate that Roosevelt actually could count only one district in Kansas.[79]

White remembered, too, that the Progressive party raised ten thousand dollars for the 1912 campaign and came out of that campaign with two or three hundred dollars in the bank.[80] If this is fact, the financial campaign must have gone over the top in the last month of the political campaign. On October 8, the Progressive party in Kansas owed fifteen hundred dollars, had fifty dollars in the bank, and would need, according to Hinshaw's estimate, six or seven thousand dollars before the campaign was over.[81]

The message of the 1912 election was writ as large on the wall for the

Progressives as it was for the standpat Republicans. Wilson received 435 electoral votes, Roosevelt 88, and Taft 8. Wilson polled 42 percent of the popular vote, Roosevelt 27 percent, and Taft 23 percent.[82] Still, the Progressives remained enthusiastic. From the letters White received, a person would have thought the Progressives were on their way to becoming the dominant political party in the United States. Roosevelt wrote to White on November 15, 1912, "No man has waged a gamer and more effective fight for the Progressive Cause than you have. Our task must now be to try to put the organization in permanent form."[83] On November 19, Roosevelt followed up that letter with another, in which he said, "We must keep our organization without a sign of faltering or compromise."[84]

It was quite true that for White the defeat of the Progressive candidates did not represent the defeat of the Progressive cause. He probably agreed with one of his more ecstatic correspondents that ". . . We are standing at the sun-rise looking forward with joy and confidence to the beauty and promise of the brightening day."[85]

After all, Wilson was Progressive in his thinking if not in his party loyalty, and after all, the Progressive party had been instrumental in beating Taft and the standpatters. (It had received substantial help from the Socialist party, by the way, Eugene V. Debs polling over a million votes.)[86] Besides, if the Progressive party did not have strength in Congress, it could set up headquarters in Washington and lobby for the Progressive legislative program.

So the mad summer waned. "Distributive justice" did have a champion, though White was uneasy about this knight of the sorrowful countenance who had unhorsed his dashing Colonel. Still, the world was going the way White wanted it to go, and he could safely pack up his family and go to California for the winter, where he would loaf on the sand, recouping his forces, and where he would get back to work on the novel that the campaign had interrupted. After all, as he had said in a Denver speech in 1911, "Only a war can shatter the sure advance of this movement of the people for distributive justice. War is the devil's answer to human progress."

9

Bull Moose Ruminant

The results of the 1912 election were so disastrous from the Progressive point of view that a less hardy group than the Lord's soldiers would probably have fled the battlefield in panic. There was some balm in the fact that if Roosevelt did not win, Wilson did; but that was all. Kansas, which had been thought of as a Roosevelt stronghold, had carried only one district for Roosevelt. Stubbs had lost his bid to the United States Senate by about eighteen thousand votes,[1] and Victor Murdock was the only Kansas Progressive congressman to survive.

Yet Roosevelt had patted White on the back and urged him back into the fray, and by December White was busy helping build a permanent Progressive organization. He issued a call for a national organization meeting in Chicago and for a state organization meeting in Topeka.[2] The response, in December 1912, was immediate and nearly unanimous.[3] It looked as if the Bull Moosers were still full of fight. On the other hand, such immediate action might have been considered a necessity. David D. Leahy, secretary to Governor Stubbs, had written White by November 15, urging immediate action "to keep the Progressive forces in solid lines."[4]

In retrospect, White's continuing enthusiasm for the Progressive cause may seem odd. He had known the hazards of bolting and had held out for a long time against even forming a third party. He had reluctantly accepted Roosevelt's decision to make a fight of it in 1912. He had seen the power of the old guard Republican organization, and he had suspected the motives of the eastern, Perkins-led wing of the Progressive party. If that were all, White's clinging to the spars of the Progressive wreckage would be strange indeed. On the other hand, White believed that the showing the Progressive party made in 1912, especially when it had such difficulty getting on the ballot at all, indicated a strength that could be developed in the next four years. He was convinced that the Progressive party would eventually supplant the Republican party, and he was out to make a strong showing in the 1914 congressional elections.[5]

The emotions generated by the Republican national convention and by the more recent, bitter election campaign acted as the mortar to hold the Progressive party together through the rest of 1912 and into 1913. In fact, it was this element of protest, not alone against the ills of society, but also against that stolen 1912 nomination, that was to keep the Progressive party vocal until the beginning of World War I. As for William Allen White, he was a man of rare optimism and resilience, and he would retain his present state of euphoria at least until after the 1914 elections.

In 1913 he wrote Senator Bristow that the Progressive party was still strong.[6] F. S. Jackson, whom White had persuaded to run for Congress in 1912 and who had been defeated, was threatening to depart for a more stable political climate, and others, too, were beginning to waver.[7] William Allen White, however, was strongly urging Bristow to announce for the presidency before the harmony talk, which was then just a murmur, destroyed Bristow's chances.[8]

By 1913 White had arrived at a position he was to hold for the rest of his life, that "practically all the Populist demands have been met by legislation—mostly federal legislation under the Roosevelt and Taft administrations."[9] A good deal more Progressive legislation was to be passed during the Wilson administration, but now at least it was official. Now Populism was respectable, and even Taft got his share of credit—now, after the election of Wilson.

It did not take long after the election for talk of fusion to begin. Neither fragment of the Republican party was entirely happy with the fragmentation. White was against fusion, however, unless the Republican party were willing to liberalize itself by adopting the rules of the Progressive party.[10] He was particularly insistent about the Progressive party rule which allowed recall of national committeemen by a majority of state committeemen. Even if the Republicans had accepted White's suggestion, it is doubtful that he would have favored fusion. He fought fusion down to the wire in 1916. As far as he was concerned, only if and when the Republican party accepted the Progressive candidate should the Progressives return to the Republican party.

If he could not see the Progressives fusing with the Republicans, neither could he accept the idea of the Progressives going into the Democratic column. For William Allen White equated the Democratic party with conservatism. Writing to Carl W. Moore in 1913, White said.

> . . . I do not regard the Democratic party as Progressive. It can never be Progressive. It must be historically and constitutionally the conservative party of this nation. Just now it is under a temporary aberration in having two Progressive leaders, Bryan and Wilson—the one being a sincere but rather second-rate man mentally, the other being a highly intellectual man without very much but intellect to recommend him. But the Democratic party, it seems to me, and I have always said so, is the inevitable residuary legatee of all conservatives in this country. I would sooner think of being a third-party Prohibitionist or a Socialist than of being a Democrat as the party is now constituted, as long as it is fettered by the ideas of states rights and free trade. These two ideas make it inexorably conservative.[11]

Since federal regulation of business was part of the Progressive philosophy, White could consider states rights a conservative doctrine. However, when he made free trade a conservative tenet, he left logic altogether. Since the conservatism of the Democratic party was one of the preconceptions White took with him into politics, he could not be shaken from that preconception, regardless of what the history of his own time was proving.

As for 1914, White did the only honorable thing he could do. In fact, he stayed with the Progressive party until it ceased to exist. He realized his power and position in the party. As he wrote in March 1914, "I see this thing nationally, and my defection or the defection of the Kansas Progressives nationally would be heralded as the cave-in of the Progressive party in one of the four states where it is strongest."[12]

None of the Progressive regulars out in the states seemed to be thinking of deserting. There were meetings and dinners and speeches right up to the 1914 elections. What White did not realize, nor did any of his fellow Progressives at the time, was that the same people kept appearing at all the meetings. The Progressives were gaining no new recruits as 1913 melted into 1914 and the elections got closer and closer.

But the surviving Progressives remained enthusiastic. White himself was writing George Perkins, probing for possible issues for the campaign. He thought the Progressive platform of 1914 ought to have planks endorsing national prohibition, women's suffrage, and national ownership of railroads.[13] While he was proferring a platform to Perkins with one hand, with the other, he was holding off Gifford Pinchot, who wanted to get rid of Perkins. White told the impatient Pennsylvanian to wait till Roosevelt got back from Brazil, and he himself took up his favorite position on the fence.[14]

Besides, there were other things to occupy White besides domestic politics. The arrest of American sailors at Vera Cruz and Admiral Mayo's demand for an apology and a salute of the American flag from the Mexican authorities interested him particularly. His University of Kansas classmate and life-long friend, General Frederick Funston, was to command the forces that bombarded Vera Cruz. Very much against his will, he was also to lead the withdrawal of American troops after arbitration under the good offices of the ABC countries, Argentina, Brazil, and Chile.

Agreeing to arbitrate represented a master stroke of Wilsonian diplomacy, but the whole affair incensed White, and he spread himself and wrote a piece for the April 25 issue of *The California Outlook:*

> MAKE HIM "SWALLER" IT
>
> Saluting the American flag is a mighty small penance to put on Huerta. What they ought to do is make him eat it–and that with a forty-foot flag pole wrapped with barbed wire; and more than that, he should be made to swallow the flag pole without chewing it, and when he is strung on it like a mud cat on a willow withe, he should be run up and down the flag pole for a couple of weeks by way of diversion to show all the cayenne pepper dictators who rule by homicide that this country, while it may be long suffering and patient, and while it may turn the other cheek for a year or two, will finally assert itself and make the punishment fit the crime. By the time Huerta gets ten or twenty feet of flag pole through his system, he would be getting an

> idea of the dignity of our American government through his head. Anyway, the experiment is worth trying.[15]

Meantime, White was fighting fusion with all his weapons. In the letter he wrote to Roosevelt, detailing what had happened in politics while the Colonel was in Brazil, White pleaded for his friend to avoid the contamination of fusion and to stay out of the New York gubernatorial race. He told Roosevelt that flirting with the fusion nomination would hurt the Kansas party, and that Henry J. Allen, "who is running for governor as a sacrifice," would not stay on the ticket if Roosevelt fused with the Republicans in New York. Running for governor of New York would localize Roosevelt's influence, White told him, and it would weaken the party nationally.[16] Roosevelt had no intention of being a Progressive candidate for governor, but the idea of fusion intrigued him. It was time, he said, for the two wings of the Republican party to find common ground again. As for the governor's race in New York, he said he would support any Republican "who would war on Republican crookedness just as much as upon Democratic crookedness."[17]

The hard fact was that the Progressive party existed from 1912 to 1916 on the strength of the supposition that Roosevelt would be its presidential candidate in 1916—this despite the fact that Roosevelt and La Follette were to have another head-on collision in 1916. Nobody but La Follette himself and the same irreconcilable group that had stuck by him in 1912 gave the man a chance. If Roosevelt was not to be the Progressive candidate, there would be no Progressive party after 1916.

Actually, there was no party to speak of after 1914. Only Hiram Johnson among the Progressive leaders of the states survived, and such Kansas Progressive strong men as Victor Murdock and Henry J. Allen went down in an avalanche of Republican and Democratic votes. The Republican and Democratic parties each tallied over six million votes. The Progressives could count less than two million.

Roosevelt wrote to White on November 7, 1914, "From the night of the election two years ago, I have felt that the chances were overwhelming against the permanence of the Progressive party."[18] That letter contrasts strongly against the one Roosevelt wrote White the week after the 1912 elections, but it is probably a truer reflection of his feelings that the 1912 letter had been. Thus in 1914, Theodore Roosevelt, in effect, pronounced the Progressive party dead. But the party would not lie down, though its head, after announcing the death, began rather obviously to try to re-attach itself to the party it had cut away from in 1912.

Regardless of the defection of his chief, William Allen White stayed with the Progressive party—because he had to. When that party went down to almost irreparable defeat in 1914, the usually optimistic Kansan was saturated in gloom. "I am cast into outer darkness politically . . ." he wrote to future senator Arthur Capper. "I am going to watch events for the next few months, and we shall see what we will see."[19] White felt this defeat more than he had felt any other political defeat in his career. He had had some inkling of what he was up against when he went around the state trying to fill a Progressive ticket before the election. It had been hard work. After the emotion-charged campaign of 1912, that of 1914 was an anticlimax, and some of the candidates who had run with Roosevelt had begun to have second thoughts about their impetuosity when there was no Roosevelt on the ticket.[20]

From the bottom of the well White wrote to Roy Bailey of the *Salina Journal*: "So far as politics are concerned, I am going to sit on the fence for a while and watch the procession go by. I don't know what the future has in store. I have no particular pride in any party, or never have had."[21] He recognized that the coming of the war had lessened public interest in reform, and he wrote to Joseph Tumulty, Wilson's secretary, "How sad it is that the war is taking the national interest away from justice."[22]

But William Allen White was not one to stay down for long. By November 23 he was writing to Hiram Johnson, the California Progressive who had been Roosevelt's running mate in 1912 and who was making plans to run for the United States Senate in 1916.[23] White used Johnson as a sounding board for his ideas about the 1916 Progressive platform. That platform should have in it, he wrote Johnson, planks endorsing government ownership of railroads, a minimum wage law, a mothers' pension, restriction of working hours for women and children, and the national adoption of the initiative, referendum, and recall.[24]

The trouble with the Progressive party as it stood in 1914, he wrote to George Perkins, was that it did not have a big issue. What that big issue should be, White himself was not sure. It should not be national prohibition, he said. The old parties would simply get on the bandwagon in states where prohibition was popular. For all his assurance to Johnson, he told Perkins he was not sure of the nationalization of the railroads as a major issue, and he had an idea that the tariff commission and the one-schedule tariff provision were a bit above the head of the average voter.[25]

The bubble on the stream of history, as White was to call himself, was resisting the current with all the strength at his command. He reported to Johnson a continuing enthusiasm for the Progressive cause in every western state but Colorado, but he also detected a notable coolness in the East.[26] The East had already felt the effects of the war in Europe, and concern for domestic reform waned as the war took more and more of the eastern seaboard's attention.

The war had put White in the middle again. By nature a pacifist, despite his occasional outbursts of jingoism, he was nonetheless caught up in Theodore Roosevelt's call for preparedness. He counsled Roosevelt to avoid criticism of the Wilson-Bryan peace propaganda, not necessarily because he favored that propaganda, but because for Roosevelt to criticize it at that time would only make Wilson stronger. "If I were you," he wrote Roosevelt, "I would discuss anything but politics; and Bryan and Wilson peace propaganda is blood-raw politics and you can't make it anything else. . . ."[27]

It was not entirely because of politics that White advised Roosevelt not to attack the Bryan-Wilson peace program. At least, White was to write in his autobiography that he was closer to Bryan's views on peace than he was to Roosevelt's, and that he suspected that he and Bryan were closer in their views than were Bryan and Wilson. Besides, White agreed that a sudden shift in policy toward preparedness would impugn the sincerity of Wilson's neutrality statements. Meanwhile, Roosevelt "would have armed to prevent war."[28]

Even then, White could not forswear his loyalty to Roosevelt. He added, "He and I disagreed, though he was probably right."[29] White could occasionally see holes in his knight's armor, however. In discussing Bryan's contribution to Progressivism and Roosevelt's intransigent distrust and dislike of Bryan, White wrote of Roosevelt, "I do not think I ever heard him say once, 'I was dead wrong; I am sorry'—seven rather difficult words for the best of us to articulate clearly."[30]

White was not spending all his time worrying about the war and getting the Progressive party in Kansas ready for the 1916 campaign. He had gone back to writing fiction. In the summer of 1912, in the midst of that first roaring Progressive campaign, he had spent his Colorado vacation working on a novel. Immediately after the 1912 election, he wrote to

Roosevelt, ". . . I was never so well in my life and never had a more beautiful time than the last six or eight months I have put in working for the Progressive cause. I hope now to get a year in which I may work on a new novel, which I have not even looked at since we began the hike for Armageddon. If the Lord and the Progressives will let me have a year to myself I believe I can turn out a real story. I have written the thing through, but revision is always the greater part of my work."[31] Though it would not see print until 1918, White whittled away at *In the Heart of a Fool* during vacations and at odd times when there was nothing more urgent in his typewriter.

In the meantime, he began to publish a series of long short stories in *The Saturday Evening Post* and in *Collier's.* He gathered them into book and Macmillan published them as *God's Puppets* in 1916.[32] Two of the stories are spin-offs from the novel to come, and it is almost as if the book of short stories had been created to give White the boost for the novel he had been working on so long.

Again White went back to the Bible for his themes, and again the stories were patently written to illustrate the moral universe White envisioned and to show what happened when the morality of that universe was violated. Two of the stories are retellings of Biblical parables. "A Social Rectangle" retells the story of the strange woman whose "feet go down to death." The woman is Lalla Rookh Longford, and the story concerns her relationship with her father, a doctor, and a professor. Lalla Rookh, an obvious Circe, turns all the men into animals before her father sees the evil in her. The story ought to end there, but it does not. Much as he tried to be a realist, White could not let a story end in negation, even when the logic of the story demanded it:

> "A strange woman," repeated Charley, sighing; "and 'her feet go down to death.'"
>
> "Oh, well, Charley, I don't know. So far as that goes, so are we all strange women–some of the time–all of us. But, Charley," cried the woman gently, "one of us was chosen as the first witness of the Great Resurrection!"[33]

The other parable is "The One A Pharisee," an explicit retelling in terms of the self-righteous, scheming, Sunday-School-teaching Boyce Kilworth and his gambling half-brother, Caleb Hale, "the one a Pharisee, the other a publican." It is also the story of Kilworth's daughter and Hale's son, the hope of the world in the new generation.[34]

The parable of the Pharisee and a story called "A Prosperous Gentleman" are the spin-off stories preparing the way for the novel, *In the Heart of a Fool.* "A Prosperous Gentleman" is Charley Herrington, son of the town banker. Charley had seduced and abandoned a poor country girl in his home town. Though the seduction did not prevent his succeeding his father in the bank, making a fortune on bogus land stocks, buying the daughter of a Crippled Greek miner for a wife, and becoming the president of the branch railroad, it did send him to his death in his seventies, a broken and demented man with the soul burnt out of him, muttering what the girl had said to him on the fatal night: "The larkspur's all faded–like me."[35] White told this story as a straight, moralistic tale. The ironic humor of it is entirely unconscious. Charley Herrington was a preliminary sketch of Thomas Van Dorn, the fool of the novel White was writing.

"The Gods Arrive" harks back to *Stratagems and Spoils.* It updates the prostituted politician and puts him in a highly untenable position, now that the Progressives are in power in his state and the reform legislation of the Progressive era has been passed.[36] "The Strange Boy" is a strange story, a wistful reaching back to boyhood, coupled with the realization that we cannot go back.[37]

These are not merely moral stories, born of White's belief in and hope for a moral universe through the actions of good men. They are moralistic. What White intended for symbols became in his typewriter sign-boards. They are what White intended all of his stories to be: fictionized editorials, sermons in print.

White was having an easier time with his fictional universe than he was with the world he lived in. The whole nation, apparently, from President Wilson through Theodore Roosevelt down to the grass-roots that William Allen White knew, thought at the beginning of the European war that America could trade with both sides and remain outside the conflict. If the German propaganda had not been so clumsy, if German sabotage of American production had not been so obvious, and finally, if it had not been for the submarine attacks on American shipping, perhaps America could have remained neutral. For the British were playing the game, too, and though they finally made some concessions in their blacklisting of American manufacturers dealing with Germany, they never did give up the principle of the blacklist. But George Sylvester Viereck was not so skillful a propagandist as was Lord Northcliffe, and German agents did sabotage American industry, and most important of all, the German U-boat attacks aroused American emotions against the Germans and made plain the vulnerability of the east coast.[38]

So it was not all Roosevelt's doing that turned Wilson from neutrality, though White credited Roosevelt's clamor for preparedness with Wilson's change of mind.[39] White heard Wilson make his preparedness speech at the Manhattan Club meeting in New York. He noted that Wilson "was taking the medicine without licking the spoon, and it was a bitter dose." What really killed any idea of neutrality in the United States, however, was Wilson's leading the Preparedness Parade down the streets of Washington, D.C., on June 14, Flag Day, 1916. "When Woodrow Wilson spoke for preparedness at the Manhattan Club, and when he marched . . . in the long Preparedness Parade," White wrote, "the bell tolled for social reform in the United States. . . ."[40]

But he did not know that at the time. In fact, William Allen White and a good many other Progressives were milling around in considerable confusion as the 1916 campaign approached. White had written to George Perkins as early as May 1915 that he feared Roosevelt was edging back into the Republican party.[41] He himself was not ready to return to the Republican party, and yet–. He really did not know what to do. As he wrote to J. L. Brady at about the same time he wrote Perkins, "I feel more deeply grounded in the Progressive faith than ever before and less like tieing up with the Republicans. I could not possibly see my way clear to being a Democrat under any circumstances, and yet it may be wise to stand by Wilson in the next campaign. I do not know. 'Sufficient unto the day is the evil thereof,' which being translated means, 'the devil is to pay and no pitch hot.'"[42]

To one person he wrote about the necessity of getting out a Progressive ticket. To another he said he would be against such a move.[43] The political picture was indeed confused, and White was in the midst of the confusion. He reported to Gifford Pinchot that Roosevelt had lost strength in the Midwest because of his stand on preparedness.[44] He even wrote privately that if he did not think Roosevelt's emphasis on preparedness was only temporary, he would not support him.[45] White should have known better, and perhaps he did. As he was forever attributing to the public his own attitudes, so this threat of disavowal may have been an attempt to make over his god in his own image. It could be also that the letter was simply an attempt to keep in line the midwestern Progressives whose first interest lay in domestic reform.

If White was confused, so was the whole Progressive movement. The diehards, of whom White, of course, was one, still hoped that Roosevelt would pull the party out of its confusion by running in 1916 and holding the party together for another try in 1920.[46] The war, meanwhile, was an irritating intrusion, and White wrote bemusedly, "The war has had a curiously reactionary effect upon public opinion all over civilization."[47] Why "curiously" it is hard to discover, for this has been the way of wars in all history. White had only to look at the American Civil War to find an example close at hand. In 1916, however, Wilson would be able to run for President on the slogan, "He kept us out of war." The world did not yet need to be saved for democracy. Rather, the United States had to be established as an example of economic justice for all the world to see and to emulate. The war was an irritating interruption, and perhaps, given the Progressives' line of sight, the reactionary effect of that war was a curious thing.

For at the moment, the problem was to defeat both the Republicans and the Democrats and make the Progressive party the new liberal party of the United States. If William Allen White could help do that, he would indeed be making his private sentiment public opinion. Such a party would be one molded after White's own ideas of middle-class liberalism. It would be the shadow of White and of the men like White who had erected it. As White wrote to J. N. Dolley of Topeka, a comrade-in-arms from the 1912 campaign, if the Republican party were defeated in 1916, either the Republican party would disappear entirely or its shell would be handed over to the Progressives.[48] All this presupposed that the United States would not become directly involved in the European war, of course, and to White, any coalition or combination which would bring about the supremacy of the Progressive party would be worth the effort. When he looked back later, he was amused at his backing and filling and wondered whether he had been a vacillating opportunist or a diabolical intriguer.[49]

Actually, he was neither of these things. He was, instead, a man who had accepted early both the pleasure and the responsibility of making his private sentiment public opinion. He had accepted the reform philosophy of the Progressive movement as wholeheartedly as some men accept religion, and he used whatever honorable political means that came to hand to bring his vision of the good life to reality. In 1916 he was also living in the past of Progressive achievement, and he had a good deal of company. Those Progressives who agreed with him that America should let the rest of the world go by and continue to develop industrial and economic justice were, like White, simply saddened that the war was taking men's minds off the main target.

White went to the 1916 Progressive convention in that frame of mind. He also went completely opposed to "harmonizing" with the Republicans, and convinced that only Roosevelt's nomination could save the Progressive party. But when the Republican and Progressive conventions met simultaneously in Chicago that June, it soon became apparent that Roosevelt, in Oyster Bay, through George Perkins in Chicago, was maneuvering to get both the Republican and the Progressive nominations, and that, if he himself did not get the nomination, he had no intention of running again against the Republican nominee.

The Progressives, led by what Roosevelt was calling "the lunatic fringe" and "wild Western radicals," were determined to nominate Roosevelt immediately.[50] Roosevelt and Perkins were just as determined that they wait until the Republican party moved. A joint committee from the two conventions met to discuss a compromise candidate. The first time they met, the Republican members said they could not name a compromise candidate until the convention had selected a nominee. By the time they met again, after the first ballot, Charles Evans Hughes was the obvious choice of the convention, with Roosevelt running a sad seventh at 65 votes. When his total had risen to only 81 on the second ballot, Roosevelt knew he did not have a chance for the Republican nomination, though he still would not allow the Progressives to nominate him at their convention.[51] He did not absolutely refuse the nomination. He simply said that he wanted to know where Hughes stood on such things as "Americanism" and preparedness before he decided whether to support the Republican nominee or not.[52]

So he kept the Progressive convention dangling, and when George Perkins read Roosevelt's letter asking the Progressives to support the Republican nominee, all hell broke loose. White remembered that delegates tore the Roosevelt buttons from their lapels and threw them on the floor with roars of rage and frustration.[53] The Progressives understandably felt betrayed. The wonder is that they did not see the betrayal coming. Throughout the 1916 conventions, Roosevelt and Perkins had been using the Progressive party as a dowsing rod in their search for the Republican nomination. White himself had had hints in his correspondence with Roosevelt that the Colonel was backing away from the Progressive party. Roosevelt could have deceived White, for he had a capacity to be to every man what that man wanted him to be. And William Allen White usually took Theodore Roosevelt at rather more than face value.

It has been said that the western Progressives themselves sabotaged any chance Roosevelt might have had to run for the presidency in 1916, by their insistence that he run as a Progressive. It has also been said that Roosevelt made an honest effort to find a true compromise candidate before he backed out entirely and supported Hughes. There was never any chance of compromise. The only name the Republican members of the fusion committee mentioned as a "compromise" candidate was Charles Evans Hughes, the man the Republican convention was already determined to nominate. When it became obvious after the second ballot that Roosevelt had no chance at the Republican nomination, he himself presented two "compromise" candidates whom the Progressives could not possibly accept. First Roosevelt suggested General Leonard Wood, former governor general of Cuba. When his advisers pointed out to him that the Progressives were unlikely to accept a military man, especially a man who had recommended a universal draft as a preparedness measure, Roosevelt went fishing again. After rejecting several possibilities, he suggested his old friend, Senator Henry Cabot Lodge of Massachusetts. If anything, Lodge was more conservative than Hughes.[54] The Progressives shouted down the nomination, and the Republicans listened to the nomination speech almost without interest, then went ahead to nominate Hughes on the next ballot, almost unanimously.

Whereas the Progressives of 1912 had gone out of their convention enthusiastically angry and ready to battle for the Lord, the same Progressives in 1916—what was left of them—went out of their convention sullen, angry, and muttering of perfidy and treachery.

There were some attempts to fight the results of the Chicago conventions on the state level, but for the most part, the erstwhile Bull Moosers went to find a place to hide and lick their wounds. Some of them became Democrats, but most of them, including White, drifted disconsolately back into the Republican herd, shedding their antlers as they went and acquiring rudimentary trunks and tusks.

When he wrote his autobiography more than thirty years after the event, White said that Perkins had kept him and the other Progressives unaware of the telephone line between Perkins' hotel room and Oyster Bay. In fact, he painted quite a scene of his telling Roosevelt about Perkins' treachery and of Roosevelt's sputtering in mighty indignation.[55] A stenographic transcription of those two-telephone conference calls indicates, however, that Hiram Johnson, Gifford Pinchot, and William Allen White himself were among those taking part in the conversations, and that it was White who tried hardest to get Roosevelt to permit the Progressives to nominate him early.[56] Maybe consciously, maybe unconsciously, by the time White wrote his autobiography, he was looking for a way out for his hero. For regardless of the way Roosevelt used White, and the other Progressives, individually and collectively, Roosevelt remained White's hero until White himself died.

Yet White could reflect ironically as he summed up Roosevelt's actions at the 1916 conventions: "For by that time," White wrote, "he had persuaded himself that he had been forced to bolt in 1912, when, as a matter of cold fact, he went into the third-party bolt in a rage. No one could have stopped him; I had tried vainly. He had persuaded himself that it was a matter of principle, and we all agreed with him after the fact; but in 1916 he felt that he had nobly led an assault on privileged plutocracy, and had done his full part in the progressive movement."[57]

When the Progressive party died, part of William Allen White died, too. This is not a melodramatic statement, for to White political affiliation and political principles were almost as sacred as those of religion, his disclaimers notwithstanding. Besides, the clay feet which he had suspected his hero of having had come into plain view. Though White was never to abandon his championship of Roosevelt, Roosevelt kept making it hard for him not to abandon it. For though White was essentially a political pragmatist, his pragmatism was framed in a set of political and social principles. The social and political program of middle-class liberalism came first, and White used political pragmatism in an attempt to achieve essentially idealistic ends. Roosevelt, on the other hand, as White came to know and to acknowledge, was a pragmatist to whom results, often purely personal results, were all-important.

White took his medicine like a man, but he did not lick the spoon, either. On September 6, 1916, he wrote to Charles H. Sessions, "I am running the Republican ticket in the paper today. But I feel, in re Hughes, that the best thing I can do is to put the muffler on my cutout."[58] As far as he could see, the rest of the Progressives felt pretty much the same as he did. On September 26, he wrote to Henry J. Haskell of the *Kansas City Star.* ". . . I talked last night to David Hinshaw, who is out for the National Republican Committee digging up the Bull Moosers," he wrote. "He says they are going to vote for Hughes—but they are going to vote for him in the beloved hope and fond expectation that he will be defeated. Not that they care to elect Wilson. They don't want to elect anybody."[59]

White's own correspondence showed the same kind of despair. "I have had two or three letters this week from prominent Bull Moosers over the state," he added, "and they are going to vote for Hughes unless they die before November, which earnest hope they are enjoying with all the enthusiasm of their ardent natures."[60]

To Hamlin Garland White wrote that he was keeping out of politics in 1916 "with all my might and main."[61] This was not altogether because of his deep disappointment over the happenings at Chicago. Already he was beginning to look ahead. He had no enthusiasm for Hughes, but he, like the other Progressives he had heard from, planned to vote for Hughes, nonetheless. He thought Hughes was a better man than Wilson, but, as he wrote another correspondent, "I don't know how much better and I could not justify myself in an argument. The Progressive convention, of course, broke my heart," he added, "and a fellow with a broken heart shouldn't try to buck up and talk sassy until he gets over a decent period of mourning."[62]

The reason he ran the Republican ticket in the *Gazette,* White said, was that it gave him a "pretty good alibi so if I want to make a fight inside the Republican party, I can do it."[63] He was sure that the fight over Progressive principles would continue somewhere, sometime after the election, and he wanted to be in it, if not in the Republican party, then somewhere else. And after that brave promise to stay in there and fight, he ended sadly, "I wish by some miracle that both Hughes and Wilson could be defeated. . . ."[64]

It was inevitable that White support Hughes, despite his protestations and despite his amazement and chagrin that Hughes showed no knowledge at all of Progressive issues.[65] His presuppositions about the Democratic party had probably been reinforced by Roosevelt's hatred of Wilson. White was infected with that hatred by close association with Roosevelt if by nothing else.

The death of the Progressive party marked the virtual end of practical political power for William Allen White. He was to be a delegate to the National Republican Convention in 1920, 1928, and 1936, and he was to be a member of the policy-making body in 1936. Yet he was always a minority member, a left-over Progressive.

His strength returned to its source. It was the voice of an articulate man whose principal amplifier was a daily newspaper in a small country town and the pages of the nation's popular magazines. He continued to use his editorial page and the magazines as pulpits and to write about reform. He still saw the political arena as the battleground for social betterment, but he began to realize, as he was to write in 1929 about liberal leaders in general, that "one of the major mistakes of the liberal leaders was that they sought to make government the *only* agency of human welfare."[66] Judging from White's activity in the Progressive era, he would have included himself in that mild indictment.

By 1929 his philosophy of justice had come out from behind the protection of his fiction and stood clear. The individual human heart was the place of the beginning of justice. Writing in the preface to *Masks in a Pageant,* a collection of political biographies, he said: "They forgot that masses who require the stimulation of a just prosperity for their happy well-being must themselves first learn to love justice in their own hearts before they can get much out of prosperity except food and clothes and shelter. Liberal governments brought much prosperity to Christendom, distributed the prosperity with something like equity—only to find that the classes they had improved materially were just as greedy and dull as their oppressors had been in the days before liberalism broke the rusted chains of economic feudalism. Government helped as an agency of human welfare," he concluded. "It failed as the only agency."[67]

It is possible to substitute an "I" for every "they" in that quotation. Only when progress by government failed to live up to his expectations did William Allen White abandon reform by legislation as a panacea for social ills. By 1925, when he wrote *Some Cycles of Cathay,* he had come to see political action as the civil arm of Christianity. The individual moral force of Christianity and the socially motivated reforming force of the government had become separate expressions of the same ethic.[68]

The semi-religious attitude was implicit in the Progressive philosophy, and not only in its revivalist fervor. But White had to live through the experiment of reform by legislation before he saw that reform must originate in the heart of the reformed. But in 1916 he did not realize that that was what he had been through. The collapse of the Progressive party was to him the twilight of the gods. The ruler of the pantheon had brought the lordly habitation crashing down about the ears of the lesser deities. A world had come to an end.

With a war on the horizon, it did not look as if there was a new world coming, either. On the other hand, with the coming of the war, White had a chance to escape the wreckage of one world and to go and report on the doings of a larger, though no more stable one. He could also look for hope in a war to end all wars.

10

World War I - An Interlude

The twilight of the Progressive gods was a relatively long one, and it might have been longer if World War I had not interrupted it. In his first administration, Woodrow Wilson oversaw the enactment of a great part of the Progressive program. With rather astonishing rapidity, Congress established the Federal Reserve system, the Postal Savings program, and the tariff and trade commissions, among other important Progressive measures. The Progressives in Congress, Republican and Democrat alike, were busy building a new heaven and a new earth.

Much to Theodore Roosevelt's chagrin, White supported Wilson's policy wholeheartedly, though he could not bring himself to vote for a Southerner and a Democrat. He even gave qualified approval to Wilson's foreign policy and probably would have agreed with it completely if it had not been for what he regarded as Wilson's diplomatic defeat in Mexico and the humiliation of General Funston at Vera Cruz.[1] Before World War I, that foreign policy was, after all, essentially pacifistic and based on Wilson's belief in the superiority of morally righteous diplomacy over force. For that reason, if for no other, White's sympathies were more with Wilson than with Roosevelt regarding the European war in 1916. He wanted the United States to stay out of the war. So did much of the Midwest, and so did many of the members of the late but still unburied Progressive party. The war was to them simply a threatened interruption of domestic progress toward a morally righteous economic and social order.

For White himself, there were other considerations. He had always thought of himself as a pacifist, and he always was a pacifist until circumstances forced him to be otherwise. He had called America's Cuban adventure "a case of tommyrot" until he had been caught up in the missionary zeal for democratizing the remains of the Spanish Empire and had become convinced that the Anglo-Saxon was destined to rule the world.

Perhaps it was even simpler than that. William Allen White saw his country go into three wars in his lifetime, and his reaction followed an almost identical pattern on all three occasions. He began by opposing absolutely any involvement of the United States in the war. Gradually, he accepted the reasoning of those who favored the war. Finally, he became fully committed to the prosecution of the war by any means that would bring victory. Ordinarily, such a pattern would not be remarkable. It was the pattern that the nation itself followed, except, perhaps in the Spanish-American War. White's case is remarkable because in the heat of the event he saw himself as man making his private sentiment public opinion. In fact, he followed and crystallized public opinion at least as much as he made it. The letters he wrote at the time show that he was as confused and bewildered as the next man who thought about politics in the midst of a war.

To W. W. Liggett of the Non-Partisan League he wrote on April 5, 1918, that while he approved of many of the economic ideas of the league, he suspected it of being anti-war, and while he said he was open-minded about it, he also said that he would not support a disloyal organization or one suspected of being disloyal.[2] Even his old Bull Moose teammate Joseph Bristow disturbed White because he was allowing other considerations to take precedence over the war. Writing about Bristow's campaign for senator, White said, "I agree with practically all of the economic part of Bristow's platform, but to inject economic issues prominently into politics at this time"–White wrote the letter April 6, 1918–"tends merely to Bolshevikism and to confusion and disintegration. There should be but one issue and that is the war and winning it."[3]

White favored the non-partisan approach, but only as a patriotic measure for a nation at war. At about the same time he was writing that letter, he was writing to George Horace Lorimer of the *Saturday Evening Post,* seeking a way to arouse the American people from their political lethargy and advocating the non-partisan approach to politics. He was not only confused and bewildered but also discouraged, saying:

> I have been watching the Non-Partisan League for several months very closely. I note what you say about the political situation and I quite agree with you that the time has come to can the partisan stuff and go down the line to try to ascertain [*sic*] some brains and weight to the next conference, but I believe the job is absolutely hopeless. Nothing would please me more than to join some sort of a movement that would have a Non-Partisan patriotic cast and intention. But the party system has grown like a great cancer on the people. They cannot think except in partisan terms. . . . Wilson has been an intense partisan and each crowd is bad because it seems to pay to be bad politically. I am sick and sore of the whole lethargic political expression in this country. Along patriotic lines in the Red Cross, in the Bond Drive, in the various other patriotic organizations, the people function beautifully and effectively, but in party politics they simply do not function. They have gone dead. Any article which I might write would be scolding and pessimistic, but if you think I ought to write it, I will try. But it is a mighty gloomy outlook toward any citilizationing [*sic*] of the political situation by non-Partisan action.[4]

Evidently, Lorimer thought better of the idea, for White did not write the piece. On the one hand he seemed to belabor politicians for seeking political solutions, while on the other hand he was bemoaning the fact that the political sensitivity of the American people was dead. The coming of the war had indeed turned the world upside down for William White.

He had seen the war zone himself by this time. He had worked mightily to get to Europe, finally succeeding in making the trip with his Wichita friend Henry J. Allen as a Red Cross observer.[5] He went to war, as he called it, in the summer of 1917 and came home in the autumn of the same year, leaving Allen in Europe working for the Red Cross. By his own admission, White did very lttle observing for the Red Cross,[6] though he did write some pieces for Red Cross publications after he returned to the States.[7] But he did meet with the American ambassadors to France and Italy, and he was able to make of the Red Cross experience a dry run for his coverage of the peace conference.[8]

He also got a book out of the experience, almost accidentally. While he was in Europe he wrote regularly to Sallie and young Bill and Mary. They were chatty, intimate letters, full of off-the-cuff observations, and having written them, White forgot about them. When he got home, however, Sallie persuaded him that the letters presented a fresh view of the war and insisted that White assemble them into a book for publication.[9]

The letters by themselves were too slight to make a book. White added a love story to give the collection a plot and sent the result off to Macmillan. *The Martial Adventures of Henry and Me* was understandably, a thin book, and White himself had little faith in it.[10] He was surprised when the public liked it and even more surprised when the book stayed in print until the beginning of World War II, when the plates were melted down—White says in his autobiography—to make bullets.

White returned from Europe in the autumn of 1917 and immediately plunged into local war work, selling bonds, raising funds for the Red Cross and for the YMCA.[11] Nor was he through with politics, despite his mercurial, up-and-down moods about it. Though he had left Henry J. Allen in Europe, working for the Red Cross, Allen's friends drafted him to run for governor of Kansas anyway. White persuaded his friend to remain in Europe and to run for office *in absentia,* with White running the campaign in Kansas.[12]

White tackled the job of getting his friend and political ally elected with the enthusiasm of a youngster and the assurance of an old campaigner. He felt pretty sure that he was backing a winner when he was able to raise more than ten thousand dollars in Allen campaign funds. "Speaking generally," he philosophized for would-be politicians in his autobiography, "I should say politicians who want to win should beware of a cause that does not speak fluently in money. People who won't give, won't vote."[13] Allen had been drafted as a "harmonizing" candidate, with White working for him from Emporia and Mortimer Albaugh, the leader of the standpatters in Kansas, working for him from Topeka.

The use of "harmonizing" Progressives was not limited to Kansas, and White was convinced at that time that the Republican party could be "purified" by harmonizing on Progressive terms. The ex-Bull Moosers were moving in everywhere, and the regulars were losing control of the party. Under the leadership of Will H. Hays of Indiana, the chairman of the Republican National Committee, the liberal wing of the Republican party was again trying to take control. At least that is the way White saw it.[14] In March 1918, he wrote to Harold Ickes that Hays had asked him to go along on a scouting trip with Hays and a standpatter among ex-Bull Moosers to see what the possibilities were for harmonizing on Bull Moose terms.[15]

Another indication that, as far as White was concerned, the Progressives were still alive and that they should merge with the Republicans on Progressive terms was that White was still tilting at his old enemy, George Perkins. He had sent a telegram to Ickes.

> Make it clear that our demands will come not from former Bull Moosers but from former Republicans and Bull Moosers who desire Republican affiliation. And then specifically declare that Perkins is trying to steal our thunder and warn Progressives of the country that our group was organized to secure new and Western leadership for Republicans. . . . Think this call should come as an intermediate call between our statement of December fifth and our final call for Republican-Progressive conference in Chicago in March.[16]

It was, in a way, the last gasp of fusion. By April the war had come, and the Roosevelt Progressives, as a viable political bloc, had ceased to wiggle and were finally buried.

Even the trip with Hays never materialized, and White smelled a rat. He wrote to Roosevelt on April 24:

> I have an idea that Hays got cold feet on me. He called me on the long distance phone, arranged the trip, got out the itinerary and then suddenly, after some consultation with his friends, withdrew the invitation to me, and went on the trip himself. Now I don't mind that in the least. . . . But if it means that he is going to run the National Committee under the auspices of Heminway and Jim Watson, and men of the Lodge type, why I am not going to run any sideshow to their circus. I want to help the crowd that is trying to move things forward and I believe the Republican party is the only vehicle now at hand which will carry the forward moving load. But the load is of vastly more importance to me than the vehicle and I want to be careful of the vehicle only because I believe it will pull the load and for no other reason. . . .[17]

In 1918 William Allen White still clung to the possibility of making the Republican party the liberal party–liberal in terms of Progressive politics–in America. He saw what he interpreted as a resurgence of Progressivism in the Senate and in several of the gubernatorial races.

He was convinced that Wilson saw the resurgency, too, and was out to embarrass Henry Allen in the Kansas primary race.

White sent Medill McCormick, the Illinois Progressive Republican, a day letter in which he accused Ivy Lee and George Case, working from inside the Red Cross, of trying to get Allen recalled from his Red Cross job.[18] That would return Allen to America in disgrace, with the back of his campaign broken. He sent a similar telegraphic message to Roosevelt,[19] and by August 14, 1918, as Allen's campaign was heating up, he wrote to Harold Chase of the *Topeka Journal* that he knew what had gotten Allen "in bad with the administration." It was, said White, "a certain declaration he made about a boy who froze to death at the Detention Camp at Camp Funston. This made the administration piping mad." White added, "Henry does not know I know this, but I got it from a confidential source."[20]

Whatever the reason, there was apparently a real danger that the administration's attitude would damage Allen's campaign, especially if Allen were to have to go home in the middle of it. White persuaded Allen to remain in Europe. Then he pulled some strings to get his candidate transferred from the Red Cross to the YMCA, which was not government-sponsored and where the wrath of the administration could not touch him. Meanwhile, White continued to run Allen's remote-control campaign, and he did it so effectively that Allen won the endangered primaries easily, carrying 100 of 105 counties. He also won the election, and that without making a single speech or appearance on his own behalf.[21]

William Allen White was to have influence and power of a sort after that 1918 campaign, but that was his last great stand as a kingmaker. What the almost always optimistic White took for the new dawn of Progressivism in the off-year elections of 1918 was really one last, bright flare of the twilight of the Progressive gods. But White continued to think of Theodore Roosevelt as the liberal hope of the Republican party. Furthermore, the letter he wrote to Roosevelt about the Bull Moose scouting trip indicates that he assumed Roosevelt would be as indignant as he was about party leadership.

He took both Hays and Chairman Simeon Davison Fess of the Congressional National Committee to task in a letter to McCormick:

> . . . Reconstruction may make as vital a crisis as war. . . . And to

> assume that we are going back to "status quo ante" is an act of assumption, which offends, and every time that Feese [*sic*] or Hays talks about the temporary economic condition and looks longingly back to the good old days before the war, a lot of Progressives turn away from the Republican Congressional ticket. It will be quite possible to elect a Republican Congress this year; the drift is all that way. . . . But the Democrats will win as surely as sunrise if Feese [*sic*] and Hays keep putting out reactionary dope.[22]

That letter was written on September 16, 1918, before the vote was in. The vote proved White wrong. The twilight was deepening. The reaction which was to bring full darkness to White's hopes had already begun to set in. Part of this White was to recognize later as not merely a political reaction, but a reaction from the high moral and emotional tension of the Progressive Era and the fighting of the war to end all wars.

Meanwhile, White's own thoughts about what the postwar world should be like continued along lines of government control and other prewar Progressive notions. He even softened his appraisal of Wilson, and in June 1918 wrote to Norman Hapgood of *Collier's*: "I read your article about the President. In the main, I agree with you. During the entire campaign of 1916, I could not find anything to say for him and nothing to say against the President. I think he is functioning beautifully as our great democratic leader. Of course," he added, as, being William Allen White, he almost had to add, "I am always afraid of the south. They are reactional and crooked and I fear their influence. Yet he has done pretty well with them so far and he may be able to go further."[23]

White wrote to George Creel, of the Committee on Public Information, that he hoped the day would come when America would have a thorough-going radical party with a thorough-going radical program. "I am weary of promises and repression, and all the mummery of agreement with smug conservatism," he wrote. "I have written a dynamiting, hell-raising book that has just been published," he added, "and I am sending it to you herewith."[24]

That dynamiting, hell-raising book had to be White's last novel, *In the Heart of a Fool*, because White did not publish anything else but magazine pieces and editorials in 1918.[25] The dynamite seems less explosive today then it might have seemed in White's own time, but *In the Heart of a Fool* is an earnest indictment of the urban industrial power structure that White saw overtaking his beloved rural America. In that, it was a new departure for White. He had never written an industrial novel before. He had never written about the relations of organized labor and management before. Otherwise, however, he went back to the one major source of his fiction, the Bible. *In the Heart of a Fool* is the retelling of the Passion of Jesus. Mark Adams, the labor organizer, is Jesus,[26] and Judge Van Dorn is variously Pontius Pilate and the Devil himself.[27] White had been reading Bouck White's *The Call of the Carpenter* as he began to work on his own book, and the influence is highly visible.[28] *In the Heart of a Fool* has all the faults of William Allen White's other fiction. It is over-written. Where it intends morality, it is moralistic. Where it intends sentiment, it exudes sentimentality. Where there ought to be a symbol, White provides a signboard instead. His intention was to prove that evil does not necessarily bring punishment nor virtue reward, and he tried as hard as he could—on his own testimony—to make sure that the villains were not all black nor the heroes all white.[29] The fact remains, however, that in this novel just as much as in the fiction that preceded it, William Allen White was using the novel as a pulpit, and his sermon was showing. White could not let the story tell its own moral. He even had Judge Van Dorn compose a motto for the occasion:

> Get onto the Prince of Peace,
> Big Boss of the Democracy of Labor.[30]

And though he gives to his Christ-figure some humanizing characteristics, his Judge Van Dorn is evil incarnate, an unrepentant John Barclay.

After the fact, White himself was not happy with the book. Although some reviewers faulted the book on its prolixity and its too-explicit preaching,[31] Everett Rich, an early biographer of White, said that none of the reviewers was as hard on the book as White was himself in conversations with Rich.[32] American reviews, generally, ran the gamut from kind to ecstatic.[33]

At the time, as far as White was concerned, it was a hell-raising book. It was the unregenerate Progressive taking one last fictional swipe at the forces of industrial power and evil. The book behind him and Henry J. Allen's campaign for governor successfully handled, White began to hunt for ways to get to Europe to cover the peace conference. He wrote on January 14, 1918, to Victor Murdock, who was by this time a member of the Federal Trade Commission, asking Murdock's help in getting him a place on the Russian commission. "I believe," he wrote, "that the Russian revolution is the greatest net gain of this war so far."[34] He was already looking ahead, and, as we have seen, he was early afraid of a post-war reaction. He was afraid of postwar unrest both from consolidating industry and from labor.

On November 13, 1918, he was writing to William H. Ingersoll, of the Committee on Public Information,

> I am known as a radical in politics and in many other activities of life. So what I say must not be read out of the mouth of the conservative. I fear there is grave danger in America of a Bolshevist movement—partly the reaction of the people against the rigors of the war, and partly a fear among laborers that after the war they will be economically declassed, that is returned to their former economic status of low wages and bad living conditions. During the war, they have plainly seen their value to society, and our need of them. They are going to insist on value received after the war, and if they do not get it, there is going to be trouble. Generally I am not timid about social disturbances, but I am timid about what is in the offing. But I think some sincere attempt should be made, not so much to thwart and suppress the movement as to prevent its culmination by intelligent discussion and by earnest consideration of the causes of the movement. Perhaps I am wrong. It may be that the iron hand is better than the soft answer which turneth away wrath. But I feel that if we drift, we are in danger.[35]

If White had followed his hunches more, and not backed off so often, as he did in the last two sentences just quoted, he would indeed have been a seer whose private sentiment could have been made public opinion. Events proved that there was considerable labor unrest after the war. There was America's first big Red scare, and the iron fist was perhaps not as effective as a soft answer might have been in remedying the trouble.

The big story was, of course, the peace conference, and White naturally wanted to cover it. In the first place, he wanted to be a member of the peace commission, and he sent identical telegrams to Henry Cabot Lodge, Will Hays, and Theodore Roosevelt, saying, "If Republicans have membership on peace commission and also minority part in organizing commission I should greatly like place in organization and would deeply appreciate any help or suggestion from you."[36]

Nothing came of the telegrams, and one wonders why White thought anything should come of them. Even if the Republicans had had any power in the organization of the American delegation to the peace conference, it is hard to image Lodge recommending this member of the Midwest "lunatic fringe" to membership. Moreover, Hays had already shown signs of backing away from Bull Moose contagion, and there can be little doubt that Roosevelt, though even then a sick man, was busily mending fences among the Regulars, with an eye on the 1920 Republican presidential nomination.

When he could not go to Versailles in an official capacity, White contracted with the Wheeler Syndicate.[37] It made little difference. White had spent his life alternating among three positions: that of participant, as in party caucuses and platform committees; that of observer, as a reporter and interpreter of events in which he was not personally involved; and that of combination participant-observer, as at a national political convention at which Delegate White sat at the press table and recorded the proceedings of which he was a part.

All that White really wanted was to be on the inside, to be in the middle of things. It did not matter to him whether he stirred or was stirred. As he wrote to George Creel, "I wish I could persuade our beloved President to give me a job in the organization of the Peace commission. I don't want to be high commissioner but I would like to be somewhere where I could stick my eye to the keyhole and see what was going on inside."[38]

Once he got to Europe, White found that reporting an international peace conference was not quite the same thing as reporting a national political convention or a precinct primary, although there were similarities. He and the other reporters found themselves caught between the Wilsonian idea of open covenants openly arrived at and Wilson's own reluctance to give those reporters a true picture of what was going on at the conference. White reported later that he and the other reporters could get straighter information from the British press officer than from the American.[39] Wilson, indeed, often embarrassed his own people by contradicting their releases.[40] This reluctance on the part of Wilson combined with the acceptance of *de facto* censorship by the European press persuaded White to lead a struggle to open up the coverage. According to Dorothy Canfield Fisher, it was White's influence at the newsmen's protest meeting that opened to the press what were to have been closed meetings of the peace conference.[41]

White's reports on the peace conference were, in the end, much like the stories he had written about political conventions. He was at least as interested in the personalities behind the news as he was in the news itself. Though he protested later that he had gone to Europe totally unprepared to cover the kind of story he found there, that was only partially true. For the peace conference was indeed a kind of magnified political meeting, more like a caucus than a convention, and White saw that Wilson was at a disadvantage because Wilson had never had to engage before in any real political in-fighting.[42]

The kind of thing that he wrote for the Wheeler Syndicate he later incorporated into his autobiography. The sketches of Clemenceau and Lloyd George, Wilson's opponents in what White called "the cosmic poker game," are good indications of the kind of insight that White brought to his reporting.

"Premier Clemenceau represented the continent of Europe," he wrote. "He knew it as well as any one man could know it. He was a cynic but not a pessimist, for he had great faith. But chiefly his faith was in France and the French way of life. At first he probably despised Wilson as a canting Presbyterian moralist."[43]

As for Lloyd George, White saw him as a "horse-trading Welsh politician" whose "eyes were greedy for advantage to the British Empire." White surmised that Lloyd George knew Wilson and his kind better than Clemenceau did, because to Lloyd George, Wilson was "a Scotch-Irish parson."

"Lloyd George, in the Council of the Three, worked more often with Wilson than with Clemenceau," White wrote, "but when the interests of the British Empire were at stake he deserted Wilson with the sweet and lovely complacency of the courtesan who has her children to support."[44] Wilson gave away everything else to get the League of Nations, White wrote. "The difference between the complacency of Lloyd George and the surrender of Wilson," White wrote, "was that the Britisher knew he was harloting, and Wilson believed he was serving the will of God."[45]

White sympathized with Wilson's position. Brought up short by the immovable fact of the secret treaties which England and France had signed before America's entrance into the war, Wilson bent enough to try to find his way around the obstacles. He got his covenant, and that was what he had come all the way to Paris to get. Never mind that most of the famous Fourteen Points that were supposed to secure honorable peace for mankind had been considerably blunted in conference. Wilson got his covenant—the hard way. "He really had only one chip in the game," White wrote, "to secure justice for humanity in some kind of vital political organism that was in his own heart. But alas," White added, "the thing he fathered has his own weaknesses. He begot it too good for this world."[46]

Meanwhile, there was to be a conference between delegates of the smaller Baltic states that had broken away from Russia on one side and either Lenin and Trotsky or their representatives on the other. The French, though frightened of the possibility of Russian power, had agreed to set up the conference. William Allen White was to be one of the American delegates at the Prinkipo Conference, to be held on the island of Prinkipo in the Marmora Sea off Turkey.[47] His partner on the delegation was to be George D. Heron, sociologist, economist, the diplomat in the cloak-and-dagger tradition who had helped pave the way for the Weimar Republic in Germany. These accomplishments were important to the proposed conference. They were also important to White, his experience in diplomatic missions being non-existent.[48] What interested the American press about the Herron appointment, however, was that some twelve years before, Herron had fallen in love with one of his students at a small independent college, persuaded her mother that there was nothing wrong with the idea, and had gone to Europe with his new love *and* her mother, leaving behind his wife and family. By the time White met him, Herron had been married four times.

Needless to say, the American press had a good time resurrecting the old story, and Sallie became worried that association with Herron would sully her Will's reputation.[49] Her Will was not worried. He was having a splendid time. The Herron scandal did not bother him. What did bother him was the fact that the French were apparently out to sabotage the Prinkipo Conference. The French, according to White's recollection, were afraid of a resurrected Germany, but they were also afraid of the emerging Soviets to the north and east. They were doing everything in their power to prevent an *entente* between the White Russians of Estonia, Lithuania, and other small states which had pulled out of the Soviet bloc and the Bolsheviki. White thought that the French were holding out for a return to monarchy in Russia or, at the very least, the re-establishment of a Kerensky type of republic.[50]

As the French went about sowing doubt among the White Russian delegates at the peace conference, White showed that he was a better diplomat than he knew. Seeing that most of the emigré delegates lived meagerly, to say the least, White suggested that he and Harron take the delegations out to dinner, one after the other. Thus, while the French sabotaged the conference by day, two mismatched Americans undid the damage at night with good talk and good food.[51]

The French won finally, when the date for the conference slipped by and the other delegations could not persuade the French to set another date. As White said, the conference "fizzled." It had so little importance in the deliberations following World War I that one has to look long and hard to find it listed in history books. But the abortive Prinkipo Conference and the Versailles Conference were both important parts of the latter-day education of William Allen White.

Although he did not like Wilson–it was much more a matter of personality than it was of politics–White was a fervent supporter of the League of Nations. He still believed that it was within the power and province of politics to establish and maintain a just peace for all mankind. He had misgivings, nevertheless, about Wilson's chances of achieving that peace. For one thing, Wilson refused to release to reporters the substance of the covenant, though White, who was an old hand at making good use of political propaganda, pleaded with Colonel Edward House, Wilson's aide, to release the news so that the newspapers could begin educating the American public in the advantages of such a league.[52]

What bothered White most about Wilson was his imperious, self-righteous attitude–that and the fact that Wilson was not Theodore Roosevelt. What White witnessed, as he watched Clemenceau and Lloyd George outmaneuver Wilson at Versailles, was not a failure of American diplomacy. It was a lack of American diplomacy. White himself called Wilson's great powers of moral righteousness and persuasion one of the three great weapons of the Allied forces in the lately concluded war, but Wilson's big mistake was believing that the moral force he generated among the people at home and the people on the streets in Europe was an effective substitute for diplomatic bargaining with professional diplomats.[53]

It is doubtful that Theodore Roosevelt could have done any better under the circumstances. He would not have been a third party making his good offices available as he had been in the negotiations following the Russo-Japanese conflict. Here he would have been a participant, to borrow White's figure, with stakes on the table. Although Wilson and Roosevelt were diametrically opposite temperaments, the choice between a cold intellect, who could not understand that politics is not necessarily a logical process, and an emotional reactor, capable of being triggered by shibboleths, is no choice at all.

While White was covering the peace conference at Versailles, he received word of Roosevelt's death. Roosevelt had been for White, a man who always needed a hero, the final hero. "I have never known another person so vital nor another man so dear," he wrote in his autobiography.[54] He wanted very much to find another such hero. Later, he tried to put Herbert Hoover and Wendell Willkie into the Theodore Roosevelt mold. Neither would fit.

So William Allen White reported the peace conference; watched not only Clemenceau and Lloyd George, but Italy's Orlando as well, chip away at Wilson's dream of a just peace; watched Wilson struggle as the other members of the Big Four wrung concession after concession out of him; saw Wilson salvage only the covenant of the League of Nations and, in a strategic error, make it a part of the treaty; and then went home to help Wilson fight for the League in America.

11

The God-Damned World

Though the death of Theodore Roosevelt had been a great emotional shock to White, even before Roosevelt's death, he had begun to look on Woodrow Wilson as Roosevelt's Progressive successor. If he had accepted Wilson reluctantly, it was more because of a difference in personalities than a difference in program.[1] In fact, when White wrote a biography of Wilson in 1924, he saw between Roosevelt's New Nationalism and Wilson's New Freedom "that fantastic imaginary difference that always existed between tweedle-dum and tweedle-dee."[2]

That was one reason that, despite his suspicions concerning this Southern Bourbon Democrat, this patrician schoolmaster who did not know the ways of practical politics, William Allen White returned from the peace conference ready to fight for the League of Nations. The other reason was that he believed completely in the League as an instrument of world government and world peace.[3] Having had a ringside seat at the peace conference, White came home as disillusioned about international politics as the next man, but he still believed that the war that had been fought to make the world safe for democracy need not have been fought in vain. So he went up and down the land, making speeches in favor of the League.[4] He fought as long and as hard for the League as did Wilson, and in the end, he wrote in his biography of Wilson that Wilson's immortality among men depended on whether the League stood or fell.[5]

It depends on whose evidence one accepts whether the failure of the

League and of the covenant of the League be blamed on the "little band of willful men" in the United States Senate or on the equally willful man who was President of the United States. White put the onus squarely on Wilson, without mitigating the part played by the irreconcilables in the Senate.[6] Wilson made the first blunder, according to White, when he asked for a Democratic Congress in 1918. Given his belief in party responsibility, it is hard to see what else Wilson could have done.[7] In fact, given White's own belief in party responsibility, the only difference that divided the two men on this issue was the difference between Democratic party responsibility and Republican party responsibility. Anyway, and more or less incidentally, the request for a Democratic Congress came first from the National Democratic Committee and not from Wilson, as White himself was quick to point out.[8] Certainly subsequent events proved that it was the divided Congress that resulted from the 1918 elections which prevented Wilson from achieving his goals in foreign relations.

And so Wilson fell, and with him went American participation in the League of Nations. If White's campaign to elect Henry Allen governor was his last great stand in state politics, his fight for the League of Nations was the last national political fight he would wage until World War II. There seemed to be no hope left for White. His political power was at low ebb, and he knew it, though he did not stop fighting.

White was a member of the National Republican Committee twice after 1918, and there is evidence that he slanted the Landon presidential campaign in 1936 toward the midwestern liberal vote.[9] Nevertheless, he really ceased to be effective nationally after the 1916 campaign. Even so, and though it may be true, as Walter Johnson has said, that from then on White kept his high place in national Republican councils as a sort of liberal window-dressing,[10] White himself either did not realize the fact or, realizing it, was still willing to be the gadfly of his party.

Certainly he fought the nomination of Warren G. Harding to the end. He held out till the last ballot for Herbert Hoover, whom he regarded as the heir to the insurgent liberal tradition in the Republican party.[11] But White voted for Harding, finally, and the taste of it never left his mouth. The National Committee knew White's feelings about the Harding nomination and sought to placate him. It named White a member of the committee to notify Calvin Coolidge of his vice-presidential nomination. White would have none of it. On July 20, 1920, he wrote to Republican

Chairman Will Hays, "I am going to hike out to Colorado Monday so I can't go to notify Coolidge. This is definite and final."

Nevertheless, White had finally voted for Harding's nomination, and he did vote for Harding in the election. His own testimony contradicts itself here. In his autobiography, White wrote, "I was faced with . . . either bolting Harding or supporting him. I did neither."[12] Yet in the *Gazette* at the time, from September 1919 to the end of March 1922, White supported Harding, at the same time rationalizing for all he was worth.[13]

Early in the Harding administration, White supported the Republican administration, and particularly Harding, hoping on what evidence it is hard to imagine, that Harding would break from his senatorial advisors and continue the prewar liberal trend.[14] But William Allen White was going against the current for the first time in his life. In his young manhood he had been a conservative Republican at a time and in a place where conservative Republicanism was in the majority and ruled the nation. He had been a member, as he said, of the governing, if not of the ruling class. In his prime he had been a rebel when rebellion was in the air. Now in his maturity, he was still a rebel, but the days of rebellion were over. In that sense he was what he was to call Calvin Coolidge—a museum piece.[15]

It is to his credit, and an answer to those who have called William Allen White a political opportunist, that he did not turn back. Having found the road to limited, middle-class liberalism, he stayed on it. Within the limits he accepted and within the framework of the Republican party which he could not again gainsay, William Allen White remained a liberal for the rest of his life.

It was a heroic stand, but, for the most part, it was an ineffectual stand. In the 1920s White did not even have a strong minority behind him within his own party. He fretted in print about what the party was doing. He remained the gadfly, but he could not change the party. Yet as late as 1936, when he wrote *What It's All About,* a rather lukewarm endorsement of Alf Landon, White maintained that the political battles in Kansas were not so much between the Republican and Democratic parties. They were rather, he said, battles between the liberal and conservative forces within the Republican party. When the conservatives took control of the party, he added, the state was likely to choose a liberal, Democratic governor and to surround him with members of the liberal faction.[16] The wish was father of the thought. William Allen White was trapped in his own preconceptions about the Republican party, about the Democratic party, and about himself.

Hence, the 1920s were a sad time for him. A little over a month after the 1920 election, White wrote this cry of anguish to his old friend Ray Stannard Baker:

> What a God-damned world this is! I trust you will realize that I am not swearing; merely trying to express in the mildest terms what I think of the conditions that exist. What a God-damned world!
>
> Starvation on the one hand, and indifference on the other, pessimism rampant, faith quiescent, murder met with indifference, the lowered standard of civilization faced with universal complaisance, and the whole story so sad that nobody can tell it.[17]

Two great personal losses obviously had much to do with the mental depression from which White was evidently trying to break free. Though Theodore Roosevelt had died on January 6, 1918, that death and the memory of the dreams that died with Roosevelt continued to haunt White. He wanted to write a biography of Roosevelt. It was a natural ambition, but White never realized it. Early in 1920, he wrote several letters asking for reminiscences,[18] and he wrote to Macmillan's that he was "grinding away on the Roosevelt book."[19] Apparently, all that survives is a twenty-page manuscript in the White collection in the William Allen White Memorial Library, on the campus of Kansas State Teachers' College, Emporia.[20]

One reason White never finished the Roosevelt book may have been that while he was working on it, someone dearer to him than Roosevelt died. The death of Mary White provided her father with what he called the "baggage for the short trip into posterity that I may take."[21] The editorial that resulted from that death not only gave William Allen White a trip into posterity, it gave to Mary White herself a kind of immortality of which she surely would have approved. That editorial became a high school classic. By 1947 it had been reprinted in over 200 books,[22] and it remains to this day the first thing to come into the minds of those who remember William Allen White.

There is not a wasted word in "Mary White." In a little more than a thousand words, William Allen White distilled the story of a vibrant, gay, questing young life. The temptation to weep must have been strong in him, but he turned away from the death that occasioned the essay to the life that ran before it and the life that came after. One paragraph detailed the death; two were for the funeral. The rest of the essay was about life, not death. It has the same tension of emotion under strong control that should characterize elegaic poetry.

MARY WHITE

May 17, 1921.

The Associated Press reports carrying the news of Mary White's death declared that it came as the result of a fall from a horse. How she would have hooted at that! She never fell from a horse in her life. Horses have fallen on her and with her—"I'm always trying to hold 'em in my lap," she used to say. But she was proud of few things, and one of them was that she could ride anything that had four legs and hair. Her death resulted not from a fall but from a blow on the head which fractured her skull, and the blow came from the limb of an overhanging tree on the parking.

The last hour of her life was typical of its happiness. She came home from a day's work at school, topped off by a hard grind with the copy on the High School Annual, and felt that a ride would refresh her. She climbed into her khakis, chattering to her mother about the work she was doing, and hurried to get her horse and be out on the dirt roads for the country air and the radiant green fields of the spring. As she rode through the town on an easy gallop, she kept waving at passers-by. She knew everyone in town. For a decade the little figure in the long pigtail and the red hair ribbon has been familiar on the streets of Emporia, and she got in the way of speaking to those who nodded at her. She passed the Kerrs, walking the horse in front of the Normal Library, and waved at them; passed another friend a few hundred feet farther on, and waved at her.

The horse was walking, and as she turned into North Merchant Street she took off her cowboy hat, and the horse swung into a lope. She passed the Tripletts and waved her cowboy hat at them, still moving gayly north on Merchant Street. A Gazette carrier passed—a High School boy friend—and she waved at him, but with her bridle hand; the horse veered quickly, plunged into the parking where the low-hanging limb faced her and, while she still looked back waving, the blow came. But she did not fall from the horse; she slipped off, dazed a bit, staggered, and fell in a faint. She never quite recovered consciousness.

But she did not fall from the horse, neither was she riding fast. A year or so ago she used to go like the wind. But that habit was broken, and she used the horse to get into the open, to get fresh, hard exercise, and to work off a certain surplus energy that welled up in her and needed a physical outlet. The need has been in her heart for years. It was back of the impulse that kept the dauntless little brown-clad figure on the streets and country roads of the community and built into a strong, muscular body what had been a frail and sickly frame during the first years of her life. But the riding gave her more than a body. It released a gay and hardy soul. She was the happiest thing in the world. And she was happy because she was enlarging her horizon. She came to know all sorts and conditions of men; Charley O'Brien, the traffic cop, was one of her best friends. W. L. Holtz, the Latin teacher, was another. Tom O'Connor, farmer-politician, and the Rev. J. H. Rice, preacher and police judge, and Frank Beach, music master, were her special friends; and all the girls, black and white, above the track and below the track, in Pepville and Stringtown, were among her acquaintances. And she brought home riotous stories of her adventures. She loved to rollick; persiflage was her natural expression at home. Her humor was a continual bubble of joy. She seemed to think in hyperbole and metaphor. She was mischievous without malice, as full of faults as an old shoe. No angel was Mary White, but an easy girl to live with for she never nursed a grouch five minutes in her life.

With all her eagerness for the out-of-doors, she loved books. On her table when she left her room were a book by Conrad, one by Galsworthy, "Creative Chemistry" by E. E. Slosson, and a Kipling book. She read Mark Twain, Dickens and Kipling before she was ten—all of their writings. Wells and Arnold Bennett particularly amused and diverted her. She was entered as a student in Wellesley for 1922; was assistant editor of the High School Annual this year, and in line for election to the editorship next year. She was a member of the executive committee of the High School Y.W.C.A.

Within the last two years she had begun to be moved by an ambition to draw. She began as most children do by scribbling in her school books, funny pictures. She bought cartoon magazines and took a course—rather casually, naturally, for she was, after all, a child with no strong purposes—and this year she tasted the first fruits of success by having her pictures accepted by the High School Annual. But the thrill of delight she got when Mr. Ecord, of the Normal Annual, asked her to do the cartooning for that book this spring, was too beautiful for words. She fell to her work with all her enthusiastic heart. Her drawings were accepted, and her pride—always repressed by a lively sense of the ridiculous figure she was cutting—was a really gorgeous thing to see. No successful artist ever drank a deeper draft of satisfaction than she took from the little fame her work was getting among her schoolfellows. In her glory, she almost forgot her horse—but never her car.

For she used the car as a jitney bus. It was her social life. She never had a "party" in all her nearly seventeen years—wouldn't have one; but she never drove a block in her life that she didn't begin to fill the car with pick-ups! Everybody rode with Mary White—white and black, old and young, rich and poor, men and women. She liked nothing better than to fill the car with long-legged High School boys and an occasional girl, and parade the town. She never had a "date," nor went to a dance, except once with her brother Bill, and the "boy proposition" didn't interest her—yet. But young people—great spring-breaking, varnish-cracking, fender-bending, door-sagging carloads of "kids"—gave her great pleasure. Her zests were keen. But the most fun she ever had in her life was acting as chairman of the committee that got up the big turkey dinner for the poor folks at the county home; scores of pies, gallons of slaw, jam, cakes, preserves, oranges, and a wilderness of turkey were loaded into the car and taken to the county home. And, being of a practical turn of mind, she risked her own Christmas dinner to see that the poor folks actually got it all. Not that she was a cynic; she just disliked to tempt folks. While there, she found a blind colored uncle, very old, who could do nothing but make rag rugs, and she rustled up from her school friends rags enough to keep him busy for a season. The last engagement she tried to make was to take the guests at the county home out for a car ride. And the last endeavor of her life was to try to get a rest room for colored girls in the High School. She found one girl reading in the toilet, because there was no better place for a colored girl to loaf, and it inflamed her sense of injustice and she became a nagging harpy to those who she thought could remedy the evil. The poor she always had with her and was glad of it. She hungered and thirsted for righteousness; and was the most impious creature in the world. She joined the church without consulting her parents, not particularly for her soul's good. She never had a thrill of piety in her life, and would have hooted at a "testimony." But even as a little child, she felt the church was an agency for helping people to more of life's abundance, and she wanted to help. She never wanted help for herself. Clothes meant little to her. It was a fight to get a new rig on her; but eventually a harder fight to get it off. She never wore a jewel and had no ring but her High School class ring and never asked for anything but a wrist watch. She refused to have her hair up, though she was nearly seventeen. "Mother," she protested, "you don't know how much I get by with, in my braided pigtails, that I could not with my hair up." Above every other passion of her life was her passion not to grow up, to be a child. The tomboy in her, which was big, seemed loath to be put away forever in skirts. She was a Peter Pan who refused to grow up.

Her funeral yesterday at the Congregational Church was as she would have wished it; no singing, no flowers except the big bunch of red roses from her brother Bill's Harvard classmen—heavens, how proud that would have made her!—and the red roses from the Gazette forces, in vases, at her head and feet. A short prayer: Paul's beautiful essay on "Love" from the Thirteenth Chapter of First Corinthians; some remarks about her democratic spirit by her friend, John H. J. Rice, pastor and police judge, which she would have deprecated if she could; a prayer sent down for her by her friend Carl Nau; and, opening the service, the slow, poignant movement from Beethoven's Moonlight Sonata, which she loved; and closing the service a cutting from the joyously melancholy first movement of Tchaikovsky's Pathetic Symphony, which she liked to hear, in certain moods, on the phonograph, then the Lord's Prayer by her friends in High School.

That was all.

For her pallbearers only her friends were chosen: her Latin teacher, W. L. Holtz; her High School principal, Rice Brown; her doctor,

> Frank Foncannon; her friend, W. W. Finney; her pal at the Gazette office, Walter Hughes; and her brother Bill. It would have made her smile to know that her friend, Charley O'Brien, the traffic cop had been transferred from Sixth and Commercial to the corner near the church to direct her friends who came to bid her good-by.
>
> A rift in the clouds in a gray day threw a shaft of sunlight upon her coffin as her nervous, energetic little body sank to its last sleep. But the soul of her, the glowing, gorgeous, fervent soul of her, surely was flaming in eager joy upon some other dawn.[23]

The death of two such persons who were so very dear to him, coupled with the apparent destruction of all that he had worked for for twenty years, made it necessary for White to stand back and reconsider. The wonder is in the resilience of the man. Even when the fortunes of all that he believed in had nearly hit rock bottom, that fact in itself engendered hope. On December 29, 1920, he had written to Victor Murdock:

> I, of course, am very unhappy politically. I suppose any man is who has any love of country or faith in its institutions, or hope for its future. I don't think we have come to the Slough of Despond yet. We are going down further. But what I fear is, or perhaps not so much what I fear as what I hope for, is that we will dam the waters of progress so that there will be a tremendous breakover flood. . . . I feel that our splurge from 1903 to 1914 was very worth while. We did get a lot of things done. Things that were worth doing; things that are permanent.[24]

In 1921, in their capacity, as White said, as "Vice-regents of God," the Federal Reserve Board deflated the currency.[25] The purpose of this move, according to White, was to slow the rising strength of labor in the country. It may have done that to some degree. What it did in White's country was to drive many cattle feeders to destruction, for the feeders depended on long-term loans to finance the purchasing and feeding of cattle for the market. When the feeder farms failed, the farm boys moved to town looking for work. They had become fair mechanics, working on cars, tractors and other machinery around the farm. They had become, in a small, Midwestern way, a part of the industrial labor supply.

So it was that when cattle shipments were down and the Emporia shops of the Santa Fe railroad felt the pinch, a shopmen's strike did not have a chance. The garage mechanics in the area moved in to take the shop jobs, and the displaced farm boys moved into the garages. The unrest put a double pinch on Emporia. The railroad shops were as important to the economy of the town as were the cattle feeders. Moreover, what was happening in Emporia was happening throughout the Midwest. Credit was tightening, stores were closing, banks were wobbly.[26]

In this situation, the men in the Emporia shops joined the nationwide shop strike. The strike was not so much for wages or working conditions as it was for the right of the shop men to join the Railroad Brotherhoods, for the shop union in 1922 was a company union. When the shop men came to White to talk about the impending strike, he did not advise them to strike or not to, but he promised them that if they did strike, they would get fair coverage in the *Gazette.* Perhaps because so much of Emporia's economy depended on the shop payroll, there was considerable sympathy among the merchants for the strikers, and the strikers asked the merchants to put placards in their windows saying "We are with the strikers 100%."[27] And there was the rub.

Although the Emporia strike was part of a national strike, Governor Henry J. Allen took it upon himself to invoke the powers of the Kansas Industrial Court, which was established to adjudicate labor disputes in essential industries. Under the powers of the legislation, he ordered the signs removed from the store windows.

In reply, White warned Allen that he was going to put a placard in the window of the *Gazette* office to say, "So long as the strikers maintain peace and use peaceful means in this community, the Gazette is with them 50 per cent, and every day which the strikers refrain from violence, we shall add 1 per cent more of approval."[28]

Allen said, "Bill, if you do that, I'll have to arrest you."[29] White did it, and the battle—a friendly one throughout, as far as the principals were concerned—was joined. White wanted to take the case to the courts to test Allen's action against the right of free speech and to publicize the issue, and since Allen and White were known to be friends and political associates, the case got national coverage.[30] Out of it also, William Allen White produced a Pulitzer prize editorial, one of the best short discussions of the meaning of freedom ever penned by an American.

In the midst of the controversy, he received a warm letter of remonstrance from Fred J. Atwood, an ex-Bull Moose friend of Concordia, Kansas. White answered the letter, and then it occurred to him that his answer to Atwood might be his answer to all those who opposed his stand in his dispute with Governor Allen. He edited the carbon copy of his letter, trimmed it, tightened it, and ran it as a front-page editorial in the *Gazette* of July 27, 1922:

> TO AN ANXIOUS FRIEND
>
> July 27th, 1922.
>
> You tell me that law is above freedom of utterance. And I reply that you can have no wise laws nor free enforcement of wise laws unless there is free expression of the wisdom of the people—and, alas, their folly with it. But if there is freedom, folly will die of its own poison, and the wisdom will survive. That is the history of the race. It is proof of man's kinship with God. You say that freedom of utterance is not for time of stress, and I reply with the sad truth that only in time of stress is freedom of utterance in danger. No one questions it in calm days, because it is not needed. And the reverse is true also; only when free utterance is suppressed is it needed, and when it is needed, it is most vital to justice.
>
> Peace is good. But if you are interested in peace through force and without free discussion—that is to say, free utterance decently and in order—your interest in justice is slight. And peace without justice is tyranny, no matter how you may sugar-coat it with expedience. This state today is in more danger from suppression than from violence because, in the end, suppression leads to violence. Violence, indeed, is the child of suppression. Whoever pleads for justice helps to keep the peace; and whoever tramples on the plea for justice temperately made in the name of peace only outrages peace and kills something fine in the heart of man which God put there when we got our manhood. When that is killed, brute meets brute on each side of the line.
>
> So, dear friend, put fear out of your heart. This nation will survive, this state will prosper, the orderly business of life will go forward if only men can speak in whatever way given them to utter what their hearts hold—by voice, by posted card, by letter, or by press. Reason has never failed men. Only force and repression have made the wrecks in the world.[31]

In the meantime, the strike was settled, and the Kansas attorney general moved to dismiss the case against White. White protested, but there was nothing else for the judge to do but to dismiss. Nevertheless, White's actions and his editorial had done their work. The editorial was reprinted almost as widely as "What's the Matter with Kansas?" had been, and once more, from a little town in the middle of the Kansas prairie, William Allen White had made his private sentiment public opinion, and he had made it count. As had happened with "What's the Matter with Kansas?" the editorial and the occasion gave White a national audience for his views, and he followed up "Industrial Justice–Not Peace" in the May 1922, issue of *Nation's Business*[32] with "William Allen White States His Own Case" in the August 2, 1922, issue of *Outlook*[33] and "W. A. White On The Kansas Court," in the December 27, 1922, issue of *Nation.*[34] He continued also to fight what looks in hindsight like a forlorn rear-guard action with articles like "Why I Am a Progressive" in the *Saturday Evening Post*[35] and "What's the Matter with America?" in *Collier's.*[36] Neither was he through with Harding. In the March 4, 1922, issue of *Collier's,* he had taken a lusty swipe at "The Best Minds Incorporated."[37]

What he had written to Victor Murdock was true to William Allen White. America was not yet at the bottom of the abyss, nor was White himself ready to hide in the darkness. He was already working on the biography of Woodrow Wilson which he would publish in 1924. He saw in Wilson a great man who had overestimated the power of his own intellectual equipment; a man who would brook no challenge to the rectitude of his actions; a man, in other words, who believed completely in himself as one of the elect of God.[38] He was, said White, as proud of his "single-track" mind as he was of his "first-rate" mind.[39] He was also a man to whom the intuitions and traditions of practical politics were as a dark country. And always, besides, he was a Democrat, a captive of the Irish city bosses, of the radical West, and of the Bourbon South. The contradictions inherent in this appraisal, in view of his own relationship with the radical West, seem never to have occurred to White.

Regardless of his political bias, White was able to appreciate and analyze Wilson's prewar and wartime contributions. He saw Wilson as a sort of patrician liberal, more premier than president. It was White's distinction, but it fit. It is the theory behind Wilson's own book, *Constitutional Government in the United States.* He also saw Wilson's moral force and the power of his words as one of the three elements most responsible for the Allied victory in World War I, ranked with the armies of General Foch and the British Navy.

Regardless of the political differences between the two men, White's *Woodrow Wilson* is cast in the same mold as is *The Autobiography of William Allen White.* There is the same insistence on the importance of heredity, the same warring of the Irish and the Puritan, the same child-is-the-father-of-the-man framework. White even traces Wilson's political development almost step by step with his own. Both White and Wilson were conservatives as young men. Both men saw the light of liberalism at about the same time in their lives. To White, Wilson was a liberal as White was a liberal, and one who tried to put that liberalism on the world stage. The main trouble with Wilson, one gathers from reading the White biography, was that he was not Theodore Roosevelt.

Another shortcoming White found in Wilson he traced to the fact that Wilson lacked practical political experience. Neither had he come up in the world by way of the ward caucus nor had he been subjected to defeat—either as a boy on the playground or as a man in the rough-and-tumble of politics—until he was thwarted by the United States Senate after World War I. All of which may seem a little strange, because when White came to write the first of his two books about Calvin Coolidge, he said that the trouble with Calvin Coolidge was that he *had* come up from the ward caucus. He had become the willing tool of the powers of plutocracy, said White, not for any venal reason, but simply because he believed as they did in the sanctity of property. White could excuse this in Coolidge because he recognized it in his old self, but the trouble with Calvin Coolidge was that he did not progress. He did not follow Theodore Roosevelt and Woodrow Wilson and William Allen White in leaving the temple of the Pharisees. Yet he was middle class, he was Calvinistically Puritan, he was a Republican, and he was an honest politician. All this White said in *Calvin Coolidge, the Man Who Is President,* which he published in 1925, making a book out of four articles that he had written earlier for *Collier's.*[40]

White may have considered himself in outer darkness, and he may have thought that the world he lived in was literally God-damned, but he continued to do what he could to disprove his own thesis. He was turning out articles telling the world outside Kansas what a Kansas man thought of the world and interpreting the world and world events to his Kansas neighbors. He may indeed have been on the wrong side of the door to the political arena, but he used his magazine articles to batter against that door. Besides, in July 1922, he began writing a weekly feature for the Sunday edition of the *New York Herald Tribune,*[41] and from November 1921, to August 1922, he wrote editorials for *Judge.*[42]

The 1920s saw a spate of books from the White workshop. Besides the Wilson and Coolidge biographies, the first of two collections of his *Gazette* editorials, *The Editor and His People,*[43] appeared in 1924, and *Politics: The Citizen's Business* in 1927.[44] That book was a citizen's primer on the uses of the pressure group, something William Allen White knew a great deal about. He pointed out to his readers that the ordinary citizen could use the pressure group just as effectively as could the special interest. All the ordinary citizen had to do was to join the groups in which his interests lay, work in the groups and with them, and he would thereby increase his effectiveness as a citizen in a democracy. It was White's own method, the most effective way he had, aside from his own writing, of making his private sentiment public opinion.

Meanwhile he put together a collection of political portraits that he had been writing for the magazines—portraits of political bosses and powers he had known, mostly, like Platt and Quay and Chicago's Big Bill Thompson—and published them in a book called *Masks in a Pageant.*[45] Sandwiched between *Politics* and *Masks* were two little books, *Boys—Then and Now* and *Conflicts in American Public Opinion,* a twenty-eight page booklet which he wrote with Walter E. Myer.[46]

All this obviously indicates prodigious production. Add to it the fact that White was at the same time running a daily newspaper and keeping up an almost unbelievable volume of correspondence.[47] But White was not really prodigal with his words. Nearly all of his books grew out of previously published editorials, articles, lectures, and short stories. This is not to say that the articles did not undergo revision before they became parts of books, nor is it to say that the books were paste-pot-and-scissors jobs. White was a good reporter, and when he had to depend on research, he was indefatigable. The Wilson book sent him scurrying across country on interviews,[48] and *A Puritan in Babylon,* which did not appear until 1938, and which was his second attempt to delineate and explain the Calvin Coolidge phenomenon, was perhaps his most thoroughly researched and most competent job of writing on a large scale.[49] The fact remains, however, that White's editorial page was his daybook, and that, in a sense, he wrote one book all his life: the life and opinions of William Allen White. In what he wrote in the 1920s, White can be seen sorting out those opinions, seeking reasons for the wrecking of the dream, trying to find out why, after the glorious vision of the teens, in the 1920s this was, after all, a "God-damned world."

Maybe he could not find the answer for the world, but a long time afterward, when he came to write his autobiography, White had found the answer about his own country. It was a matter of relaxation, of reaction, after twenty years of straining toward the good. As he put it:

> The country, after eight years of Wilson and the four short years of breathing space with Taft before Wilson, and seven years of Roosevelt—almost twenty years in which people were keyed up on principles, years in which causes were followed and battles were fought for issues rather than men—was tired of issues, sick at heart of ideals, and weary of being noble. . . . In 1920 also, the fact that we were a creditor nation sobered us down. Our vast national debt of twenty-four billion gave us pause. And we kicked off our pilgrim's shoes, unbuttoned our strait-laced raiment with the odor of sanctity about it, and slumped.[50]

This would explain the election of Harding and Coolidge. They were what the people ordered. White saw the election of Harding as a seizure of power by the Senate, but he also saw the election of both Harding and Coolidge as a manifestation of spiritual relaxation of a people stretched too tightly and too long on the rack of reform and war.

What he said about the people at large was also a projection from White himself. Consider what he said in his autobiography about his own behavior at the nomination of Harding:

> I have wondered . . . why I faltered that hot afternoon in Chicago. . . . I believe that the death of Theodore Roosevelt and the rout of his phalanx of reform, together with the collapse of Wilsonian liberalism . . . and the eclipse of the elder La Follette's leadership, all created in my heart a climax of defeat. . . . Indeed the whole liberal movement of the twentieth century which had risen so proudly under Bryan, Theodore Roosevelt, and La Follette, was tired. . . . The spirits of the . . . Progressives were bewildered . . . I was too tired to rise and fight. I hope now, looking back to that sordid hour in Chicago, that I am not merely rationalizing my conduct to justify its turpitude.[51]

Very well, he was tired and disillustioned, but there were still some fights to be fought, and he had one other qualified victory in this period of desolate despondency besides his victory in the railroad strike. He beat the Ku Klux Klan in Kansas.

There is some evidence that the Klan influence was on the wane in the Midwest before White became a major factor in the fight against it.[52] Perhaps. The fact remains that in 1924 in the state of Kansas, both the Democratic and the Republican candidates for governor tacitly accepted Klan endorsement. It is also a fact that the Klan was reorganizing in Kansas in the early 1920s, and that, within a week after a Klan organizer arrived in Emporia, White went after the organization with all the weapons in his arsenal. He wrote:

> The Ku Klux Klan is said to be reorganizing in Emporia. It is an organization of cowards. Not a man in it has the courage of his convictions. It is an organization of traitors to American institutions. Not a man in it has faith enough in American courts, laws and officials, to trust them to maintain law and order. . . . It is a menace to peace and decent neighborly living and if we find out who is the Imperial Wizard in Emporia, we shall guy the life out of him. He is a joke, you may be sure. But a poor joke at that.[53]

But the Klan proved to be stronger and more numerous than White had anticipated, even to the point of holding a regional meeting in Emporia. White sent a reporter to the hotel where many of the Klansmen were staying, instructing his reporter to get the names off the hotel register. The desk clerk refused to release the information. White sent his reporter back with instructions to tell the manager that if the register was not made available, the name of the hotel would never again appear in the columns of the *Gazette.* White got the list and printed it. He also printed an editorial praising the accommodations of the hotel and its cooperation. "When you have to spank the baby," he told the reporter, "it's a good idea to give it a piece of candy afterwards."[54]

But chastisement and candy were not enough to stem the Klan influence, and before long Emporia had a Klansman for mayor and enough weight that both the Republican candidate and the Democratic candidate for governor were willing to accept Klan endorsement.[55]

William Allen White had built his political and journalistic careers on a foundation of political chastity, knowing that political influence declined when trading for office began. He and Sallie had hurried to Washington in the first flush of his political power to plead with McKinley not to give White a post office appointment.[56] He did not want to be governor of Kansas in 1924 any more than he had wanted to be Emporia postmaster in 1897, but someone had to oppose the Klan.

So it was that on September 20, he announced as an independent candidate for governor. His reasons?

> I want to offer Kansans afraid of the Klan and ashamed of that disgrace, a candidate who share their fear and shame.
>
> The issue in Kansas this year is the Ku Klux Klan above everything else. It is found in nearly every county. It represents a small minority of the citizenship and it is organized for purposes of terror, directed at honest law-abiding citizens; Negroes, Jews and Catholics. These groups in Kansas comprise more than one-fourth of our population. They menace no one. Yet because of their skin, their race, or their creed, the Ku Klux Klan is subjecting them to economic boycott, to social ostracism, to every form of harassment, annoyance, and every terror that a bigoted minority can use.
>
> Kansas, with her intelligence and pure American blood, of all states should be free of this taint. I was born in Kansas and lived my life in Kansas. I am proud of my state. And the thought that Kansas should have a government beholden to this hooded gang of masked fanatics, ignorant and tyrannical in their ruthless oppression, is what calls me out of the pleasant ways of my life into this disgraceful but necessary task. I cannot sit idly by and see Kansas become a byword among the states. . . . I call to my support all fair-minded citizens of every party, of every creed, to stop the oppression of this minority of our people. It is a national menace, this Klan. It knows no party. It knows no country. It knows only bigotry, malice and terror. Our national government is founded upon reason, and the Golden Rule. This Klan is preaching and practising terror and force. Its only prototype is the Soviet of Russia.[57]

Of course, campaigning was not nearly so distasteful to him as his editorial made it sound. It was disgraceful that someone outside the party structures had to challenge the Klan, certainly; but as to the campaigning itself, William Allen White was back in harness, happy as a reactivated fire horse. With Son Bill chauffeuring him, he covered the length and breadth of Kansas, speaking, bargaining, politicking, fighting the good fight in the arena he liked best, the arena of grassroots, midwestern American politics.[58]

Ben Paulen, the Republican candidate, won the election; but William Allen White polled about as many votes as did the Democratic candidate, and he polled more votes than there were Klansmen in the state.[59] Thereafter the Ku Klux Klan was not an effective political force in Kansas. The Klan did continue to try. On May 5, 1926, White took this one last, glorious swipe at the cow-pasture klaverns:

> Doctor Hiram Evans, the Imperial Wizard of the Kluxers, is bringing his consecrated shirt tail to Kansas this spring, and from gloomy klaverns will make five Kansas speeches. We welcome him. Enter the Wizard—sound the bull-roarers, and the hewgags. Beat the tom-toms.
>
> He will see what was once a thriving and profitable hate factory and bigotorium now laughed into a busted community; where the cock-eyed he-dragon wails for his first-born, and the nightshirts of a once salubrious pageantry sag in the spring breezes and bag at the wabbly knees.
>
> The Kluxers in Kansas are as dejected and sad as a last year's bird's nest, afflicted with general debility, dizziness on going upstairs, and general aversion to female society.[60]

White had won the battle, but he certainly had not won the war, and he knew it. Indeed, things seemed to have returned to *status quo ante* Theodore Roosevelt. The nation was again worshipping at the altar of Mammon, as it had under Hanna and McKinley. "What a sordid decade is passing!" White wrote in 1926. ". . . Corruption is rampant in high places. Special privilege is unleashed and shameless. The fourth-rater is coming into prestige and power in business, in politics, in religion."[61]

Maybe, he wrote to reformer-novelist Brand Whitlock, the whole time was epitomized in the life of Warren G. Harding. Whitlock had suggested that White undertake Harding's biography, and White was tempted. Predictably, he saw the story as another retelling of the Prodigal Son parable. This time, however, society itself would be the impatient spendthrift, wasting its substance in riotous living. But the time was not ripe for such a book, said White. Too many people were still alive who might be hurt in the telling of the story of Harding the "he-harlot."[62]

Too many people might be hurt—and to no purpose. White was a good enemy, but he hardly ever attacked persons except to get at institutions he disliked or feared. When the Daughters of the American Revolution blacklisted him—along with a long list of liberals and pacifists—in 1928, White was delighted. He said its leaders had been "hypnotized by the brass buttons of the retired Army officers and lured into this red-baiting mania by the tea-gladiators of Washington."[63] When Mrs. Alfred Brosseau, then president of the DAR, demurred in kind and with spirit, White replied, "The DAR has yanked the Klan out of the cow pasture and set it down in the breakfast room of respectability, removing its hood and putting on a transformation." Then he added, with a courtly bow, "Mrs. Brosseau is a lovely lady with many beautiful qualities of heart and mind, but, in her enthusiasm, she has allowed several lengths of Ku Klux nightie to show under her red, white and blue."[64]

At the same time, White was fighting the same kind of a rear guard action on the literary front, though now that fight took the form of reviewing fiction rather than creating it, White's own fictional output having dwindled to nothing after World War I. And no wonder. White's literary heroes were Ralph Waldo Emerson, Mark Twain, and, most of all, William Dean Howells, who had insisted on a realism that dealt with the "smiling aspects of life."[65]

By 1918, White himself had said all he had to say about the world as it was and the world as it ought to be. Then the world blew up in his face. It would never again be the glorious world in which good fought laughing in the face of evil. Perhaps the problems of the world could no longer be explained in the retelling of Biblical parables. For one thing, the world was no longer made up of small towns where foibles, virtues, and vices of society could be gently satirized and delineated in miniature as White had done in *In Our Town.*

Sinclair Lewis had demolished Main Street, and though White had praised the novel, he had also come to the defense of the street and the people who worked on it. He defended his Main Street, especially in a city whose population had reached five thousand, but he added, when he wrote to Lewis:

> It has been years since I have read anything so splendidly conceived and so skillfully executed as "Main Street."

> If I were a millionaire, I would buy a thousand of those books and send them to my friends, and then I would go and bribe the legislature of Kansas to make "Main Street" compulsory reading in the public schools. No American has done a greater service for his country in any sort of literature, than you have done.[66]

On the other hand, in reviewing *Main Street* and Dorothy Canfield Fisher's *The Brimming Cup,* White wrote:

> Mr. Lewis seems to be dealing with facts; but he has only the facts about the side [of Main Street] containing the hardware stores, the grocery stores, the pool hall and drug stores; he omits the facts about . . . the side which contains the drygoods stores, the millinery and suit shops, the music store and the book store.[67]

In 1906 he had written sternly to a Miss Kate Delano:

> I assume that you want a frank answer to your letter . . . and you may as well know that your stuff is exactly the kind that makes me madder than any other kind that is written. It is a bad kind and miserably bad of its kind. . . . A certain decency of heart and soul are [*sic*] required for the real stuff. . . . If you wish to get anywhere in the world of writing, get it out of your head that smart stuff counts. Until you see that goodness, decency and wholesomeness is not dull [*sic*] but that it is all that is worthwhile, you will not amount to much in the writing way. . .
>
> . . . Forget it; cut it out; do household hints, cooking recipes, religious notes, heart to heart talks with indigent idiots, but cut out the erotic. There is nothing in it when it is well done, and you do it badly.[68]

There is, incidentally, no evidence that Miss Delano ever published.

Clearly, a man who believed in decency and wholesomeness and in a moral order in fiction as well as in fact had to dig for his faith in this "sordid decade." In 1925, White delivered the Weil Lectures on American Citizenship at the University of North Carolina, published as *Some Cycles of Cathay.* In one of those lectures, White said sadly, "In literature leadership is falling into the hands of a cult that is clearly on the side of the devil's own angels, the side that scoffs at any theory that there is a moral purpose guiding our universe."[69]

In literature as in politics and social philosophy White was the man in the middle, and in the sad days between the two world wars he sometimes found that middle ground lonely. In an undated manuscript called "What About the Novel?" he stated his literary position like this:

> And "Sister Carrie" is as false as "Pollyanna" in its philosophy. Life is doubtless highly carrieful—to coin a word for Mr. Dreiser, and for Mrs. Porter it is surely pollyanneous; but for a lot of us it is neither. We trek along the middle plane. . . . Possibly this middle average toddles about with "Alice Adams."[70]

In 1926 White helped bring about a greater dissemination of books in the land, and he also put himself in position to make his literary tastes known in yet another way. He became one of the founding judges of the Book-of-the-Month Club and remained a judge until his death, along with Heywood Broun, Henry Seidel Canby, Dorothy Canfield Fisher, and Christopher Morley. Those years of judging books for wide distribution, especially the later years of his life, pretty well epitomized White's life and attitudes. As Canby wrote in the *Saturday Review of Literature* at the time of White's death:

> If he could not come [to the judges' meeting in New York], there would be a lengthy yellow sheet of telegram, a masterpiece of epigrammatic criticism of the books he had read. All the solid Middle West would be in those telegrams—its background of Puritanism, cracking down on the flippantly indecent, surprisingly appreciative of frank honesty, scornful of piddling sophistication. All its liberalism, too, the liberalism of a man who hated equally reaction and the radical dogmatism of writers who had never tried to make politics or economics do useful work.[71]

In the memorial brochure in which the Canby tribute was reprinted, Harry Scherman, president of the Book-of-the-Month Club, reproduced some of White's telegrammatic criticism, charitably omitting the names of authors whom White chastised or of authors of whom White approved but whose books were not chosen for Book-of-the-Month Club distribution. The telegrams Scherman quotes are from the 1940s, but White indicated one of the facets of his critical judgment earlier, when he wrote that he preferred the novels of Harold Bell Wright to those of Jack London.[72]

Still, he knew what he liked and what he did not like. For instance, he telegraphed his colleagues in New York:

> Seems to me by all odds the best buy is DeVoto's THE YEAR OF DECISION. It will stand up with REVEILLE IN WASHINGTON . . . although not so interesting a period and of course with no great figure in it but still it is a dignified job of which we will all be proud.[73]

In the same telegram, White said:

> ——— is the dirtiest book I ever read. Not that I was shocked by it. The fences, barns and outhouse walls of childhood's golden hour gave me great familiarity with the general idea of the book.[74]

Above all, White had a keen eye for the false, the over-written, and the manufactured book. Of one book he wrote that it was "one of those books that bewildered me. As I read," he continued, "I thought, 'Well, maybe this is symbolism,' but I got to thinking, 'No, this is alcoholism.' My final conclusion is that it is gibberish."[75]

Literary embroidery got this reaction: "The decorative writing of first half makes it pretty terrible. I mean those lugged-in and pinned on metaphors similes and tropes which are like pimento strips on a salad or paper panties on a mutton chop."[76] And about one scissors-and-paste job he said that it was "just a paper from a woman's club on Flemish art done as a cyclorama. It reads as well forward as backward and up as well as down."[77] He was easily bored by the marital musical chairs game which had already become stock material in the popular novels. "The adulteries become too monotonous after the first half-dozen," he complained. "They are repetitious and one longs somehow for good vigorous criminal assault and battery."[78]

He grew weary of "books out of books, research stuff," and longed for good first-hand adventure, searching also for the great American novel. His criteria were somewhat tougher than they had been when, as a young man, he had been lifted off his feet by the verse of James Whitcomb Riley, tougher than they had been when, try as he might, he could not squeeze the sentimentality out of his own fiction.

Thus, as a judge for a book club, William Allen White was again busy making his private sentiment public opinion. He would accept neither the inverted sentimentality of Dreiser nor the explicit sentimentality of Mrs. Porter. Rather, he "toddled along" with the genteel realism of Booth Tarkington. It was, after all, at least in the world of letters, neither a good nor a bad world, and certainly not the "God-damned" world that White had pictured to Ray Stannard Baker. But that was the political world, and this was the literary world.

And in the political world, the great time was over. All that was left was to reminisce, as White did in *Masks in a Pageant:*

> Those were truly Cromwellian times—from 1901 to 1917. What a lot of liberty we bought "with lance and torch and tumult" in those days from Roosevelt to Wilson! In those days the America of *laissez faire,* the Jeffersonian America, passed. The morality of the people restated itself in the laws and institutions needed by a complex civilization. If ever our land had a noble epoch, America enjoyed it in those days of the Great Rebellion.[79]

Now, if ever, things were indeed in the saddle and rode mankind, as Emerson had said. Literature was cheap, politics in the hands of the hated plutocracy, and the whole nation playing the part of the Prodigal Son. To make it worse, there seemed no way for the Prodigal Son to return to the house of his father. And so it was that the warrior from Armageddon could write wearily, as early as 1926, "What a sordid decade is passing!" He added, at the end of an editorial that was a long lamentation:

> What a joy it would be to get out and raise the flaming banner of righteousness! Instead of which we sit in our offices and do humdrum things and go home at night and think humdrum thoughts.
>
> What a generation!

When Russell Fitzgibbon reprinted the editorial in 1937 in a compilation of White's editorials called *Forty Years on Main Street,* White added this footnote: "Well, six years brought the man. And when he came, I some way did not 'get out and raise the flaming banner of righteousness.'"[81] There is no need to wonder why. The New Deal was not the Square Deal, and Franklin Roosevelt was not Theodore Roosevelt.

12

The Other Roosevelt

Though White remembered that he had longed for a leader for whom he could shake out the flaming banner, and though he remembered that when the leader appeared, he did not cheer, his letters and editorials tell the story differently. He was convinced that Franklin Delano Roosevelt had no consistent domestic policy at all, and that the whole New Deal was a matter of trial and error. Still, he supported most of the social legislation that resulted from that trial and error. After all, he pointed out, considering the circumstances in which the country found itself, a policy of trial and error was better than no policy at all. He had high hopes for the new administration from the beginning, calling Roosevelt's speech at his nomination the most exciting acceptance speech he had ever heard. Besides, no government which included in its cabinet such old-time Progressive friends as Harold Ickes, Frances Perkins, and Henry Wallace could be all bad.

As the New Deal developed, White was by turns convinced that Franklin D. Roosevelt was returning the country to the Progressive path, bewildered by the speed and variety of FDR's actions, and increasingly concerned about the methods Roosevelt was using to achieve his ends, no matter how Progressive those ends might be.[1]

Once again, William Allen White was caught in the trap which he himself had spent an adult lifetime making. He might approve of most of FDR's domestic policy. By the summer of 1935, however, when he had to choose between acceptance of the program and loyalty to his Kansas-based Republican party, he chose the party. He chose the party, indeed, every election year; and he was embarrassed when Roosevelt singled him out in the crowd during an Emporia stopover, for his support "three and a half years out of every four."[2] There was little else White could do. By 1936 he saw that no Republican candidate on the horizon could beat Roosevelt unless the Republicans made some substantial changes in their attitudes and pronouncements. Certainly the Republican party could not defeat Roosevelt simply by indicting him.

If he favored most of the New Deal domestic program, and if he was so out of sympathy with the Hamilton wing of the Republican party, why then did William Allen White support Alf Landon in the 1936 presidential election? He supported Landon out of friendship for Alf's father, a fellow Bull Moose.[3] He supported him out of loyalty to his Kansas friends who had initiated the Landon Presidential boom.[4] He supported him because, after all, Landon was a Republican, one of the few Republican governors to survive in a predominantly Democratic era, and a Kansas Republican at that.[5]

William Allen White supported Alf Landon's candidacy from the beginning, but from the beginning that support was ambiguous. In letters to those who wanted to know his opinion of Landon, White wrote that Landon had as much political experience as Coolidge had had when he became vice president. But then in *A Puritan in Babylon,* White was to call Coolidge a "museum piece," a political "troglodyte." It may be that he saw in Landon what columnist Raymond Clapper saw in the conference that got away from White and Henry Allen, a candidate midway between Hoover conservatism and the New Deal.[6]

White supported Landon, that is, but not very stoutly. In fact, if some of the eastern newspapers accused White of being lukewarm,[7] it was only because he was. Consider this from an editorial published in late 1936 and reprinted by W. L. White in the *Autobiography:*

> . . . Political geography has taken him where he is; a successful Republican governor of a midwestern state who, as La Follette's Monthly declares, is not too progressive to offend the conservatives, nor too conservative to lose the support of the liberals.
>
> But political geography does not make a man President. He must measure up to certain spiritual requirements. . .[8]

White then detailed the political and spiritual requirements of a President and vacillated between pride in the fact that a Kansan had been nominated for the presidency and an unspoken fear that Alf Landon did not have the necessary presidential equipment.[9]

Nevertheless, and in spite of the fact that his conference to liberalize the Republican party had been captured by John Hamilton and the Old Guard, White went to Cleveland as a Landon delegate to the National Convention and served on the platform committee of that convention.[10] He also wrote a campaign book, *What It's All About,* but it was a perfunctory performance; White's heart was not in it.[11] After all, he did support at least the purpose of most of the New Deal social legislation, and from 1933 forward he was a strong and unequivocal supporter of the Roosevelt foreign policy.

It was the means that Roosevelt used to activate his domestic policy that bothered White, not the ends. What he had been proud to call distributive justice under Theodore Roosevelt he called Hamiltonian feudalism when Franklin Roosevelt proposed a similar program.[12] Nor was this entirely campaign rhetoric. He firmly believed that most social and economic reforms could be and should be achieved at the local level, or at the farthest distance, the state level.[13] He did not approve of federal aid unless its functions were performed and its funds distributed by the state or local governments—the closer to the people the better. On the other hand, when the states would not or could not do what he knew was the right thing, White supported a federal program. This he did joyfully, for instance, when Roosevelt fought for the Child Labor Amendment.[14]

Moreover, in 1930, he put himself at the service of the government again. He went to Haiti as a member of a presidential commission to get the U.S. Marines off the island.[15] Though he protested again his lack of diplomatic experience, he was, by all accounts, one of the most effective members of the commission.[16] Largely on the groundwork that the commission laid, Haiti and the United States signed a treaty in 1932 and by 1934 the last U.S. Marine had left the island.[17]

Meanwhile, White was still in demand as a syndicated columnist. In 1933, he and Sallie went to England, where he covered the London Economic Conference for the North American Newspaper Alliance. For the most part, White wrote, the conference was a waste of time, chiefly because the United States was in the process of devaluing the dollar at the same time that the conferees were trying to find a way toward international monetary stabilization.[18] From London Will and Sallie White went to Russia, where they discovered, but could not report, the great famine in the south caused by the collectivization of the farms and the slaughter of the Kulaks.[19]

Back home, he was still "froggy in the middle." He liked this later Roosevelt and was "glad he came," but he still wondered whether it was possible to "establish a new revolution of free men with their dollars in shackles."[20] He was pleased that a Kansan could become the standard bearer of the Republican party; still he was unhappy to see that standard bearer become the captive of the Old Guard.

But though he might say to himself and to others, from time to time, that he was just going to sit on the fence and watch the political world go by, natural inclination and long habit made it inevitable that he be in the fight somewhere. One of his favorite devices in the 1930s was to buy newspaper advertisements in the Kansas press to persuade and exhort his fellow Kansans. He thus advertised his support for the Kansas Civil Service Amendment,[21] and in 1938, he used advertising to expose and denounce the Reverend Gerald P. Winrod, a Wichita demagogue who was seeking nomination to the United States Senate. Typical of White's campaign against Winrod was a four-column ad which appeared in the *Iola Register* for July 22, 1938. In it, White called attention to the dangers inherent in Winrod's nomination. Winrod was, he pointed out, violently anti-Semitic, anti-Catholic, and anti-Negro. Besides which, White's advertisement continued, Winrod was also opposed to, and opposed by, twenty-two Protestant churches in his home town.[22]

There remained, however, White's greatest contribution to his country and the kind of democratic society he espoused. It came in his participation in the making and propagandizing of American foreign policy. The pattern was by this time familiar. White hated war. It was "the Devil's joke on humanity," he said.[23] Because, above all things, he wanted to keep America out of war, he supported the Neutrality Act of 1935, his desire for peace overcoming his usually pragmatic approach to public affairs.[24] It was not until 1939 that he saw that the Neutrality Act, because it forbade arms shipments to *any* nation, actually made aggression more attractive and defense against aggression more difficult.[25] Aside from that one defection, White supported the Roosevelt foreign policy, both before and during the war. He was particularly ardent in his support of the Good Neighbor policy and of the reciprocal trade treaties.[26] But if he was leading the parade on those two issues of foreign policy, he was just one of the midwestern troops in his belief that America could stand aloof from what was going on in Europe and in Asia in the early 1930s. From 1935 to 1939, William Allen White was no leader of public opinion; he was its reflector. He was like a released homing pigeon, circling to get his bearings.

When Germany invaded Poland on September 1, 1939, White stopped circling. Even before the invasion, he had modified his position from one that insisted on strict neutrality and embargo to one favoring cash-and-carry sale of armaments.[27] He intensified his support of such a position in editorials written immediately after the invasion. Thus he was ready when Clark Eichelberger called him from New York on September 26, 1939, to ask him to head a Non-Partisan Committee for Peace through Revision of the Neutrality Law.[28] Eichelberger was director of the League of Nations Association and of the Union for Concerted Peace Efforts.[29] The committee White was to head was an outgrowth of the UCPE.

Though events from the first of September had made White psychologically ready for the job Eichelberger wanted him to do, he was at first reluctant to accept it. He was working on his autobiography, and he was seventy-one years old.[30] He wanted to devote the time he had left to the book. But the friendly persuasion he had used over the years to get his friends to do things in public life was turned on him, and old friends like Dorothy Canfield Fisher finally convinced him that he could and should take the job.[31]

Thus began William Allen White's last great exercise in making his private sentiment public opinion. Here was a chance to fight for cash-and-carry help to the Allies. Here was a chance to help beat Hitler. And finally, here was a way, he hoped, to keep America out of the war.

Once at the head of the Non-Partisan Committee, he polished up his old armament: telegrams, letters, editorials and news stories. He even added a new weapon, national radio broadcasts.[32] In order to get Congressional support for cash-and-carry, White also went on a buttonholing campaign in Washington, D.C.[33] It was tough work. He found the Republican contingent in Congress almost solidly opposed to any revision of the Neutrality Act. One hundred forty Republicans, including a Kansas delegation whom White did not even bother to try to persuade, voted against the revision when it finally passed.[34] But pass it did, and on the testimony of Franklin D. Roosevelt and Cordell Hull, White and his committee were greatly instrumental in its passing.[35]

September 1, 1939, had polarized White's thinking. Before that time, peace was paramount. Afterwards, peace for America and the defeat of Nazism had equal priority. The Non-Partisan Committee and the American Union for Concerted Peace Efforts were one thing; some of the other committees that sprang up like mushrooms in a rainy forest were something else. As hard as White worked for the first two, he worked against the Anti-War Mobilization, the Women's International League for Peace, the National Council for the Prevention of War, the Keep America Out of War Congress, and World Peaceways.[36] By now White was as opposed to peace at any price as he was to war.

By now, also, Roosevelt knew what he had to do. His problem was to get the American people to go along. On December 14, 1939, he wrote a long letter to White. He examined his alternatives and found none good. He wrote:

> Here is the thought for you to devote thought to. Taking things in their broadest aspect, the world situation seems to me to be getting progressively worse as the weeks go by. No human being, with the best of information, has the slightest idea how this war is going to come out. But the fact remains that there are four or five possibilities, each leading to greater chaos, or to the kind of truce that can last only a short period.
>
> As you know, I do not entertain the thought of some of our statesmen of 1918 that the world can make, or we can help the world to achieve a permanently lasting peace. . . . On the other hand, I do not want this country to take part in a patched-up, temporary peace which would blow up in our faces in a year or two.
>
> There are several schools of thought about the Russian-German arrangement. One thinks that Germany could take hold of the Bear's tail to keep England and France out of the war and that Germany today is much concerned over Russia's unexpected policy of action. . . .
>
> The other school of thought, with equal reason, believes that there is a fairly definite agreement between Russia and Germany for the division of European control and with it the extension of that control to Asia Minor, Persia, Africa, etc., etc.
>
> If that latter is true and Germany and Russia win the war or force a peace favorable to them, the situation of your civilization and mine

> is indeed in peril. Our world trade would be at the mercy of the combine, and our increasingly better relations with our twenty neighbors to the south would end—unless we were willing to go to war in their behalf against a German-Russian dominated Europe.
>
> What worries me, especially, is that public opinion over here is patting itself on the back every morning and thanking God for the Atlantic Ocean (and the Pacific Ocean). We greatly underestimate the serious implications to our own future and I fear most people are merely going around saying "Thank God for Roosevelt and Hull—no matter what happens, they will keep us out of war."
>
> The Lord and you know perfectly well that Roosevelt and Hull fully expect to keep us out of war—but on the other hand, we are not going around thanking God for allowing us physical safety within our continental limits.
>
> Things move with such terrific speed these days, that it is really essential to us to think in broader terms and, in effect, to warn the American people that they, too, should think of possible ultimate results in Europe and the Far East.
>
> Therefore, my sage old friend, my problem is to get the American people to think of conceivable consequences without scaring the American people into thinking that they are going to be dragged into this war . . .[37]

White, too, was in a quandary. For a man of his temperament and experience, America's situation in the world in December 1939 presented a real Gordian knot. In his answer to Roosevelt, on December 22, he reflected the indecision of the American people. "I fear our involvement before the peace," he wrote, "and yet I fear to remain uninvolved, letting the danger of a peace of tyranny approach too near."[38]

But if December was a time of doubt, by May the doubt had left White's mind. Through the winter and into the spring of 1940, the troops of Adolf Hitler's Nazi Germany rolled like a seemingly unstoppable wave across Europe. By May, White and his friends on the Non-Partisan Committee for Revision of the Neutrality Law were convinced that unless what was still free in Europe were aided positively by America, America herself would be nearly defenseless against Nazi invasion.

Using the Non-Partisan Committee as a base, White, Eichelberger, and others began to organize the Committee to Defend America by Aiding the Allies. They enlisted newspaper editors, publicists, clergymen, educators–influential persons from all walks of public life. With White as chairman, they encouraged the formation of local groups within the Committee to Defend America by Aiding the Allies, hoping to crystallize and channel opinion from the grass roots.

The idea caught fire immediately, and by May 25 he was asking Roosevelt for "sailing orders." He had an enthusiastic nation-wide organization, and he was not sure what to do with it. He was all dressed up, he told the President, with no place to go.[39] Apparently, the President was not too ready with a road map, for early in June, White sent him a telegram saying, "As an old friend, let me warn you that maybe you will not be able to lead the people unless you catch up with them."[40]

White worked hard at his chairmanship. Whatever else White was, he was not the figurehead that the pro-German groups and the isolationists called him.[41] He wrote, he spoke, he arranged. It was all in the familiar pattern, and to make the pattern complete, he was right where he had been most of his public life–in the middle.

In less than a month, he was denying British bias in a letter to Oswald Garrison Villard. ". . . I hold no brief for the British Government," he wrote, "but I do believe that if it falls, we will be in pretty bad shape and all I am doing is trying to prevent the fall of the British Government by selling, cash on the barrelhead, the material we are legally allowed to sell and to amend the laws if need be so that we can sell her some second string, rather old fashioned destroyers."[42]

On July 25, the Century Group inside the Committee to Defend America by Aiding the Allies–a group which included among its members Eichelberger, Herbert Agar, and Ward Cheney–issued a Declaration calling for immediate declaration of war on Germany. Said the Declaration, in part: "The United States should immediately give official recognition to the fact and to the logic of the situation–by declaring that a state of war exists between this country and Germany. Only in this constitutional manner can the energies be massed which are indispensable to the successful prosecution of a program of defense."[43]

Roosevelt met with members of the Century Group on August 1, but he was non-committal about the Declaration. When White heard about the meeting, he wrote that the President seemed to him, since the renomination, to have "lost his cud." Roosevelt, White thought, had become hazy and apathetic.[44]

Then there were those who wanted to use White's committee to fight political battles. White felt constrained to send a long night letter to Phillip Degarmo, of Poughkeepsie, New York, telling Mr. Degarmo why the committee should not fight Congressman Hamilton Fish, a vocal and powerful isolationist. White wired:

> . . . it happens I have known Hamilton Fish's father and Hamilton for many years. Personally, I like him. Factionally, we disagree inside the Republican party. But our committee has no business, as a committee taking any stand whatever against Mr. Fish because if we begin to fight Fish, we have got to fight the entire Republican membership in Congress, which would land us right square in the Democratic camp and absolutely annul our influence. Fish is no worse than the rest, and supposing every local committee started to fighting its Republican congressmen. We would be nothing but a Democratic sideshow. And when I heard our committee's name was being used, even indirectly, in the fight against Fish, I had to disavow it, and in disavowing it I had to make it plain that personally Mr. Fish and I are friends and politically we belong to the same party and have the same party hopes.[45]

In one respect, that night letter represents a strange position for William Allen White to take. Hamilton Fish was, after all, one of the most highly vocal isolationists in Congress. He was, besides, leading the fight against leasing destroyers to Great Britain. He opposed White's committee. Yet, though we can never discount the appeal to White of personal friendship and party loyalty, the heart of his argument was sound. There was no point in fighting nearly the entire Republican party, and the Republican party, generally, was isolationist.

So White found himself between those who wanted an immediate declaration of war and those who wanted the United States to take no action at all, bombarded on one side by the propaganda of the William Pelleys and the Gerald Winrods, which called White a figurehead for warmongers, and the propaganda of those who wanted immediate war, which accused White of wanting peace at any price.[46]

The second group got a big boost from Robert Sherwood, presidential speech-writer, friend of White, author of the Pulitizer-prize winning play

There Shall Be No Night, which was inspired by W. L. White's broadcast from Finland, "The Last Christmas Tree." Sherwood took out a full-page advertisement in *The New York Times,* and in that space he presented, with all the skill and passion at his command, the argument for immediate declaration of war:

"Stop Hitler now!" he pleaded, pointing out that every step the British and French fell back brought "war and world revolution closer to the Americans." Hitler's was "a desperate gamble," he said, with the stakes "nothing less than the domination of the whole human race."

He saw the world of the future placed on a permanent war footing, with the business of living reduced to "primitive self-defense."

"'Government of the people, by the people, for the people'–if Hitler wins," Sherwood warned, "this will be the discarded ideal of a discarded civilization."[47]

The less of Europe that remained free, the more White was convinced that America could not survive the collapse of Europe. As early as June 1940, he was writing in an official letter of the Committee to Defend America by Aiding the Allies:

> If we have the good will of the Allies when they are defeated, which seems likely, we can make arrangements to get their fleets. If we have their fleets, we can defy Hitler with our fleet in the Atlantic Ocean and theirs in the Pacific Ocean. If we do not help the Allies, if we turn our backs on them now, they will see no reason for helping us by giving us their fleets. In which case, if these fleets go to Hitler, he will have the power to take the British possessions in the West Indies. These islands control the Panama Canal. In a few months he could build air and naval bases and make much trouble for us. If we let him move in after defeating the British, he would be violating the Monroe Doctrine. He will not move in without the British and French fleets. But he will move in then and war will be certain."[48]

In a radio interview given in that same fateful 1940, White defended his position and the position of his committee. "All my life," he said, "I have fought war. I hate war. I believe it never settled anything but when all that we cherish is threatened with attack I feel that we must, in the name of peace, help stop this war and by helping the Allies defend America. . . . I believe in peace. But there can be no peace in the world except as there is justice in the world. And justice comes through reason and never through force. Justice grows out of the give and take of men and nations. . . . The Nazis have proved their scorn of the compromise and give and take of nations. Their solution to all problems is force. And because the Allies represent the forces of reason, I feel that we should help them and thereby establish the rule of reasoned justice in the world. So we may secure the blessings of peace to ourselves and our posterity."[49]

White stated his position clearly and repeatedly, and while he continued to resist pressures from both the isolationists and those who wanted an immediate declaration of war against Germany, he worked hard on practical ways to aid the Allies.

On August 2, 1940, the Cabinet met to discuss finding ways to sell, "directly or indirectly," as Roosevelt's notes on the meeting put it, fifty or sixty over-age destroyers to Great Britain. The Cabinet agreed unanimously that the very survival of Britain might depend on her getting the destroyers, and that legislation was necessary to legalize the transfer.[50] The members of the Cabinet were also aware, however, that if Roosevelt were to ask for such legislations without preparing public opinion for it, such legislation would be defeated or at least delayed, perhaps beyond the time when it would help the British.[51]

Two things concerned the Cabinet in this discussion. If, through Lord Lothian, the British ambassador, the United States could be assured that the British navy would under no circumstances fall into the hands of the Germans, the expected congressional opposition to the destroyer deal might be considerably dampened.[52] Secondly, the plan needed the support of Wendell Willkie, the Republican presidential nominee, and through him the approval of Republican congressional leaders, Charles McNary in the Senate and Joseph Martin, minority leader in the House of Representatives.[53]

Roosevelt wrote a long note to himself that evening, while the events of that Cabinet meeting were still fresh in his mind. "After discussing the disposition of the British fleet in the event of the defeat of Britain," he wrote, "it was agreed that I would call up William Allen White, who had recently talked with Willkie on this; ask White to come to Washington immediately to see Hull, Knox and Stimson, and after that to see me, and then returning to see Willkie and seek to get, with Willkie's approval, the support of Joe Martin and Charlie McNary for such a plan. It was agreed that if this procedure went through successfully, that I would, at once, send a definite request to the Congress for the necessary legislation."[54]

W. L. White wrote about his father's work as chairman of the Committee to Defend America by Aiding the Allies, "Probably his principal service to the committee was in connection with the campaign of 1940 when, on several occasions, he served as a liaison between Willkie and the President in a largely successful attempt to prevent the Roosevelt foreign policy from becoming the principal issue of the campaign."[55]

Be that as it may, his success with Willkie concerning the over-age destroyers was somewhat less than complete. White was his usual optimistic self when Roosevelt called him at 8:30 P.M. on August 2. From his vacation home in Estes Park, Colorado, he assured the President that Willkie's attitude was the same as Roosevelt's; Roosevelt pointed out that Willkie's attitude was not what counted, but rather the Republican policy in Congress.[56] Willkie had already spoken several times strongly in favor of all practical aid for Great Britain, and White's initial report to Roosevelt was correct.[57] Willkie was personally in favor of the destroyer deal. Whether he could or would influence the Republicans in Congress, however, was another question.

After more telephone conversations on August 2 and 3, with both Roosevelt and Cordell Hull, White conferred with Willkie, who was also vacationing in Colorado, and thought he had obtained a commitment.[58] On August 9, however, Wendell Willkie released a statement which was a model of non-commitment.

"My general view on foreign policy and the vital interests of the United States in the present international situation are well known," Willkie said, "having been stated by me several times. As to specific executive or legislative proposals, I do not think it appropriate for me to enter into advance commitments and understandings. If the National Administration, through any of its accredited representatives, publicly takes any given position with reference to our foreign policy, I may on appropriate occasion comment thereon."[59]

That was about as flat a rejection of support for Roosevelt's attempt to line up Republican help as White could have heard, yet he remained optimistic, cautiously so, but optimistic nonetheless. Two days after Willkie released his statement, White wired Roosevelt:

"It's not as bad as it seems. I have talked with both of you on this subject during the past ten days. I know there is not two bits difference between you on the issue pending. But I can't guarantee either of you to the other," White added quizzically, "which is funny, for I admire and respect you both."[60]

On August 13, White was still hoping to get from Willkie a public pronouncement in favor of lending the destroyers to Britain in exchange for American leased bases on British islands in the western hemisphere. On that date, Henry L. Stimson recorded in his diary that "While Willkie would not commit himself to say anything before his speech of acceptance next Saturday, White was confident that he would not say anything in criticism of the destroyer transaction and might say something affirmatively favorable to it."[61]

In this instance, surely, White was involved in keeping foreign policy out of the 1940 campaign. Willkie never did commit himself. When Saturday came and he accepted the Republican nomination as candidate for President, he said,

> We must admit that the loss of the British Fleet would greatly weaken our defense. That is because the British Fleet has for years controlled the Atlantic, leaving us free to concentrate in the Pacific. If the British Fleet were lost or captured, the Atlantic might be dominated by Germany, a power hostile to our way of life, controlling in that event most of the ships and shipbuilding facilities of Europe. This would be a calamity for us. We might be exposed to attack on the Atlantic. Our defense would be weakened until we could build a navy and air force strong enough to defend both coasts. Also, our foreign trade would be profoundly affected. That trade is vital to our prosperity . . .[62]

And that was about as close as Wendell Willkie ever got to committing himself on foreign affairs during the 1940 presidential campaign. White tried, but if he achieved anything as liaison, it was apparently only the negative achievement of assuring no involvement.

Moreover, being a political animal himself, White could analyze Willkie's position and justify it. "Willkie ducked for several good reasons," he wrote. "First, the legislation has not been introduced; second, whatever Willkie's personal views are, he has not conferred about the specific legislation with House and Senate Republican leaders Martin and McNary, and he feels a natural diffidence about assuming Congressional leadership before his ears are dry."[63]

It is difficult to imagine that White misunderstood the role that

Roosevelt wanted him to play, but surely, if we are to believe Roosevelt's memorandum to himself, he told White that he wanted to be assured of Republican Congressional support *before* he introduced the lend-lease legislation. That was the whole purpose of bringing White in as a go-between in the first place.

Nevertheless, the propaganda work of the Committee to Defend America by Aiding the Allies was effective; and by September, public opinion was such that the necessary legislation could be passed and the lend-lease arrangements for the destroyers could be made. To William Allen White, as head of that committee, must go major credit for winning a great uphill fight against the generation-long, ingrained habit of American isolationism, and for so altering the nature of public opinion that Congress was forced to do what, in hindsight, was the only prudent thing to do. Naturally, Robert Wood's America First Committee, the *Chicago Tribune,* Charles Lindberg, and other ultra-isolationists protested bitterly, and the legislation passed only narrowly, with no help from the isolationist Congressmen of White's own Midwest.[64]

The New York chapter of the Committee to Defend America by Aiding the Allies, by advocating, among other things, the convoying of American supply ships to England, was putting White in an untenable position.[65] In his entire career, he had never gotten too far ahead of current public opinion. Besides, he knew that the convoys would sometime have to fire on their attackers if they were to do any good at all, and that was too close for actual warfare to him.

He was tired, he was harried, and he was bewildered. There seems to be no other explanation for the letter that he wrote to Roy Howard, president of Scripps-Howard Newspapers, on December 20. In that letter, White said, "The only reason in God's world I am in this organization is to keep this country out of war." He denied favoring convoying British or American ships; he denied favoring repeal of the Johnson Act, which forbade loans to or sales of securities in the United States of nations who had defaulted or were in arrears on their payments on their war debts from World War I; and he denied favoring the repeal of the Neutrality Law. Moreover, he gave Howard permission to print the letter.[66]

The America Firsters gleefully welcomed White to their side, and his friends on the committee were deeply dismayed. Bruce Barton had written to Roy Roberts of the *Kansas City Star* four days earlier:

> . . . and I think he is being misused and exploited, and that some

> time soon he ought to have a show-down with the crowd who are cloaking themselves with his good name.
>
> He has said repeatedly to the American people that he is against the participation of this country in the war, but the men and women who are running his operation, at least some of them, make no bones of their purposes to get the country into war as quickly as they can.[67]

That and Howard's threatened attack on the committee prompted White's letter. In it, White pointed out that the country was not prepared yet to take the steps that some of the more eager members of that committee were advocating, but the qualifying sentences in the letter were lost in the great furor that followed its publication.

So it was that on December 28, White sent a "brief for the defense" to Lewis Douglas, and asked him to read it to the policy committee:

> . . . Two weeks ago Mr. Eichelberger told me that Roy Howard had told Mr. Coudert that he intended to go after our Committee. . . . For the Scripps-Howard Newspapers across the country to go after our Committee seemed to me a sinister sign of some strong influence at work either upon public opinion or behind the scenes. . . . I don't know yet. But I felt that such an attack would hurt us and because I have known Roy Howard for twenty-five years . . ., I sat down and wrote him a personal letter. . . . I felt it proper to deny the common charges of our opponents that we were in favor of four dangerous proposals: First, deliberately aiming at war; second, espousing proposals that would immediately lead to war, the three proposals being, convoys, sending American ships with contraband of war into belligerent waters, and the repeal of the Johnson Act. I denied that we were in favor of either of those four things. I cannot see how by any stretch of the imagination the denial of those four things in any way controverted our policy of November 26.
>
> It seemed to me then and it seems now, wise to make that denial as the price of an attack by the Howard Newspapers. I did not consult the Executive Committee or the Policy Committee because I . . . still think, that I was entirely inside of the intentions of the Committee. . . . I have always said that when we seemed headed for war my usefulness to the Committee is over for I do not believe we should get into the war,

> not so much from philosophical reasons as for practical reasons at the present time. And so far as I can see present events clearly, to get into the war would hurt Great Britain more than help her. And after all our Committee is organized to defend America and to do so by aiding the Allies. And I don't see how our entrance into the war would defend America, and certainly it would not aid Great Britain.
>
> . . . My resignation seems inevitable if even a minority of the Committee feel that this policy is unwise. . . . I have asked Mr. Eichelberger to let the matter ride until I come to New York . . . when the Churchman will honor our Committee by giving me an award for the work the Committee has done. That will be a good springboard from which to announce that a younger man is needed in this place; that a year's strain has taken its toll upon my mind and body and that I want to be relieved from the work.
>
> Which is the God's truth, and which I have told many friends, including some of our closest friends in this group.
>
> I shall be happier than you can know to be relieved from the dreadful responsibility that has been a shadow on my heart since I began this work. I have been happy in it. I am proud of it. The associations I have made have been more than friendships. But I desire to close this chapter pleasantly and with the least possible shock to the work of the Committee. I earnestly hope that no statement or commitment will be made which will force this issue at this time.[68]

That was William Allen White's swansong as chairman of the committee that he had helped organize and whose course he had tried to steer between the twin rocks of isolationism and involvement in European war. Truly sick and truly tired, he resigned the active chairmanship of the committee, though his friends persuaded him to stay on as honorary chairman. Because the Committee to Defend America by Aiding the Allies was also the White Committee, however, he continued to bear the brunt of attacks on the committee itself. Finally even that burden became too great for him.

He resigned the active chairmanship on January 1, 1941, and on April 3, he resigned as honorary chairman.[69] The immediate reason for the final resignation was the abuse he took when the Committee came out finally for convoying supplies to the Allies.[70] In the meantime, however, Sallie had become so ill that even the customary trip to the desert had not improved her condition, and she had gone to the Mayo Clinic. White himself was exhausted and discouraged and unwell.[71] Besides, what he had set out to do with the committee, he had done; what the committee was doing now he could not condone, even though he recognized its new course as inevitable. He had to quit. That job was finished.

That job was finished, but his job was not. He was sick and tired, and he slowed down; but he dictated an hour and a half a day on his autobiography, he wrote editorials, and he was in the middle of Kansas Republican politics. Most of all, after Pearl Harbor, he was in the middle of the war effort. If Hitler won, he said, one of the first people he would hang would be William Allen White.

He foresaw the end of the war, and he wrote of the necessity for an effective world organization to preserve the peace that was to follow.[72] He saw the Western powers policing the world for a hundred years, and he saw Russia waiting in the wings to be the next disturber of the peace.[73] Even when he knew he was dying—the doctors at the Mayo Clinic gave him four months to live—he continued to write letters, continued to plan for the world he would not see.

He wanted, above all else, to finish his autobiography before he died, but he could not do it. And regardless of the fact that he was slowing down, one of the biggest reasons that his son had to finish the book for him after William Allen White died was that the subject of the book was too busy living his life to spend enough time writing about it. He was, as he wanted to be, "a part of things" until the end.[75]

13

The Final Philosophy

William Allen White did not live to see the end of the war. He died on January 29, 1944.[1] He foresaw its end, however, and because he had been through the same cycle of events before, he predicted the reaction that would follow the war. He had seen the fortunes of the things he believed in ebb and flow in the endless battle between people and property. He himself, from the time of his conversion to the gospel according to St. Theodore, was on the side of the people. His Republicanism hampered him, because it gave him a case of political tunnel-vision. On the other hand, it helped him, because that Republicanism, in his time and place, gave him the power to make his private sentiment public opinion to a greater degree than would have otherwise been possible. White himself assessed his work clearly when he said that it was for the most part topical and therefore ephemeral.[2] Still, by 1974, most of his books were in reprint, and William Allen White remains a bridge between the old rural America and the new, complicated, urban, world-bound America.

That he looked back to the simpler, more explicit, less subtle civilization of his youth and early maturity is understandable. That he did not shrink, even in age, from learning of the new problems and coming to grips with them represents something of the measure of the man. In his youth he lived in darkness and knew it not; in his manhood he lit a candle and forbore to curse.

The world William Allen White lit with that candle was essentially the world he created out of his own mind and heart, and as he grew, his world grew to fit. White took his world into himself and reconstituted it. Therefore when he was convinced that he had been, rather paradoxically, a Pharisee in the temple of Mammon, he had repented and had set out to convert the world. Still, for all of his progressing, and the belief in social action that his progressing meant to him, White had become convinced rather early that the way to social salvation lay through regeneration of the individuals who made up that society.[3]

Here is the true paradox in the career of William Allen White. He was completely committed to the Progressive program of ameliorative social legislation. He was a master propagandist for social betterment through political action. Yet from "The Regeneration of Colonel Hucks" through *A Puritan in Babylon,* the Prodigal Son haunted him. In the end, though White continued to work for what he believed in through political means, the Prodigal Son won out. Even in his politics, and regardless of his party regularity, White was interested more in the candidate's personality than in his policies. White tried his best, from the time of Warren Harding, to recast every Republican candidate into a middle-class liberal. In the end, he was creating candidates in his own image.

William Allen White was never as liberal as he thought himself; certainly he was never the radical he called himself.[4] Nevertheless, the recurring and increasing references to the individual do not represent a retrogression to the Hanna-McKinley conservatism of White's youth. What bothered him was that the liberalism he saw around him in the 1930s and 1940s had gotten out of bounds. It no longer depended on individual regulatory reforms in which the individual citizen had some control of the reform and the results of it.[5] Reform like the initiative, referendum and recall, and like the state labor court, could be tested in the individual states, and the individual citizen could participate directly and have some direct control.[6] White still had high faith in that kind of reform, in that kind of liberalism. That way, he thought, man could rule himself, but not "in the padded chains of New Deal paternalism."

The basic and mature philosophy of William Allen White is, after all, not hard to isolate and classify. David Hinshaw, his lieutenant in the Progressive wars, called it pure pragmatism, which it is not.[7] A reviewer called it a vague and dreamy sort of New Thought, which it is not, either.[8]

White was a pragmatist, but he was a pragmatist with a difference. To him, the criterion was not whatever works is good. Rather it was whatever works for good is good. The difference is vital. It takes White's pragmatism out of the cash-register class, and it takes his idealism out of the vague and wistful class. And always, there was the Prodigal Son. For undergirding White's pragmatism was his belief in the possibility, even the necessity, of the regeneration of the individual. That regeneration had to occur before democracy could truly succeed. In view of this, it is not surprising that White equated democracy with religion. He interpreted religion to be the social extension of the Sermon on the Mount and the Golden Rule. Conventional religion interested him very little, and he seemed to feel something akin to horror at the idea of being thought pious. He protested in a letter that his correspondent had erred in thinking that White's parents were church members. As a boy, he added, he had attended the various Sunday schools in Eldorado and Emporia "on my own hook" more for the social contacts available than for any Christian indoctrination.[9]

Yet a letter he wrote to a Christian minister demonstrates strong faith in Christianity and in the power of Christianity to remake the social order:

> I believe the world is growing better because the world is becoming more and more capable of understanding the social and spiritual message of Jesus Christ. It seems to me that Christ is not only the only living God but the only growing God in all the world.[10]

"The only growing God"—that was the major point. As long as God continued to grow because of man's continually increasing ability to understand God's message, progress was not only possible, but inevitable.

The church itself was an agency for social progress because it was an agency for spiritual progress. White's description of the purpose of the church corresponds closely, in fact, with his ideas about the purposes of politics and journalism. Writing to the Reverend John H. Jones in 1916, White had said:

> As I see it, the church has changed as everything else has changed in the past 30 years. The church now is the only organization in which purely social functions of life, the altruistic forces, find recognition. I think the job of the church today is to make a public opinion that

> will so revolutionize our industrial, commercial and political life that it will be possible for a man to live a generous, unselfish, Christian life without hurt or harm to himself or family. I think men should go to church to add their influence to the one force on earth that can regenerate society and build a better social order.[11]

Here is the "use" of the church. It is a purely pragmatic institution for a better society. Far from calling forth sacrifice for personal redemption, the church should make it possible for a man to live a Christian life without the possibility of getting hurt. The public social forces, political, literary, journalistic, and religious, overlapped in their uses, and their aims should be identical.

The goal of all religious, social, and political activity was evolutionary progress toward the triumph of altruistic humanity. In 1913, White had stated the proposition this way:

> My hope for social evolution is something like this: By a step-at-a-time process to secure for the working classes better environment, better environment in the play-grounds, schools, housing, wages, and shop conditions under the present system that you call capitalistic; then after a generation or two of workers bred in the newer, cleaner environment, a new vision will come to the workers—a vision that will justly solve the inequities of the capitalistic system. I believe capital may be harnessed for the common good as well as for the private greed.[12]

This, of course, is the Progressive talking. It epitomizes the Progressive program of environmental improvement. It also reiterates White's belief in the importance of heredity, and it is undergirded with a social Christianity, an institutionalizing of individual altruism. It was more than pragmatism. Pragmatism provided the means; idealism defined the ends.

What politics could do in this respect, White indicated in his synopsis of Kansas reforms to *Outlook Magazine.*[13] The Kansas reforms that he had listed were environmentalist reforms. They simply put roadblocks in the way of greed. The job of the competent politician who had the welfare of his neighbors at heart was to keep both business and politics honest. The Kansas Progressive reforms under Roscoe Stubbs had been the work of a group of practical politicians, at least one of whom was trying to erect a practical Christian society within a political framework. In his youth, William Allen White had been attracted to the writings of Ralph Waldo Emerson. That attraction never left him, and when he discovered higher criticism, he said that "it interested me, as an Emersonian, to know that my theory of spiritual gravitation toward the triumph of righteousness in human relations was not dependent on any script or text."[14]

For White was skeptical always of what he called "the theology of the Sunday School of my boyhood, and the protracted meetings, pulpit pounding and howling of the itinerant preachers who came along through my boyhood at home."[15] He traced his religious faith to a chance meeting with an unknown man in the street, with whom he walked and talked through a long summer night in his seventeenth year. Remembering, he wrote in his autobiography:

> He held Jesus up to me as the greatest hero in history and asked me to read the story of the two thousand years that had followed his death and to watch how slowly and yet how inexorably the world had changed, veering to human happiness as it accepted little by little, phrase by phrase, the philosophy he preached and made a part . . . of human institutions. Then my companion turned the talk to the futility of force and the ultimate triumph of reason in human affairs . . .[16]

William Allen White wrote those words at the end of his career, yet in this instance it is not necessary to make allowances for hindsight. For this became the core of White's philosophy; and with this as its core, that philosophy cannot easily be set aside as merely opportunistic and pragmatic. White stated his philosophy of progress through Christian democratic action explicitly in three books. He published *A Theory of Spiritual Progress* in 1910.[17] He had delivered it before publication to the Phi Beta Kappa Society of Columbia University.[18] He reiterated some of his ideas in the Weil Lectures on American Citizenship, delivered at the University of North Carolina and published in 1925 as *Some Cycles of Cathay.*[19] Finally, in 1939, he published *The Changing West: An Economic Theory About Our Golden Age.*[20]

His philosophy had led him down the Road to Damascus, which White made the road to the alleviation of human ills by social and political means. His philosophy informed his estimate of the leaders of his times, and it was the basis of the fictional world he created in the days of his conversion. It led him to accept diplomatic assignments to Prinkipo and Haiti. It led him to fight for the League of Nations after World War I and to try to keep his country out of World War II by founding the Committee to Defend America by Aiding the Allies.

William Allen White provides the perfect example of the life that extends itself in ever-widening circles from the self to the world. Still, and perhaps paradoxically, he was the center of his own universe, a universe which was in good part of his own making. In contrast, at least, to the ultra-conservative McKinley Republican that he was at the beginning of his career, White grew into a liberal, middle-class, small "d" democrat. The basis of his democracy was the social and political expression of the Christian ethic. Moreover, he remained optimistic that the world was progressing toward the same kind of democracy, based on that same ethic.

Perhaps most of all, what Henry Seidel Canby wrote about him in his *Saturday Review* memorial piece sums up what he was and what he tried to accomplish. White's liberalism, wrote Canby, was "a liberalism of a man who hated equally reaction and the radical dogmatism of the writers who had never tried to make politics or economics do useful work."

In that phrase is perhaps the key to the public life of William Allen White. All his life, he tried to make politics and economics do useful work toward the regenerated human society he envisioned. All his life, he stood in the broad middle way of Midwestern liberalism, throwing brickbats at the extremists on either side of the highway. Because democratic liberalism has so many shades and because William Allen White felt free to move over the whole spectrum of that liberalism, he confused his friends and enraged his enemies.

Part of that confusion resulted from a very simple fact. The liberalism which White espoused was based on the agrarian revolt of White's youth and early maturity. It was rooted, though he opposed their ideas at the time, in the Farmer's Alliance and the Populists, in William Jennings Bryan, and, finally, in Theodore Roosevelt. White put his faith not only in the middle class, but specifically in the middle class made up of farmers and of small-town business men. He never trusted the city nor city politicians. The city was to him, almost because it was the city, a stronghold of reactionary capitalism and boss-ridden politics.[21]

So it was that the liberalism of William Allen White became solidified by 1917. It was a liberalism meant to solve the problems of his kind of people and his kind of country. It was not a liberalism for the urban society he saw taking over his world well before he died. What had been liberal in the teens of the century had become conservative by the 1930s, so that perhaps Oswald Garrison Villard was right when he said, "Of all the American Liberals, Bill White of Emporia is . . . the most . . . generally maddening and altogether loveable conservative in the whole country . . ."

Yet is is worth noting that White's own life showed his inconsistency to be a surface thing. Below it ran the solid philosophy of a man who believed in the progress of the human animal. For all the emphasis White put on making politics and economics work for the easing of human ills, the progress he hoped for could come only through spiritual evolution. That evolution, in turn, would be based on a pragmatic Christian ethic, and it would depend on regeneration of the individual extending itself to the society in which the individual lived.

Perhaps, after all, what can be said about the world in which White worked and the world he envisioned, he summed up himself in the *caveat* he wrote as foreword to his autobiography:

> This autobiography, in spite of all the pains I have taken and the research I have put into it, is necessarily fiction. The fact that names, dates, and places seem to correspond with such things that occurred in real life does not guarantee the truth of these stories. . . . For only God knows the truth. I am trying, in my finite way, to set down some facts which seem real and true to me.[22]

White might very well have said the same thing about the society he envisioned. He was the individual whose shadow was the institutions he desired. Though he recognized himself as "a bubble on the stream of history," he did what he set out to do. He was, in the end, the person he foresaw when he wrote his salutatory editorial in the *Emporia Gazette* at the age of twenty-seven. More than most men, he was able to shape his own life and to impress that shape upon the life around him. Over a considerable period of his life, he was able to make much of his private sentiment public opinion and to push his society a little way toward his ideal for that society.

Notes

Chapter 1: Prairie Princeling

1. Oswald Garrison Villard, "A Long and Foolish Life," *Nation* 144 (April 24, 1937), p. 467.

2. Russell H. Fitzgibbon, ed., *Forty Years on Main Street* (New York: Farrar & Rinehart, 1937).

3. Villard, p. 467.

4. In an address delivered February 22, 1952, at the dedication of the William Allen White School of Journalism and Public Information Building, University of Kansas, Lawrence, and reprinted at that time together with "Newspapers and the Survival of a Free Society," by Erwin D. Canham, then editor of the *Christian Science Monitor,* p. 19.

5. White, *The Autobiography of William Allen White* (New York: The Macmillan Company, 1946), pp. 22-26.

6. Ibid., p. 23.

7. Ibid., p. 24-25.

8. Ibid., pp. 27, 45-47.

9. Ibid., p. 43.

10. Ibid.

11. Ibid., p. 37.

12. Ibid., p. 66.

13. Ibid., p. 132.

14. White, "Two Famous Questions," *Forty Years on Main Street,* Russell H. Fitzgibbon, ed., pp. 75-76.

15. White, *Autobiography,* pp. 44-45.

16. See the short stories that make up White's first book, *The Real Issue; A Book of Kansas Stories* (Chicago: Way & Williams, 1896).
17. White, *Autobiography,* p. 51.
18. Ibid., p. 3.
19. Ibid., p. 61.
20. Ibid., p. 84.
21. Ibid., p. 62.
22. Ibid.
23. Ibid.
24. Ibid., p. 61.
25. Ibid.
26. Ibid., p. 64.
27. Ibid., pp. 21-22.
28. Ibid., p. 72.
29. Ibid., p. 69.
30. Ibid., pp. 3-23.
31. Ibid., p. 61.
32. Ibid., pp. 67-68.
33. Ibid., p. 61.
34. Ibid., p. 69.
35. Ibid., pp. 6, 60, 136.
36. *The Emporia Gazette*, "Mary A. White," May 7, 1924.
37. White, *Autobiography,* p. 6.
38. Ibid., p. 136.
39. Ibid., p. 66.
40. Ibid., p. 60.
41. Ibid.
42. Ibid.
43. Ibid., p. 95.

Chapter 2: "Multitudes in Me"

1. White, *Autobiography,* pp. 89, 92.
2. Ibid., p. 131.
3. Ibid.
4. Ibid., p. 102.
5. Ibid., passim.
6. Ibid., p. 162.
7. Ernest Hunter Wright, "James Hulme Canfield," *Dictionary of American Biography,* Allen Johnson, ed. (New York: Charles Scribner's Sons, 1929), III, 472.

8. White, *Autobiography,* pp. 144-45.
9. Ibid., p. 144.
10. Ibid., p. 108.
11. Ibid., p. 321.
12. Ibid., p. 180.
13. Ibid., pp. 98, 126.
14. Ibid., pp. 237-40.
15. Ibid., pp. 131-32.
16. Ibid., pp. 214-64 et passim.
17. Ibid., p. 229.
18. Ibid., pp. 237-40.
19. Ibid., pp. 237-38.
20. Ibid., pp. 255-56.
21. Ibid.
22. Ibid., p. 263.

Chapter 3: The Emerging Image

1. White, *Autobiography,* p. 258.
2. Ibid., pp. 253-54.
3. Ibid., p. 257.
4. *Life* 4:11 (February 28, 1938).
5. This editorial, besides appearing in the June 3, 1895, issue of the *Gazette,* was reprinted in 1924 in *The Editor and His People,* in 1937 in *Forty Years on Main Street,* and in 1946 in the *Autobiography.*
6. Ibid., p. 630.
7. See William Allen White to Olin W. Meacham, July 14, 1904, White Collection, Library of Congress.
8. *The Editor and His People,* p. 3, n.
9. White, *Autobiography,* p. 261, n.
10. Ibid., p. 188.
11. John D. Hicks, *The Populist Revolt* (Minneapolis: The University of Minnesota Press, 1937), pp. 442-43.
12. Ibid., pp. 427-35, passim.
13. Ibid., p. 219.
14. White characterized Simpson as a powerful intellectual. Ibid., pp. 218-219.
15. Ibid., p. 198.
16. White, *The Real Issue: A Book of Kansas Stories,* pp. 178-79.
17. White, *Autobiography,* p. 198.
18. Ibid., pp. 198-99.

19. White, *The Real Issue,* pp. 39-58.

20. White to Brand Whitlock, in Walter Johnson, *Selected Letters of William Allen White, 1899-1943* (New York: Henry Holt and Company, 1947), p. 260.

21. White, "Patriotism or Anarchy," cited in *The Editor and His People,* Helen Ogden Mahin, ed. (New York: The Macmillan Company, 1924), p. 257.

22. *The Emporia Gazette,* August 11, 1896.

23. White, *Autobiography,* p. 278.

24. William Jennings Bryan and Mary Baird Bryan, *The Memoirs of William Jennings Bryan* (Philadelphia: The United Publishers of America, 1925).

25. Ibid., pp. 496-514, passim.

26. White, *Autobiography,* p. 278.

27. White, *The Editor and His People,* p. 237.

28. Ibid., p. 244, n.

29. White, *Autobiography,* pp. 275-75.

30. Ibid., p. 192.

31. Ibid., pp. 291-92.

32. White, *Masks in a Pageant* (New York: The Macmillan Company, 1928), p. 44.

33. White, *Autobiography,* p. 322.

34. White to Congressman E. H. Madison, April 8, 1911, White Collection, Library of Congress.

35. White, *Autobiography,* p. 273.

36. Ibid., p. 266.

37. Ibid., pp. 279-80.

38. David Hinshaw, *A Man From Kansas* (New York: G. P. Putnam's Sons, 1954), p. 76. See also White, *Autobiography,* p. 279.

39. *The Emporia Gazette,* July 13, 1896.

40. White, *The Editor and His People,* p. 244, n.

41. Walter Johnson, "William Allen White: Grassroots American," *Selected Letters,* p. 6.

42. White to Doubleday & McClure, September 22, 1899, *Selected Letters,* p. 6.

43. White correspondence, Library of Congress, passim.

44. White, *Autobiography,* p. 289.

45. Ibid.

46. Ibid., p. 291.

47. Ibid., pp. 300, 307.

48. Attributed to Christopher Morley in Anon., "The King of

Boyville's Own Story," *William Allen White: In Memoriam* [New York: Book-of-the-Month Club, n.d.], [n.p.].

49. White, *The Real Issue,* pp. 75-77.
50. Ibid., pp. 104-22, 22-38.
51. Ibid., p. 118.
52. Ibid., pp. 104-22.
53. Ibid., p. 22.
54. This was in 1899. See White, *Autobiography,* p. 322.
55. Cited by Hinshaw, *A Man from Kansas,* p. 75.
56. See the letters for the period in the White Collection, Library of Congress.
57. White, *Autobiography,* p. 322.
58. The importance of White's conception of the middle class to his social and political philosophy can be seen from this statement: "It is democracy, capitalism, and Christendom, one in three and three in one. And for short let us call the trinity The American Middle Class." *The Changing West: An Economic Theory About Our Golden Age* (New York: The Macmillan Company, 1939).
59. See White, *Masks in a Pageant,* p. 276.

Chapter 4: The Road to Damascus

1. White, *Autobiography,* pp. 297-99.
2. White, *Masks in a Pageant,* p. 238, n.
3. See Henry F. Pringle, *Theodore Roosevelt: A Biography* (New York: Harcourt Brace and Company, a Harvester Book, 1956), pp. 106-14 passim.
4. White, *Autobiography,* pp. 297-99.
5. Ibid.
6. Pringle, *Theodore Roosevelt,* p. 113.
7. Ibid., pp. 113-14.
8. Ibid., pp. 84-92, 93-106.
9. Ibid., p. 107.
10. Ibid., p. 110.
11. Ibid., p. 112.
12. Ibid., p. 114.
13. This attitude was not limited to politics. See Pringle throughout for quotations which reveal a lord-of-the-manor attitude concerning such things as military affairs, public morals, literature—even spelling.
14. White, *Autobiography,* pp. 297-99.

15. Ibid., p. 163.

16. Ibid., p. 188.

17. Roosevelt, *American Ideals and Other Essays, Social and Political* (New York: G.P. Putnam's Sons, 1900), p. 38.

18. Ibid., p. 51.

19. Ibid., pp. 93-115.

20. Ibid., pp. 41-42.

21. Ibid., pp. 223-59.

22. Roosevelt to Knox, June 17, 1901, White Collection, Library of Congress.

23. White, *Stratagems and Spoils: Stories of Love and Politics* (New York: Charles Scribner's Sons, 1901), pp. vi-viii.

24. Ibid.

25. White to Roosevelt, June 6, 1902, White Collection, Library of Congress.

26. White to Cyrus Leland, August 15, 1901, White Collection, Library of Congress.

27. Ibid. See also Roosevelt to Henry Cabot Lodge, August 20, 1901, *The Letters of Theodore Roosevelt,* III, in Etting E. Morison, ed. (Cambridge: The Harvard University Press, 1951), 128-29.

28. White, *Autobiography,* p. 388.

29. Ibid., p. 322.

30. White, *Masks in a Pageant,* p. ix.

31. White to W. Edwin Ulmer, June 29, 1899, White Collection, Library of Congress.

32. White, "A Crate of Tommyrot," *Forty Years on Main Street,* in Russell H. Fitzgibbon, ed. (New York: Farrar & Rinehart, 1937), pp. 191-92.

33. "McKinley's Message," *The Editor and His People,* pp. 303-04.

34. "The Gaiety of War," *Forty Years on Main Street,* pp. 348-49.

35. "What Is to Be Will Be," *The Editor and His People,* pp. 304-05.

36. Perhaps the best and most detailed account of the rise of the Populist discontent in the agrarian states is found in John D. Hicks' *The Populist Revolt.* The gradually gathering strength of the revolt is paralleled by a consistency in the demands of the rebelling organizations.

Chapter 5: A Case of Galloping Insurgency

1. Johnson, *Selected Letters,* p. 6.

2. Hinshaw, *A Man from Kansas,* p. 81.

3. Ibid.

4. White, *Autobiography*, p. 274.

5. See his reports for the North American Newspaper Alliance about the 1924 conventions, reprinted in *Politics: The Citizen's Business*, and his reports of the 1936 conventions, written for the Bell Syndicate, the *New York Times Sunday Magazine* and the *Saturday Evening Post*, reprinted in *What It's All About* (New York: The Macmillan Company, 1936).

6. See dispatches White filed for the Wheeler Syndicate from the Paris Peace Conference in 1918, White MSS., William Allen White Memorial Library, Emporia, Kansas.

7. White, *Autobiography*, pp. 288-89.

8. *The Emporia Gazette*, bound volumes, 1895-1944. White Memorial Library, Emporia, Kansas.

9. White, *Autobiography*, p. 269.

10. One of the continuing laments running through the *Autobiography* concerns the death of journalism as a craft with the coming of mechanization. Almost every book on White, including the *Autobiography*, quotes his bitter obituary on Frank Munsey, pioneer consolidator of newspaper property:

> Frank Munsey, the great publisher, is dead.
>
> Frank Munsey contributed to the journalism of his day the talent of a meat packer, the morals of a money changer and the manners of an undertaker.
>
> He and his kind have about succeeded in transforming a once-noble profession into an eight percent security.
>
> May he rest in trust!—*Gazette*, December 23, 1925.

11. White to National Advertising Co., August 14, 1899, White Collection, Library of Congress.

12. White, *Autobiography*, p. 394.

13. Ibid., p. 325.

14. Hinshaw, *A Man from Kansas*, p. 83.

15. White Collection, Library of Congress.

16. White to Roosevelt, June 20, 1899, White Collection, Library of Congress.

17. Ibid.

18. White to Cyrus Leland, Jr., August 15, 1901, White Collection, Library of Congress.

19. White to Roosevelt, October 30, 1901, White Collection, Library of Congress.

20. White to E. Montgomery Reily, September 3, 1901, White Collection, Library of Congress.

21. White to Leland, August 15, 1901, White Collection, Library of Congress.

22. White to M. M. Lee, October 14, 1901, White Collection, Library of Congress.

23. White to Roosevelt, October 29, 1901, White Collection, Library of Congress.

24. Ibid., June 2, 1902.

25. Ibid.

26. Ibid.

27. White to D. S. Henderson, November 15, 1899, White Collection, Library of Congress.

28. White to Charles F. Scott, May 25, 1900, White Collection, Library of Congress.

29. "Bryan," *McClure's Magazine* 15:232-37 (July 1900) and "Hanna," ibid., 16:56-64 (November 1900).

30. These stories appeared in *Scribner's* intermittently from June 1899 through October 1901.

31. White, *Stratagems and Spoils,* p. 6.

32. The Cornbelt Railroad is to appear again in *A Certain Rich Man.*

33. Roosevelt to White, February 6, 1900, White Collection, Library of Congress.

34. White Collection, White Memorial Library.

35. "Platt," *McClure's Magazine* 18:145-53 (December 1901).

36. White, *Autobiography,* p. 348.

37. Ibid.

38. Ibid., pp. 346-48.

39. White Collection, Library of Congress.

40. White to "Dear Charles," December 20, 1901, White Collection, Library of Congress.

41. Informal remarks at the annual Roosevelt Memorial Association dinner, 1939, cited by Hinshaw in *A Man from Kansas,* p. 118.

42. If the newspaper clippings of the Platt affair, preserved in the White Memorial Library, Emporia, are any criterion, the press was in favor of White and against Platt almost unanimously.

43. Roosevelt to White, December 31, 1901, *The Letters of Theodore Roosevelt,* III, 214.

44. Most of these, with some additions, were reprinted in 1928 in *Masks in a Pageant.* In his preface to that book, White said that the chapters were written from "old reporter's notes."

45. "Croker," *McClure's Magazine* 16:317-26 (February 1901).

46. Roosevelt to White, March 12, 1901, *The Letters of Theodore Roosevelt,* III, 10-11.

47. Oscar Theodore Barck, Jr., and Nelson Manfred Blake, *Since 1900,* rev. ed. (New York: The Macmillan Company, 1953), p. 44.

48. Roosevelt to White, *The Letters of Theodore Roosevelt,* III, 132.

49. Ibid.

50. Barck and Blake, *Since 1900,* p. 45.

51. Ibid., p. 46.

52. White, *Masks in a Pageant,* p. 276.

53. William Jennings Bryan and Mary Baird Bryan, *Memoirs,* pp. 123-24.

54. White, *Autobiography,* p. 302.

55. See Walter Lippmann, *U.S. Foreign Policy: Shield of the Republic* (New York: Little Brown, 1943), for a full discussion of the implications to American foreign policy of the Spanish-American War.

56. See n. 35, p. 210, above.

57. White to Roosevelt, December 19, 1904, White Collection, Library of Congress.

58. Roosevelt to White, *Letters,* III, 136-37.

59. See *The Letters of Theodore Roosevelt,* III, 134-35, n., for a concise character sketch.

60. Barck and Blake, *Since 1900,* pp. 46-48.

61. White to George W. Perkins, April 15, 1914, White Collection, Library of Congress.

62. H. C. Sourbeer to White, August 11, 1910, White Collection, Library of Congress.

63. White to Roosevelt, December 19, 1904, White Collection, Library of Congress.

64. Ibid.

65. White to Hugh Brown, August 15, 1904, White Collection, Library of Congress.

66. White to Roosevelt, February 12, 1904, White Collection, Library of Congress.

67. White to B. R. Waggoner, attorney for the Missouri Pacific Railroad, February 2, 1903. See also White to W. H. Simpson, November 9, 1906, in which White agrees with the Interstate Commerce Commission in its ruling that newspaper advertising represents an uncertain value and that "therefore contracts payable in a commodity of uncertain value may be discriminating in their nature." White added, "Believing as I do there is just one thing for me to do—to stop asking for transportation either for myself, the Gazette employees or my family on the advertising contract now existing between the Gazette and the Santa Fe road."

68. White to Mark Sullivan, August 13, 1908, White Collection, Library of Congress.

69. Ibid.

70. White to Parks Helmick, May 6, 1908, White Collection, Library of Congress.

71. White, *Autobiography*, p. 346.

72. White to Robert M. La Follette, April 13, 1907, White Collection, Library of Congress.

73. Ibid.

74. Roosevelt to White, January 5, 1907, White Collection, Library of Congress.

75. White to La Follette, June 20, 1908, White Collection, Library of Congress.

76. White Collection, Library of Congress.

77. Ibid.

78. White to Joseph L. Bristow, June 13, 1908, White Collection, Library of Congress.

79. White to Roosevelt, August 15, 1908, White Collection, Library of Congress.

80. White, *Autobiography*, pp. 368-69..

81. White to Joseph Folk, August 12, 1908, White Collection, Library of Congress.

82. White, *Autobiography*, pp. 424-25.

83. White to Henry J. Allen, August 11, 1908, White Collection, Library of Congress.

84. White, *Autobiography*, p. 368.

85. See telegrams to and from White and the selected editors, setting up the running of the anti-Long stories, White Collection, Library of Congress.

86. White to Thomas J. Norton, January 27, 1908, White Collection, Library of Congress.

87. White Collection, Library of Congress.

88. Roosevelt to White, July 30, 1907, White Collection, Library of Congress.

89. Victor Murdock to White, December 9, 1909, White Collection, Library of Congress.

90. William Rockhill Nelson to White, August 17, 1909, White Collection, Library of Congress.

91. White to J. M. Oakinson, December 15, 1908, and White to Ray Stannard Baker, March 25, 1909, White Collection, Library of Congress.

92. Murdock to White, December 9, 1909, White Collection, Library of Congress.

93. Taft to White, March 12, 1909, White Collection, Library of Congress.

94. Ibid.

95. White to Hamilton Wright Mabie [n.d.], White Collection, Library of Congress.
96. Ibid.
97. Ibid.
98. White to John S. Phillips, September 24, 1909, White Collection, Library of Congress.
99. White to Baker, March 25, 1909, White Collection, Library of Congress.
100. W. Roscoe Stubbs to White, October 5, 1909, White Collection, Library of Congress.
101. White to N. T. Scribner, July 23, 1908, White Collection, Library of Congress.
102. White to W. C. Bobbs, October 24, 1908, White Collection, Library of Congress.
103. Letterpress book, 1908, White Collection, Library of Congress.
104. White, *The Old Order Changeth: A View of American Democracy,* (New York: The Macmillan Company, 1910).
105. White, *In Our Town* (New York: The Macmillan Company, 1906).
106. See J. B. Kerfoot, *Life*, August 16, 1906, clipping, White Collection, White Memorial Library.
107. Conversation of W. L. White with the author, July 10, 1957.
108. White, *Autobiography,* p. 423. An advertising poster for the motion picture made from the book is preserved in the White Memorial Library.
109. Clippings, White Collection, White Memorial Library.
110. William Lyon Phelps to White, March 18, 1910, White Collection, Library of Congress. Phelps called the book "a true work of realistic art; it tells the truth and at the same time shows a strong moral grasp of life."
111. "He tells the truth unwinkingly, but with the reassuring poise and geniality of those who in the most dubious times believe in a slowly bettering world." *The Nation,* August 1909. Clipping, White Collection, White Memorial Library.
112. White, *Autobiography,* p. 302.
113. Vernon Lewis Parrington, *Main Currents of American Thought,* III, (Harcourt Brace and Company, 1938), 374.
114. White to W. R. Stubbs, November 6, 1908; White to Ralph Stout, *Kansas City Star,* November 6, 1908, White Collection, Library of Congress.
115. Ibid.
116. White to William E. Borah, August 11, 1908, White Collection, Library of Congress.
117. White to Ben B. Lindsey, August 31, 1908, White Collection, Library of Congress.
118. White to Kate Bernard, November 24, 1908; White to Roscoe

Stubbs, December 3, 1908, White Collection, Library of Congress.

119. White to John S. Phillips, May 25, 1908, White Collection, Library of Congress.

120. Cited in *Forty Years on Main Street,* p. 400.

121. Ida M. Tarbell to White, September 29, 1909, White Collection, Library of Congress.

122. Edward J. Statom to White, September 29, 1909, White Collection, Library of Congress.

123. White to Roosevelt, August 4, 1910, White Collection, Library of Congress.

124. White to H. C. Sourbeer, August 16, 1910, White Collection, Library of Congress.

125. White to Professor Frank W. Blackmar, February 10, 1912, White Collection, Library of Congress.

126. W. E. Davis to White, January 10, 1910; Albert J. Beveridge to White, July 4, 1910; Robert M. La Follette to White, March 25, 1910, White Collection, Library of Congress.

127. White to Victor Murdock, July 20, 1910; J. M. Colley (two letters), July 22, 1910; U. S. Guyer, August 4, 1910; W. E. Davis, August 5, 1910, White Collection, Library of Congress.

128. White to Congressman E. H. Madison, April 18, 1911, White Collection, Library of Congress.

129. White to E. Montgomery Reily, April 26, 1910, White Collection, Library of Congress.

130. White to Taft, February 3, 1910, White Collection, Library of Congress.

131. White to Mark Sullivan, June 5, 1910, White Collection, Library of Congress.

132. White to Victor Murdock, November 29, 1911, White Collection, Library of Congress.

133. White to Bristow, June 20, 1910; to Dante Barton, June 6, 1910; to William Rockhill Nelson, September 23, 1909, White Collection, Library of Congress.

134. White to Bristow, December 28, 1911, White Collection, Library of Congress.

135. Ibid.

136. Ibid.

137. See Barck and Blake, *Since 1900,* pp. 66-67.

138. See Taft to White, March 12, 1909, White Collection, Library of Congress.

139. Barck and Blake, *Since 1900,* pp. 63-64.

140. In a speech at Winona, Minnesota, Ibid., p. 64.
141. Ibid., p. 71.
142. See Taft to White, n. 139, above.
143. Barck and Blake, *Since 1900,* p. 72.
144. Ibid., p. 65-66.
145. Ibid., p. 66.
146. Eric F. Goldman, *Rendezvous with Destiny: A History of Modern American Reform* revised and abridged (New York: Vintage Books, 1956), p. 132.

Chapter 6: Bull Moose Resistant

1. White to Mark Sullivan, August 8, 1908, White Collection, Library of Congress.
2. Roosevelt to White, October 24, 1911. See also Roosevelt to White, December 12, 1910, January 2, 1911, and January 24, 1911, White Collection, Library of Congress.
3. Roosevelt to Frank Munsey, January 16, 1912, White Collection, Library of Congress.
4. White, *Autobiography,* p. 447.
5. Ibid., p. 448.
6. Ibid.
7. Ibid., pp. 448-49.
8. Ibid., p. 449. For an independent view of La Follette's debacle, see George E. Mowry, *Theodore Roosevelt and the Progressive Movement* (New York: Hill and Wang, 1960), pp. 106-107. Professor Mowry's is an excellent study of the diverse elements that made up the Progressive movement. See also Henry F. Pringle, *Theodore Roosevelt,* p. 388.
9. White, *Autobiography,* p. 450.
10. Mowry, *Theodore Roosevelt,* p. 210.
11. Ibid., pp. 188-90.
12. Roosevelt, "The Trusts, the People and the Square Deal," *Outlook* 99: 649-56 (November 18, 1911).
13. Mowry, *Theodore Roosevelt,* p. 188.
14. Quoted by Fitzgibbon in *Forty Years on Main Street,* p. 290.
15. Herbert Croly, *The Promise of American Life* (New York: The Macmillan Company, 1909).
16. Eric F. Goldman, *Rendezvous with Destiny,* pp. 162-63.
17. Frank A. Munsey to Roosevelt, February 13, 1912, Roosevelt MSS. Cited by Mowry, *Theodore Roosevelt,* p. 212, n. 85.

18. White, *Autobiography,* p. 438.

19. White, *Autobiography,* pp. 437-38. See also White to Dante Barton, August 24, 1910; White to Senator Jonathan Bourne, August 8, 1910; White to "Mr. Townsend," [*Outlook*] (November 16, 1911).

20. Mowry traces the estrangement step by step in *Theodore Roosevelt,* pp. 183-226, passim.

21. Elihu Root to Roosevelt, February 12, 1912; Roosevelt to Root, February 14, 1912; Roosevelt to Nicholas Longworth, February 13, 1912, Roosevelt MSS. All cited by Mowry, *Theodore Roosevelt,* p. 211, n. 80 and 81. White, *Autobiography,* p. 450.

22. Ibid., p. 466. Mowry, *Theodore Roosevelt,* p. 253.

23. Mowry, *Theodore Roosevelt,* p. 193. Mowry goes on to analyze Roosevelt's reasons for running, however, and concludes that the only logical answer lay in Roosevelt's increasing irritation at the policies of Taft, p. 197.

24. White, *Autobiography,* p. 452.

25. Mowry, *Theodore Roosevelt,* p. 210.

26. White, *Autobiography,* p. 451.

27. Ibid., p. 452.

28. Ibid.

29. Mowry, *Theodore Roosevelt,* pp. 172-73.

30. Ibid., p. 172, n. 59.

31. White, *Autobiography,* p. 453.

32. Ibid.

33. Ibid., pp. 453-54.

34. Herbert S. Hadley to Roosevelt, January 16, 1912, Roosevelt MSS; *Kansas City Star,* January 11, 1912; Archie Butt, *Taft and Roosevelt,* II (Garden City, N.Y.: Doubleday, 1930), 813. All cited in Mowry, p. 209. n. 77.

35. This was particularly true of the Southern states, which, while they could not win Taft the election, could hold the convention for him. See Mowry, pp. 209, 227.

36. Theodore Roosevelt, "Judges and Progress," *Outlook* 100:42 (January 6, 1912), cited in Mowry, p. 216, n. 95.

37. Mowry, *Theodore Roosevelt,* p. 213.

38. White, *Autobiography,* p. 456.

39. White to Charles F. Scott, Iola, Kansas, December 10, 1913. White went even further than Roosevelt in this letter. "I have almost come to the belief that, instead of the recall of judicial decision and of the judicial recall for anything but malfeasance in office, it would be better to take away entirely the legislative function of all courts but the United States

Supreme Court, and to grant it only under a restriction of unanimous agreement, and the right to annul any law passed by the congress or passed by any state and upheld by a unanimous supreme court of any state."

40. Mowry, *Theodore Roosevelt,* p. 217.

41. White, *Autobiography,* p. 456.

42. Mowry, *Theodore Roosevelt,* p. 215.

43. White, *Autobiography,* p. 353.

44. Henry F. Pringle, *Theodore Roosevelt,* p. 338.

45. White to "Mr. Townsend" [Outlook], (November 16, 1911), White Collection, Library of Congress.

46. White, *Autobiography,* pp. 177-78.

47. Ibid., p. 456.

48. The Clapp committee, investigating pre-nomination expenditures, found the following: Roosevelt spent $611,118, Taft $449,527, Wilson $219,104, Harmon $150,496, and Underwood $52,000 as reported in *The New York Times,* October 15, 1912, and cited by Mowry, *Theodore Roosevelt,* p. 225, n. 23.

49. Mowry, *Theodore Roosevelt,* pp. 226-27.

50. White to Victor Murdock, April 29, 1912, White Collection, Library of Congress.

51. White, *Autobiography,* p. 457; C. G. Roseberry to White, August 8, 1912, White Collection, Library of Congress.

52. R. W. Farrar to Ormsby McHarg, February 24, 1912, letters to Roosevelt from C. A. Lindbergh, March 7, 1912, and Thomas Thorson, March 21, 1912, cited in Mowry, *Theodore Roosevelt,* p. 213, n. 43; White, *Autobiography,* pp. 457, 459, 472.

53. Ibid.

54. Ibid., and Pearl Wight to Joseph M. Dixon, April 17, 1912, Roosevelt MSS., cited in Mowry, *Theodore Roosevelt,* p. 227, n. 29.

55. Mowry, *Theodore Roosevelt,* p. 238.

56. Ibid., pp. 223-26.

57. Ibid., p. 225.

58. White, of course, as his letter files for this whole period indicate, was in communication with most of the reformers and sympathetic with the reforms.

59. Clippings in the White Collection indicate that many of the Kansas newspapers were in the fight, e.g., the *Iola Enterprise,* the *Abilene Chronicle,* the *Arkansas City News.* White handled everything from state financing of the Roosevelt campaign to making arrangements for Roosevelt's private railroad cars. (See J. M. Connell [General Passenger Agent, AT&SF]

to White, September 2, 1912, White Collection, Library of Congress).

60. Mowry, *Theodore Roosevelt,* p. 225.

61. White to J. W. Thomas, White Collection, Library of Congress.

62. Mowry, *Theodore Roosevelt,* p. 30.

63. White, *Autobiography,* p. 473.

Chapter 7: The Battle

1. White, *Autobiography,* p. 462.

2. Ibid., pp. 462-63.

3. Mowry, *Theodore Roosevelt,* pp. 231-32.

4. John D. Hicks, *The Populist Revolt,* pp. 427-35.

5. *The New York Times,* June 18, 1912, cited in Mowry, *Theodore Roosevelt,* p. 244, n. 22.

6. Ibid., p. 243, n. 19.

7. White, *Autobiography,* pp. 464, 466.

8. Ibid., p. 464.

9. White, *The Changing West: An Economic Theory of Our Golden Age,* (New York: The Macmillan Company, 1939), pp. 41-45.

10. White, *Autobiography,* p. 465.

11. Ibid., p. 469.

12. Mowry, *Theodore Roosevelt,* pp. 244-45.

13. Ibid., p. 245.

14. Roosevelt to Dixon, May 23, 1912, and to Hadley, May 24, 1912, and Hadley to Roosevelt, June 13, 1912, Roosevelt MSS., cited in Mowry, *Theodore Roosevelt,* p. 242, n. 14.

15. Ibid., p. 242.

16. White, *Autobiography,* p. 469.

17. Mowry, *Theodore Roosevelt,* p. 246.

18. Ibid.

19. White, *Autobiography,* p. 469.

20. Ibid., p. 470.

21. Ibid.

22. Mowry, *Theodore Roosevelt,* p. 245.

23. Ibid., p. 246.

24. Ibid., n. 29, pp. 246-47.

25. Ibid., p. 247.

26. White, *Autobiography,* pp. 471-72.

27. Ibid., p. 472.

28. Ibid.

29. Mowry, *Theodore Roosevelt,* pp. 238-39 and n. 6, p. 239.

30. White, *Autobiography,* p. 468; Mowry, *Theodore Roosevelt,* pp. 250-51.
31. White, *Autobiography,* p. 472.
32. Ibid.
33. Ibid.
34. Ibid., pp. 473-74.
35. Ibid., p. 473.
36. Mowry, *Theodore Roosevelt,* pp. 255-56.
37. W. H. Bell to White, July 16, 1912; C. C. Booker to White, July 17, 1912; O. D. Bates to White, July 20, 1912; W. H. Hollenshead to White, July 17, 1912; C. W. Hollenbeck to White, July 19, 1912; J. J. Pearley to White, July 22, 1912; W. M. Slopansky to White, July 16, 1912, White Collection, Library of Congress. Representative of the drift to Wilson, see George O. Sutton to White, July 19, 1912, White Collection, Library of Congress.
38. White, *Autobiography,* p. 474.
39. Ibid.
40. A perusal of the letters of this period indicates the pulling and hauling that White's correspondents were giving him.
41. Ibid., p. 475.
42. Claude G. Bowers, *Beveridge and the Progressive Era* (Boston: Houghton Mifflin, 1932), pp. 419-20; *The New York Times,* June 21, 1912. Cited in Mowry, *Theodore Roosevelt,* p. 249, n. 38.

Chapter 8: Bull Moose Rampant

1. White, *Autobiography,* pp. 476-82, passim.
2. Ibid., pp. 478-79.
3. Ibid.
4. White, *Woodrow Wilson, the Man, His Times and His Task* (Boston and New York: Houghton Mifflin, 1924).
5. White, *Autobiography,* pp. 480-81.
6. Ibid., p. 477.
7. White, "Fifty Years of Kansas," *World's Work* 8:4870-72 (June 1904); "The Glory of the States: Kansas," *The American Magazine* 81:41, 65 (January 1916).
8. For example, C. S. Ritter to White, July 6, 1912, White Collection, Library of Congress.
9. White, *Autobiography,* p. 482.
10. John M. Wayde to White, July 29, 1912, White Collection, Library of Congress.

11. Anonymous to White, July 17, 1912, White Collection, Library of Congress.

12. Mitchener to White, July 12, 1912, White Collection, Library of Congress.

13. Isley to White, July 9, 1912, White Collection, Library of Congress.

14. Ibid., July 5, 1912, White Collection, Library of Congress.

15. Elsizer to White, July 29, 1912, White Collection, Library of Congress.

16. White to W. L. Cunningham, White Collection, Library of Congress.

17. White to Oswald Garrison Villard, September 23, 1912; White by David Hinshaw to J. L. Sargent, October 5, 1912, White Collection, Library of Congress.

18. L. A. Millspaugh to White, July 19, 1912; T. W. Sickels to White, August 15, 1912, White Collection, Library of Congress.

19. White by David Hinshaw to E. M. Blomberg, September 21, 1912, White Collection, Library of Congress.

20. L. A. Millspaugh to White, July 19, 1912; letter from Hinshaw (by White) to E. M. Blomberg, July 21, 1912; White to O. G. Villard, September 23, 1912.

21. Undated news release, White Collection, Library of Congress.

22. Ibid.

23. Ibid.

24. Ibid.

25. Ibid.

26. See n. 17 above.

27. See examples in White Collection, Library of Congress.

28. A letter which White wrote to George P. Brett, the editor with whom he dealt at Macmillan, though it was written after the "Progressive Republican" gambit failed, gives some idea of the scope of White's activities: "I am, as you know," White wrote, "the National Committeeman for Kansas for the Progressive party. I am also State Treasurer and State Chairman for the Progressive party for Kansas. We are running a Speaker's bureau here and distributing tons of literature, and conducting a press bureau as well. Incidentally I am printing a daily newspaper and am getting two columns of copy out daily. I am writing a syndicate article once a week for the Chicago Tribune, and another article on the 'Kansas Situation' for the Kansas City Star, and still another for Will Irwin's highbrowed Bull Moose syndicate. . . ." White to Brett, October 12, 1912, White Collection, Library of Congress.

29. White's letters for the period point out that though the Progressives could take the case of the electors to court, the decision would be too late to do them any good. His letters also show that he struggled

mightily to oust the delegates of the regulars, and that he did not give up until the Kansas secretary of state certified the Taft-Sherman electors. See White to electors, September 18, 1912; White by David Hinshaw, September 21, 1912; White to "Mr. Day," September 23, 1912; White to Oswald Garrison Villard, September 23, 1912; White by Hinshaw to B. B. Boone, September 30, 1912. White Collection, Library of Congress.

White remembers his actions quite differently in his *Autobiography,* p. 492.

30. George M. Adams to White, August 7, 1912, White Collection, Library of Congress.

31. "From the night of the election two years ago I have felt that the chances were overwhelming against the permanence of the Progressive party." Roosevelt to White, November 7, 1914, White Collection, Library of Congress.

32. White was proud of his grass-roots financial campaign, but his letter files for this period attest the struggle that went into money-raising. The bulk of the funds had to come from Munsey, Perkins and Co.

33. White, *Autobiography,* p. 492.

34. White to Roosevelt, June 17, 1914, White Collection, Library of Congress.

35. Ibid.

36. White to Roosevelt, telegram [n.d.], White Collection, Library of Congress.

37. White, *Autobiography,* p. 483.

38. White to E. T. Manning, December 21, 1914, White Collection, Library of Congress.

39. White, *Autobiography,* p. 483.

40. White to Charles M. Sheldon, September 16, 1912, White Collection, Library of Congress.

41. White, *Autobiography,* p. 485.

42. Ibid.

43. Ibid.

44. Ibid., pp. 485-86; Mowry, *Theodore Roosevelt,* pp. 270-71.

45. White, *Autobiography,* p. 484. According to the *Chicago Tribune,* cited by Mowry, *Theodore Roosevelt,* p. 273, the songs were "The Battle Hymn of the Republic" and the Doxology. Either way, the convention had the flavor of a revival meeting.

46. White, *Autobiography,* pp. 490-91.

47. See n. 35 above.

48. O. K. Davis, *Released for Publication* (Boston: Houghton Mifflin, 1925), cited by White, *Autobiography,* p. 491.

49. See n. 18 above.

50. See n. 29 above.

51. Robert Stone to White, September 4, 1912, White Collection, Library of Congress.

52. White to Blomberg, as cited in n. 18 above.

53. Undated open letter, White Collection, Library of Congress.

54. Campaign letter under Progressive party letterhead, August 15, 1912, White Collection, Library of Congress.

55. Dolley to White, September 4, 1912, White Collection, Library of Congress.

56. White to Hawkins, September 24, 1912, White Collection, Library of Congress.

57. White to A. M. Breese, September 21, 1912, White Collection, Library of Congress.

58. See White to George P. Brett, October 12, 1912, n. 27 above.

59. White by Hinshaw, White Collection, Library of Congress.

60. White to Samuel Lieberson, September 23, 1912, White Collection, Library of Congress.

61. White to McNay, September 20, 1912, White Collection, Library of Congress.

62. Robert Good to White, July 19, 1912; White to U. S. Sartin, October 8, 1912; White to J. W. Thomas, September 21, 1912, White Collection, Library of Congress.

63. George O. Sutton to White, July 19, 1912, White Collection, Library of Congress.

64. W. H. Bell to White, July 16, 1912, White Collection, Library of Congress.

65. See White to Sartin, n. 61 above.

66. See White to J. W. Thomas, ibid.

67. Bristow to White, telegram, July 19, 1912, White Collection, Library of Congress.

68. C. E. Carroll to White, December 12, 1912, White Collection, Library of Congress.

69. White, open letter, July 23, 1912, White Collection, Library of Congress.

70. Ibid.

71. See as an example of many such letters in White's file, E. E. Spencer to White, May 12, 1912, "I am enclosing my check for $2.00 to help elect Colonel Roosevelt. . . ." White Collection, Library of Congress.

72. W. T. Brown to White, August 12, 1912, White Collection, Library of Congress.

73. Crop failure in 1912 is mentioned again and again in letters to

White, explaining the lack of contributions; and see White by Hinshaw to B. B. Boone, September 27, 1912, White Collection, Library of Congress.

74. White to D. K. Bean, October 8, 1912, White Collection, Library of Congress.

75. White to Fred J. Bayles, October 4, 1912, White Collection, Library of Congress.

76. Hinshaw to J. B. Edwards, October 8, 1912; to Frank Allison, September 26, 1912; to James L. Jackson, September 30, 1912, White Collection, Library of Congress.

77. White to F. C. Wade, October 9, 1912; White by Hinshaw to George Tucker, September 21, 1912, White Collection, Library of Congress.

78. White, *Autobiography,* p. 496.

79. White to Roosevelt, November 14, 1912, White Collection, Library of Congress.

80. White, *Autobiography,* p. 492.

81. Hinshaw to J. B. Edward, October 8, 1912, White Collection, Library of Congress.

82. Barck and Blake, *Since 1900,* p. 83.

83. Roosevelt to White, White Collection, Library of Congress.

84. Ibid.

85. W. M. Gray to White, November 13, 1912, White Collection, Library of Congress.

86. Barck and Blake, *Since 1900,* p. 83.

87. White, *Autobiography,* p. 496.

Chapter 9: Bull Moose Ruminant

1. White, telegram, to G. W. Perkins, November 8, 1912, White Collection, Library of Congress.

2. White, circular letter, December 1, 1912, White Collection, Library of Congress.

3. See, for example, E. D. Ashley to White, December 12, 1912; B. J. Alexander to White, December 6, 1912; George W. Beverley, December 12, 1912, White Collection, Library of Congress.

4. Leahy to White, White Collection, Library of Congress.

5. White, *Autobiography,* p. 507.

6. White to Joseph Bristow, August 25, 1913, White Collection, Library of Congress.

7. White to F. S. Jackson [n.d.], White Collection, Library of Congress.

8. White to J. R. Harrington, November 1, 1913, White Collection, Library of Congress.

9. White to George W. Hanna, November 18, 1913, White Collection, Library of Congress.

10. White to J. R. Harrington, October 28, 1913; to George W. Hanna, November 18, 1913, White Collection, Library of Congress.

11. White to Moore, November 15, 1913, White Collection, Library of Congress.

12. White to Senator Kinkel [no initials], March 16, 1914, White Collection, Library of Congress.

13. White to Perkins, April 15, 1914, White Collection, Library of Congress

14. White to Gifford Pinchot, April 20, 1914, White Collection, Library of Congress.

15. *The California Outlook* 16:2 (April 25, 1914).

16. White to Roosevelt, June 17, 1914, White Collection, Library of Congress.

17. Cited by Pringle, *Theodore Roosevelt,* p. 403.

18. Roosevelt to White, November 7, 1914, White Collection, Library of Congress.

19. White to Arthur Capper, November 6, 1914, White Collection, Library of Congress.

20. White, *Autobiography,* pp. 503-504.

21. White to Roy Bailey, November 17, 1914, White Collection, Library of Congress.

22. White to Joseph Tumulty, September 4, 1914, White Collection, Library of Congress.

23. White to Hiram Johnson, November 23, 1914, White Collection, Library of Congress.

24. Ibid.

25. White to George W. Perkins, December 21, 1914, White Collection, Library of Congress.

26. White to Hiram Johnson, November 25, 1914, White Collection, Library of Congress.

27. White to Roosevelt, December 28, 1914, White Collection, Library of Congress.

28. White, *Autobiography,* p. 508.

29. Ibid.

30. Ibid., p. 510.

31. White to Roosevelt, November 14, 1912, White Collection, Library of Congress.

32. White, *God's Puppets* (New York: The Macmillan Company, 1916).

33. White, "A Social Rectangle," *God's Puppets,* p. 71.
34. White, *God's Puppets,* pp. 199-200.
35. Ibid., p. 212.
36. Ibid., pp. 246-91.
37. Ibid., pp. 292-309.
38. Barck and Blake, *Since 1900,* pp. 161-62.
39. White, *Autobiography,* p. 513.
40. Ibid., p. 516.
41. White to Perkins, May 13, 1915, White Collection, Library of Congress.
42. White to J. L. Brady, May 8, 1915, White Collection, Library of Congress.
43. White to J. R. Harrison, June 17, 1915, White Collection, Library of Congress.
44. White to Gifford Pinchot, February 10, 1916, White Collection, Library of Congress.
45. White to Tom M. Neil, May 27, 1916, White Collection, Library of Congress.
46. White, *Autobiography,* p. 517.
47. White to F. DuMont Smith, January 10, 1916, White Collection, Library of Congress.
48. White to J. N. Dolley, March 14, 1916, White Collection, Library of Congress.
49. White, *Autobiography,* p. 518.
50. Ibid., pp. 520-21; see also Mowry, *Theodore Roosevelt,* p. 351.
51. Ibid., p. 350.
52. Ibid., p. 354.
53. White, *Autobiography,* pp. 526-27.
54. Mowry, *Theodore Roosevelt,* p. 352.
55. White, *Autobiography,* pp. 523-27, passim.
56. John A. Garraty, ed., "T. R. on the Telephone," *American Heritage* 9:99-108 (December 1957).
57. White, *Autobiography,* p. 521.
58. White to Charles H. Sessions, September 6, 1916, White Collection, Library of Congress.
59. White to Henry J. Haskell, September 26, 1916, White Collection, Library of Congress.
60. Ibid.
61. White to Hamlin Garland, September 22, 1916, White Collection, Library of Congress.
62. White to Rodney Elward, October 16, 1916, White Collection, Library of Congress.

63. Ibid.

64. Ibid.

65. White, *Autobiography,* pp. 529-30.

66. White, "Introduction," *Masks in a Pageant,* p. viii.

67. Ibid.

68. White, *Some Cycles of Cathay* (Chapel Hill: The University of North Carolina Press, 1925), passim.

Chapter 10: World War I—An Interlude

1. White, "Make Him 'Swaller' It," *The California Outlook* 16:2 (April 25, 1914).

2. White to Liggett, White Collection, Library of Congress.

3. White to Rodney Elward, White Collection, Library of Congress.

4. White to Lorimer, April 8, 1918, White Collection, Library of Congress.

5. White to John Buchan, December 8, 1917, White Collection, Library of Congress.

6. White, *Autobiography,* p. 535.

7. "The Highbrow Doughboy," *Red Cross Magazine* 16:73-74 (August 1919); "The YMCA Huts, 'Safety Valves' for Our Boys in France," *Touchstone* 2:344-50 (January 1918).

8. White, *Autobiography,* pp. 436-37.

9. Ibid., p. 535.

10. White, *The Martial Adventures of Henry and Me* (New York: Macmillan 1918); White, *Autobiography,* p. 536.

11. In fact, as early as 1914, White took time out to help raise $75,000 for the YMCA. He also worked on Belgian Relief and plumped for a displaced persons program. See White to J. S. Boyer, May 21, 1914, and White to Norma Hapgood, December 9, 1914, White Collection, Library of Congress.

12. White, *Autobiography,* p. 546.

13. Ibid., p. 541.

14. Ibid., p. 546.

15. White to Harold Ickes, March 30, 1918, White Collection, Library of Congress.

16. White to Ickes, January 20, 1917, White Collection, Library of Congress

17. White to Roosevelt, April 24, 1918, White Collection, Library of Congress.

18. White to Medill McCormick, day letter [n.d.], White Collection, Library of Congress.

19. White to Roosevelt, July 1, 1918, White Collection, Library of Congress

20. White to Harold T. Chase, August 14, 1918, White Collection, Library of Congress.

21. White Collection, Library of Congress.

22. White to McCormick, September 16, 1918, White Collection, Library of Congress.

23. White to Norman Hapgood, June 25, 1918, White Collection, Library of Congress.

24. White to George Creel, November 13, 1918, White Collection, Library of Congress.

25. White, *In the Heart of a Fool* (New York: The Macmillan Company, 1918).

26. Ibid., pp. 569-70.

27. Ibid., p. 601.

28. White, *Autobiography,* p. 446.

29. Ibid.

30. White, *In the Heart of a Fool,* p. 605.

31. See *New York Globe,* November 9, 1918, as example.

32. Everett Rich, in conversation with the author, July 11, 1957.

33. *Boston Herald,* November 16, 1918; H. E. Jacobs, *Brooklyn Eagle,* November 23, 1918; Marguerite Wilkinson, *Touchstone,* June 1919. *The New York Evening Sun,* November 16, 1918, called the book the Great American novel and "greatly American"; *The New York Times,* November 10, 1918, called it "epic"; and the *Kansas City Star,* December 3, 1918, was enthusiastic for three columns.

34. White Collection, Library of Congress.

35. Ibid.

36. Ibid.

37. White remembered it as McClure's Syndicate (*Autobiography,* p. 550), but see Wheeler dispatches, White Collection, White Memorial Library.

38. White to Creel, November 13, 1918, White Collection, Library of Congress.

39. White, *Autobiography,* p. 566.

40. Ibid.; White, *Woodrow Wilson,* p. 393.

41. "Country Editor . . . and Cosmopolite," *William Allen White: In Memoriam* (New York: Book-of-the-Month Club [n.d.]), [n.p.].

42. White, *Woodrow Wilson,* p. 391.

43. White, *Autobiography,* p. 557.

44. Ibid.

45. Ibid.

46. Ibid., p. 558.

47. Ibid., p. 560.

48. Ibid., pp. 559-62.

49. White to Victor Murdock, Franklin P. Adams, and Murdock Pemberton, February 11, 1918, White Collection, Library of Congress.

50. White, "What Happened to Prinkipo," *Metropolitan,* 51:29, 30, 67-70 (December 1919). For another view of Prinkipo, see M. P. Briggs, "George D. Herron and the European Settlement," *Stanford Publications in History and Social Science,* III (Palo Alto: Stanford University Press, 1932). See also White to Upton Sinclair, July 29, 1919, White Collection, Library of Congress.

51. White, *Autobiography,* p. 562.

52. White to Isaiah Bowman, c/o American Geographical Society, September 12, 1919, White Collection, Library of Congress; *Autobiography,* pp. 570-78.

53. White, *Woodrow Wilson,* p. 486.

54. White, *Autobiography,* p. 551.

Chapter 11: The God-Damned World

1. White, *Woodrow Wilson,* pp. 322-70, passim.

2. Ibid., p. 264.

3. White, *Autobiography,* pp. 577-78.

4. Ibid.

5. White, *Woodrow Wilson,* p. 486.

6. Ibid., pp. 455-56.

7. See Walter Lippmann's introduction to Woodrow Wilson, *Congressional Government: A Study in American Politics* (New York: Meridian Books, 1956), p. 7. See also Wilson's preface to the fifteenth edition of *Congressional Government,* pp. 22-23.

8. White, *Woodrow Wilson,* p. 366.

9. Charles A. and Mary E. Beard, *American in Midpassage* (New York: The Macmillan Company, 1939), p. 303. See also White, *What It's All About.*

10. "William Allen White: Grassroots American," *Selected Letters of William Allen White,* p. 12.

11. White to Hays, July 20, 1920, White Collection, Library of Congress.

12. White, *Autobiography,* p. 595.

13. See the *Gazette,* September 13, 1919; June 14, 1920; September 3, 1920.

14. Ibid.

15. White, *A Puritan in Babylon* (New York: The Macmillan Company, 1938), p. 22.

16. White, *What It's All About,* p. 50.

17. White to Ray Stannard Baker, December 8, 1920, in Johnson, *Selected Letters,* p. 213.

18. See, for example, White to Joseph Dixon, January 1, 1920, White Collection, Library of Congress.

19. White to Edward Marsh, March 3, 1920, White Collection, Library of Congress.

20. White Collection, White Memorial Library.

21. Quoted in *William Allen White: In Memoriam,* [n.p.].

22. Johnson, *Selected Letters,* p. 216.

23. The *Gazette,* May 17, 1921.

24. White to Victor Murdock, *Selected Letters,* p. 212.

25. White, *Autobiography,* p. 610.

26. Ibid.

27. Ibid., p. 612.

28. Ibid.

29. Ibid.

30. *The New York Times,* for example, ran stories almost daily from July 21, when White first defied the industrial court, until December 20, when the presiding judge dismissed the case.

31. The *Gazette,* July 27, 1922.

32. *Nation's Business* 10:14-16 (May 1922).

33. *Outlook* 131:560 (August 2, 1922).

34. *Nation* 115:718 (December 27, 1922).

35. *Saturday Evening Post* 193:3, 4, 52, 54 (April 23, 1921).

36. *Collier's* 70:3, 4, 18 (July 1, 1922).

37. *Collier's* 60:5, 6, 19, 28 (March 4, 1922).

38. White, *Woodrow Wilson,* passim.

39. Ibid., pp. 267-89.

40. *Calvin Coolidge, the Man Who is President* (New York: The Macmillan Company, 1925); "Calvin Coolidge," *Collier's,* 75:5, 6, 38-40 (March 7, 1925); 13, 14, 36, 37 (March 21, 1925); 9, 10, 47, 48 (April 4, 1925); 9, 10, 44-46 (April 18, 1925).

41. "As I See It," *New York Herald Tribune Magazine,* July 16, 1922-March 4, 1923.

42. In a *Gazette* editorial, December 12, 1921, he reassured the home folks. He would not be going to New York, he said. He would write the *Judge* pieces in Emporia. On August 11, 1922, White resigned his editorship of *Judge* in a disagreement over Prohibition. See "W. A. White Resigns Editorship of Magazine Judge," *The New York Times,* August 11, 1922; "W. A. White Resigns from Staff of Judge Because of Stand on Prohibition," ibid., August 12, 1922; White, "Editorial on Attitude Toward Prohibition,"

ibid., August 14, 1922. See also, Frank C. Clough, *William Allen White of Emporia* (New York: Whittlesy House, 1941), p. 164.

43. White, *The Editor and His People,* Helen Mahin, ed. (New York: The Macmillan Company, 1924).

44. White, *Politics: The Citizen's Business* (New York: The Macmillan Company, 1927).

45. White, *Masks in a Pageant* (New York: The Macmillan Company, 1928).

46. White and Myer, *Conflicts in American Public Opinion* (Chicago: American Library Association, 1925).

47. The White Collection in the Library of Congress contains 324 boxes of correspondence. While that includes both in-coming and out-going mail, most of it is letters from White. Moreover, the Library of Congress collection does not include the correspondence in Johnson, *Selected Letters,* nor does it include the correspondence deposited in the White Memorial Library in Emporia, Kansas.

48. White, "Introduction," *Woodrow Wilson,* pp. xiv-xviii.

49. Irving Dillard, then editorial page director of the *St. Louis Post-Dispatch,* recalled in 1957 that to him, and to White, the use of previously unpublished letters of William Howard Taft provided the most newsworthy part of the book. Irving Dillard, *The Editor I Wish I Were: Eighth Annual William Allen White Lecture, Delivered February 11, 1957, William Allen White School of Journalism and Public Information, University of Kansas, Lawrence,* p. 7.

50. White, *Autobiography,* p. 597.

51. Ibid., pp. 287-88.

52. Yet Barck and Blake estimate a national Ku Klux Klan membership of between four and five million as late as 1925. *Since 1900*, p. 370.

53. Quoted by W. L. White, "The Last Two Decades," *Autobiography,* p. 630.

54. Clough, *William Allen White of Emporia,* pp. 151-53.

55. W. L. White, "The Last Two Decades," *Autobiography,* p. 630. See also Hinshaw, *A Man From Kansas,* pp. 243-44.

56. White, *Autobiography,* pp. 293-94.

57. *Gazette,* September 20, 1924.

58. Hinshaw, *A Man From Kansas,* pp. 247-48.

59. Ibid., p. 248.

60. *Gazette,* May 5, 1926.

61. Quoted by W. L. White, "The Last Two Decades," *Autobiography,* p. 632.

62. White to Brand Whitlock, July 15, 1925, in Johnson, *Selected Letters,* p. 260.

63. Quoted by W. L. White, "The Last Two Decades," *Autobiography*, p. 633.

·64. Ibid., pp. 633-34.

65. White, *Autobiography*, passim.

66. White to Sinclair Lewis, November 23, 1920, in Johnson, *Selected Letters*, pp. 211-12.

67. White, "The Town and the Triangle: A Festive Discussion of the Literary Invasion of the Country Town," undated MS, White Collection, White Memorial Library.

68. White to Miss Delano, November 5, 1906, White Collection, Library of Congress.

69. White, *Some Cycles of Cathay*, p. 24.

70. White Memorial Library.

71. Reprinted in *William Allen White: In Memoriam*, [n.p.].

72. White to Robert Bridges, March 14, 1916, White Collection, Library of Congress.

73. *William Allen White: In Memoriam*, [n.p.].

74. Ibid.

75. Ibid.

76. Ibid.

77. Ibid.

78. Ibid.

79. White, *Masks in a Pageant*, p. 282.

80. Quoted by W. L. White, "The Last Two Decades," *Autobiography*, p. 633.

81. White, *Forty Years on Main Street*, p. 322, n.

Chapter 12: The Other Roosevelt

1. For a summary of these views, excerpted from White's writing by his son, see William Lindsay White, "The Last Two Decades," *Autobiography of William Allen White*, pp. 635-44.

2. Ibid., pp. 639-40.

3. Ibid., p. 638.

4. Ibid.

5. Ibid.

6. White, *What It's All About* (New York: The Macmillan Company, 1936), p. 40.

7. Boston *Herald*, February 8, 1936.

8. William Lindsay White, "The Last Two Decades," *Autobiography*, pp. 638-39.

9. Ibid.

10. Ibid, p. 639.

11. White, *What It's All About,* passim, and especially p. v.

12. Ibid.

13. Ibid., p. 49. See also William Lindsay White, "The Last Two Decades," *Autobiography,* p. 629.

14. "It is the sort of thing that makes the people love him. . . ." Quoted in William Lindsay White, "The Last Two Decades," *Autobiography,* p. 636.

15. White, "Haitian Experience," Problems of Journalism: Proceedings of the Eighth Annual Meeting, American Society of Newspaper Editors, Washington, D.C., April 17-19, 1930, pp. 103-108.

16. "Haiti Finds a Champion," *The Portland* (Maine) *Evening News,* March[n.d.] 1930; "Mr. White Captures Haiti," The Kansas City (Missouri) *Star,* March [n.d.] 1930; "W. A. White Gesture Wins," Ibid., March 3, 1930; Melancholy Jacques, "Mr. White in Haiti," *New York Herald-Tribune,* March 4, 1930; "A Hoover Commission That Made Good," *New York World Telegram,* March 17, 1930.

17. Barck and Blake, *Since 1900,* pp. 462-63.

18. See Barck and Blake, pp. 580-83, for corroboration. Barck and Blake also allude to the very limited agenda the U.S. Congress insisted on, and the limits the agenda place on the conference.

19. William Lindsay White, "The Last Two Decades," *Autobiography,* p. 636.

20. Ibid., p. 637.

21. Hutchinson (Kansas) *News,* October 25, 1940, White Collection, White Memorial Library.

22. Iola (Kansas) *Daily Register,* July 22, 1938, White Collection, White Memorial Library.

23. *Gazette,* editorial, November 11, 1933.

24. William L. Langer and S. Everett Gleason, *The Challenge of Isolation,* I (New York: Harper Torchbooks, Harper and Rowe, 1946), p. 225.

25. Ibid.

26. Ibid., II, 753.

27. Ibid., I, 470.

28. White, "Non-Partisan Committee for Peace" (news release), October 3, 1939, White Collection, White Memorial Library.
Kansas.

29. Langer and Gleason, *The Challenge of Isolation,* I, 225.

30. But according to his managing editor, there was no such hesitation on White's part. See Clough, *William Allen White from Emporia,* p. 187.

31. Everett Rich, *William Allen White: The Man From Emporia* (New York: Farrar & Rinehart, Inc., 1941), p. 317.

32. See script of 1940 radio interview [n.d.], White Collection, White Memorial Library.

33. Langer and Gleason, *The Challenge of Isolation,* I, 486.

34. Ibid.

35. Ibid.

36. Ibid., 225.

37. Roosevelt to White, December 14, 1939, cited by Langer and Gleason, ibid., I, 346-47 and by Johnson, *The Battle Against Isolationism,* p. 60, from Franklin D. Roosevelt, *FDR: His Personal Letters,* Elliott Roosevelt and others, eds., II (New York: Duell, Sloan and Pearce, 1947-1950), 767-68.

38. White to Roosevelt, in Johnson, *Selected Letters,* pp. 402-03.

39. White to Roosevelt, May 25, 1940, in Johnson, *Selected Letters.*

40. White to Roosevelt, June, 1940, cited in Johnson, *The Battle Against Isolation,* p. 82.

41. Rich, *The Man from Emporia,* pp. 326-27.

42. White to Oswald Garrison Villard, July 12, 1940, White Collection, Library of Congress.

43. Century Group Declaration, July 25, 1940. See William Langer and S. Everett Gleason, *The Challenge to Isolation,* II, 507 and n. 21.

44. Ibid., 749 and n. 17.

45. White to Philip Degarmo, night letter [n.d.], 1940, White Collection, Library of Congress.

46. Rich, *The Man From Emporia,* pp. 328-29.

47. *The New York Times,* Sec. 1, p. 3, August 12, 1940, cited in Langer and Gleason, I, 487.

48. Johnson, *Selected Letters,* pp. 407-08.

49. Radio interview, 1940, White Collection, Library of Congress.

50. The president's notes on the Cabinet meeting, dated 9:37 P.M., August 2, 1940 (*FDR: His Personal Letters,* II, 1050-51), cited in Langer and Gleason, *The Challenge to Isolation,* II, 750.

51. Ibid.

52. Ibid.

53. Ibid.

54. Ibid.

55. William Lindsay White, "The Last Two Decades," *Autobiography,* p. 642.

56. Langer and Gleason, *The Challenge to Isolation,* II, 751.

57. Ibid., p. 753.

58. Ibid., p. 754.

59. *The New York Times,* August 10, 1940, in ibid., n. 29.

60. White to Roosevelt, telegram, August 11, 1940, *Roosevelt Papers,* ibid., p. 754, n. 30.

61. *The New York Times,* Sec. 1, p. 33, August 18, 1940, cited in ibid., p. 758.

62. Ibid., p. 762.

63. Johnson, *The Battle Against Isolation,* pp. 127-28, cited by Langer and Gleason, II, 754.

64. Barck and Blake, *Since 1900,* pp. 633-34.

65. Bruce Barton to Roy Roberts, *Kansas City Star,* December 16, 1940, White Collection, Library of Congress.

66. Rich, *The Man From Emporia,* pp. 227-28.

67. Bruce Barton to Roy Roberts, *Kansas City Star,* December 16, 1940, White Collection, Library of Congress.

68. White to Lewis Douglas, December 28, 1940, White Collection, Library of Congress.

69. Rich, *The Man From Emporia,* p. 330.

70. Ibid., p. 329.

71. See White to Lewis Douglas, December 28, 1940, White Collection, Library of Congress.

72. William Lindsay White, "The Last Two Decades," *Autobiography,* p. 644.

73. Ibid., p. 643.

74. Ibid., p. 644.

75. See Hinshaw, *A Man From Kansas,* pp. 292-93.

Chapter 13: The Final Philosophy

1. White would have read some significance, no doubt, into the fact that he died on Kansas Day, just twelve days before his seventy-sixth birthday.

2. See, for example, his prefaces to *Politics: The Citizen's Business* and *What It's All About.*

3. One sees this most clearly in White's repeated use of the Prodigal Son in his fiction. See also his *Some Cycles of Cathay,* pp. 16-21, passim. Indeed, any man who spends his life making his private sentiment public opinion is a walking example of his thesis.

4. White to J. Willis Gleed, January 15, 1916; White to William H. Ingersoll, Committee on Public Information, November 13, 1918, White Collection, Library of Congress.

5. This is the theme of *What It's All About.*

6. White's letters as reflected by the Library of Congress collection are full of support for reforms like referendum and recall which would give the people such direct control.

7. Hinshaw, *A Man From Kansas,* p. 140.

8. Review of *The Old Order Changeth* [n.d.], Sidney, Australia, *Morning Herald.* Clipping, White Collection, White Memorial Library.

9. White to Eugene Bryan, November 23, 1914, White Collection, Library of Congress.

10. White to Clifford A. Cole, June 3, 1914, White Collection, Library of Congress.

11. White to the Reverend John H. Jones, September 26, 1916, White Collection, Library of Congress.

12. White to Fred D. Warren, September 20, 1913, White Collection, Library of Congress.

13. White to Mr. Townsend, November 16, 1911, White Collection, Library of Congress.

14. White, *Autobiography,* p. 107.

15. Ibid., p. 103.

16. Ibid., pp. 107-108.

17. White, *A Theory of Spiritual Progress* (The Gazette Press, 1910).

18. The fact is included in the subtitle of the book.

19. White, *Some Cycles of Cathay* (Chapel Hill: The University of North Carolina Press, 1925).

20. White, *An Economic Theory about Our Golden Age* (New York: The Macmillan Company, 1939.

21. This can be seen in his portraits of Croker, Quay, Big Bill Thompson of Chicago, Platt and others in *Masks in a Pageant.* It explains in part his refusal to take funds from the national Progressive organization to run the Kansas campaign of 1912. Further, it provided, in White's eyes, an automatic limitation on the socio-political effectiveness of any Democrat, as White illustrates explicitly in his *Woodrow Wilson.*

22. White, *Autobiography,* [n.p.].

Selected Bibliography

Included in this bibliography are two types of material: that used directly in the preparation of this book, and that which supplements the direct references. There are two reasons for limiting the list in this way. First, a complete bibliography of the works by and about William Allen White would be far beyond the physical scope of this book. The Johnson-Pantle bibliography cited below contains 576 titles. Even so, the authors have omitted all of White's editorials except those contained in *The Editor and His People* and *Forty Years on Main Street.* Moreover, they included only those book reviews by White which they considered "real literary or interpretative essays." Hence, they did not include Book-of-the-Month Club "blurbs" or other book-launching pieces. Nor did they include White's syndicated articles.

Secondly, an extensive bibliography already exists, done by the Kansas State Teachers College. *A Bibliography of William Allen White* is a two-volume work listing all the White material, manuscripts, letters, books, articles and realia housed in the William Allen White Memorial Library on the campus of Kansas State Teachers College in Emporia. Beyond these limits a truly definitive bibliography—one containing everything that White wrote and everything that has been written about him—may never be done. William Allen White not only wrote news and comments on the news, but he made news wherever he went, and a complete bibliography would entail, one must assume, research in nearly every newspaper morgue in the United States.

BOOKS BY WILLIAM ALLEN WHITE

The Autobiography of William Allen White. New York: The Macmillan Company, 1946.

Boys–Then and Now. New York: The Macmillan Company, 1926.

Calvin Coolidge, The Man Who Is President. New York: The Macmillan Company, 1925.

A Certain Rich Man. New York: The Macmillan Company, 1909.

The Changing West: An Economic Theory About Our Golden Age. New York: The Macmillan Company, 1939.

Conflicts in American Public Opinion (with Walter E. Myer). Chicago: The American Library Association, 1925.

The Court of Boyville. New York: Doubleday & McClure Company, 1899.

Defense for America: The Views of Quincy Wright, Charles Seymour, Barry Bingham [and others]. Edited with Introduction by William Allen White. New York: The Macmillan Company, 1940.

The Editor and His People: Editorials by William Allen White, Selected from the Emporia Gazette by Helen Ogden Mahin; Introduction and Footnotes by Mr. White. New York: The Macmillan Company, 1924.

Forty Years on Main Street, Compiled by Russell H. Fitzgibbon From the Files of the Emporia Gazette. New York: Farrar & Rinehart, Inc., 1937.

God's Puppets. New York: The Macmillan Company, 1916.

In Our Town. New York: McClure, Phillips & Company, 1906.

In the Heart of a Fool. New York: The Macmillan Company, 1918.

_____ and T. F. Doran, eds. *Sunflowers.* Lawrence Journal Publishing Company, 1888.

_____ and G. B. Wilson. *Letters of William Allen White and a Young Man.* New York: John Day, 1948.

The Martial Adventures of Henry and Me. New York: The Macmillan Company, 1918.

Masks in a Pageant. New York: The Macmillan Company, 1928.

The Old Order Changeth: A View of American Democracy. New York: The Macmillan Company, 1910.

Politics: The Citizen's Business. New York: The Macmillan Company, 1927.

A Puritan in Babylon: The Story of Calvin Coolidge. New York: The Macmillan Company, 1938.

The Real Issue: A Book of Kansas Stories. Chicago: Way & Williams, 1896.

Selected Letters of William Allen White, 1899-1943. Edited with an introduction by Walter Johnson. New York: Henry Holt and Company, 1947.

Some Cycles of Cathay. Chapel Hill: The University of North Carolina Press, 1925.

Stratagems and Spoils: Stories of Love and Politics. New York: Charles Scribner's Sons, 1901.

A Theory of Spiritual Progress: An Address Delivered Before the Phi Beta Kappa Society of Columbia University in the City of New York. Emporia: The *Gazette* Press, 1910.

What It's All About: Being a Reporter's Story of the Early Campaign of 1936. New York: The Macmillan Company, 1936.

Woodrow Wilson, The Man, His Times, and His Task. Boston: Houghton Mifflin Company, 1924.

ARTICLES BY WILLIAM ALLEN WHITE

"The Abuse of the Direct Primary." *Independent* 113:18 (July 5, 1924).

"Address of the President." *Kansas State Historical Quarterly* 8:72-82 (February 1939).

"Al Smith, City Feller." *Collier's* 77:8 ff. (August 21, 1926).

"Annihilate the Klan." *Nation* 120:7 (January 7, 1925).

"The Anti-Saloon League." *Saturday Review of Literature* 4:961-62 (June 16, 1928).

"An Appreciation of the West." *McClure's* 11:575-80 (August 1898).

"Are Human Forces Independent of Wars?" *Journal of Social Forces* 3:393-95 (May 1925).

"Are Movies a Mess or a Menace?" *Collier's* 77:5 ff. (January 16, 1926).

"As Kansas Sees Prohibition." *Collier's* 77:23 (July 3, 1926).

"The Average American." *New York Times Magazine*, January 4, 1931, 1-2.

"Beefsteak as I Prepare It." *Better Homes and Gardens* 12:97 (April 1934).

"Be of Good Cheer, Little Guy!" *Rotarian* 63:10-13 (July 1943).

"The Best Minds, Incorporated." *Collier's* 71:5 ff. (March 4, 1922).

"Bill's School and Mine." *Journal of Education* 75:257-58 (March 7, 1912).

"Blood of the Conquerors." *Collier's* 71:5ff. (March 10, 1923).

"Books of the Decade." *Yale Review* 29:419-20 (December 1939).

"Books of the Fall." *Saturday Review of Literature* 14:16 ff. (October 10, 1936).
"The Boom in the Northwest." *Saturday Evening Post* 174:1-3 (May 21, 1904); 1-2 (May 28, 1904).
"Boys–Then and Now." *American Magazine* 101:7 ff. (March 1926).
"The Brain Trust." *Saturday Evening Post* 175:1-3. (March 21, 1903).
"A Brief for the Defendant." *Collier's* 9-10 (March 4, 1908).
"Bryan." *McClure's* 15:232-37 (July 1900).
"Building up the Prairie West." *Collier's* 29:10 (May 10, 1902).
"The Business of a Wheat Farm." *Scribner's* 22:531-48 (November 1897).
"Calvin Coolidge." *Collier's* 75:5 ff. (March 7, 1925); 13 ff. (March 21, 1925); 9 ff. (April 4, 1925); 9 ff. (April 18, 1925).
"Caring in a Nightmare." *Survey Graphic* 27:402 (August 1938).
"Certain Voices in the WIlderness." *Kansas Magazine* 1-5 (January 1909).
"Carrie Nation and Kansas." *Saturday Evening Post* 173:2-3 (April 6, 1909).
"Cheer Up, America." *Harper's* 154:405-17 (April 1927).
"Cleveland." *McClure's* 18:322-30 (February 1902).
"Concerning 'Art for Art's Sake'." *Agora* 3:290 (April 1894).
"The Confederate Colonel as a Political Issue." *Agora* 2:27-31 (July 1892).
"The Conflict Between Important and Interesting in Newspapers." *Proceedings,* American Society of Newspaper Editors, 34-36 (April 1935).
"The Country Boy." *Saturday Evening Post* 176:18 (December 19, 1903).
"The Country Editor Speaks." *Nation* 128:714 (June 12, 1929).
"Croker." *McClure's* 16:317-26 (February 1901).
"Cuban Reciprocity." *McClure's* 19:387-94 (September 1902).
"The Dawn of a Great Tomorrow." *Collier's* 71:11 ff. (March 17, 1923).
"The Democratic Survival." *Saturday Evening Post* 177:6-7 (August 13, 1904).
"A Democratic View of Education." *Craftsman* 21:119-30 (November 1911).
"The Dollar in Politics." *Saturday Evening Post* 177:8-9 (July 2, 1904).
"Don't Indulge in Name-Calling with Press Critics." *Editor and Publisher* 72:14 ff. (April 22, 1939).
"A Dry West Warns the Thirsty East." *Collier's* 70:3 ff. (September 2, 1922).
"An Earlier Cycle of American Development." *Social Forces* 4:281-85 (December 1925).
"Edna Ferber." *World's Work* 59:36 ff. (June 1930).
"Educational Services of the Library." *School and Society* 18:55-56 (November 10, 1923).

"The End of an Epoch." *Scribner's* 79:561-70 (June 1926).
"England in Transition." *Collier's* 74:9 ff. (September 27, 1919).
"Esther the Gentile." *University Review* 9:161-63 (March 1888).
"The Eternal Bounce in Man." *Vital Speeches* 3:606-08 (July 15, 1937).
"The Ethics of Advertising." *Atlantic* 164:665-71 (November 1939).
"A Eulogy of the Santa Fe and Santa Fe Men." *Santa Fe Employes' Magazine* 4:45 (May 1912).
"Ever Been in Emporia?" *New Republic* 22:348-49 (May 12, 1920).
"The Fair Play Department." *Saturday Evening Post* 175:1-2 (May 2, 1903).
"The Farmer and His Plight." *Survey* 62:281-83 (June 1, 1929).
"Farmer John and the Sirens." *Saturday Evening Post* 194:10 ff. (November 28, 1922).
"The Farmer Takes His Holiday." *Saturday Evening Post* 205:6 ff. (November 26, 1932).
"The Farmer's Votes and Problems." *Yale Review* 27:433-38 (March 1939).
"Farmington." *Saturday Evening Post* 177:20 (January 21, 1905).
"Fifty Years of Kansas." *World's Work* 8:870-72 (June 1904).
"Folk." *McClure's* 26:115-32 (December 1905).
"Forty Years: New Men, Old Issues." *New York Times Magazine,* August 9, 1936, 1 ff.
"Four-Cornered Fight for Statehood." *Collier's* 32:7-8 (January 16, 1904).
"Free Kansas." *Outlook* 100:407-14 (February 24, 1912).
"From Harrison II to Roosevelt II." *Saturday Review of Literature* 11:121 ff. (September 22, 1934).
"From One Country Editor to Another." *Saturday Review of Literature* 76:121 ff. (January 29, 1938).
"Funston—The Man from Kansas." *Saturday Evening Post* 173:2 ff. (May 18, 1901).
"The Futility of Reports." *Review of Reviews* 82:46 (April 1931).
"Gay Life of a Pinfeather Rooster." [*Autobiography*]. *Scholastic* 49:17-18 (September 23, 1946).
"The Gentle Art of Knocking." *Kansas Knocker* 1:23-24 (April 1900).
"The Glory of the States: Kansas." *American Magazine* 81:41-56 (January 1916).
"God Only Knows." *Homiletic Review* 107:303-5 (April 1934).
"Good Newspapers and Bad." *Atlantic* 153:581-86 (May 1934).
"Government of the People, by the People, and for the People." *Independent* 135:187-90 (February 7, 1916).
"Governor Smith and Myself." *Commonweal* 9:402 (February 6, 1929).

"Grafting and Things." *Saturday Evening Post* 176:4 (May 7, 1904).
"The Great Political Drama of St. Louis." *Collier's* [St. Louis Convention Extra], 2 ff.
"Greatheart." *World Review* 7:85-86 (December 22, 1928).
"Haitian Experience." *Proceedings,* American Society of Newspaper Editors, April 1930, 203-08.
"Hanna." *McClure's* 16:56-64 (November 1900).
"Harrison." *Cosmopolitan* 32:489-96 (March 1902).
"Herbert Hoover–The Last of the Old Presidents or the First of the New?" *Saturday Evening Post* 205:6 ff. (March 4, 1933).
"Here was a Man." *Saturday Review of Literature* 8:257 ff. (November 7, 1931).
"The Highbrow Doughboy." *Red Cross Magazine* 14:19-24 (August 1919).
"Hot from the Griddle." *Saturday Review of Literature* 9:73-74 (September 3, 1932).
"How Far Have We Come?" *Survey Graphic* 24:669-72 (December 1937).
"How Free is Our Press?" *Nation* 147:693-95 (January 18, 1938).
"How Free is the Press?" *Collier's* 103:16 ff. (April 8, 1939).
"How Kansas Boarded the Water Wagon." *Saturday Evening Post* 187:3 ff. (July 11, 1914).
"How May the West Survive?" *Christian Science Monitor Magazine,* May 20, 1931, 1 ff.
"How the West May Survive." *North American Review* 248:7-17 (Autumn 1939).
"How We Buried Him." *Graduate Magazine* 7:260-61 (August 1909).
"I Cover the Pacific Waterfront." *Proceedings,* American Society of Newspaper Editors, April 1, 1936, 39-44.
"If I Were Dictator." *Nation* 133:596-98 (December 2, 1931).
"Immortal Insult." *Scholastic* 46:20 (March 12, 1945).
"Incorruptible Colonel." *Scholastic* 51:16 (October 27, 1947).
"Industrial Justice–Not Peace." *Nation's Business* 10:14-16 (May 1922).
"In Kansas, the Landon Home State." *Review of Reviews* 93:55 (April 1936).
"Journalism–Its Good and Its Gray Side." *World Review* 8:104 (March 18, 1929).
Judge. Editorials from November 26, 1921, to August 12, 1922, inclusive.
"Just Wondering." *Kansas Magazine,* 1934, 86-88.
"Kansas and Prohibition." *Kansas Magazine,* 1937, 50-52.

"The Kansas Conscience." *Reader Magazine* 6:488-93 (October 1905).
"The Kansas Fight." *La Follette's Weekly Magazine* 1:5 ff. (January 6, 1900).
"Kansas: Its Present and Future." *Forum* 23:75-83 (March 1897).
"The Kansas Red Scare." *Kansas Magazine,* 1938, 130-131.
"Landon: I Knew Him When." *Saturday Evening Post* 209:5 ff. (July 18, 1936).
"The Larger Cycle of American Development." *Social Forces* 4:1-5 (July 1925).
"The Last of the Magic Isles." *Survey* 56:176 ff. (May 1, 1926).
"Lawton–The Metropolis of the Wilderness." *Saturday Evening Post* 174:3 ff. (September 7, 1901).
"The Leaven of the Pharisees." *Saturday Evening Post* 192:20 ff. (May 29, 1929).
"Liberalism for Republicans." *Review of Reviews* 87:27 (January 1933).
"The Librarian, A Community Engineer." *Libraries* 32:183-84 (April 1927).
"Lincoln and Our Democracy." *Collier's* 49:10-11 (February 15, 1908).
"Litmus Papers of the Acid Test." *Survey* 44:343-46 (June 5, 1920).
"The Lone Lion of Idaho." *Collier's* 74:6 ff. (September 12, 1926).
"Make Him 'Swaller' It." *The California Outlook* 16:2 (April 25, 1914).
"A Man of Courage." *Saturday Review of Literature* 60: 185-86 (October 22, 1932).
"The Man Who Rules the Senate." *Collier's* 76:10 ff. (October 3, 1925).
"Mary Elizabeth McCabe." *Kansas Newspaperdom* 1:2 (May 1894).
"Mary White." *Scholastic* 44:21 ff. (May 1, 1944).
"McKinley and Hanna." *Saturday Evening Post* 174:1-2 (March 12, 1904).
"Memoirs of the Three-Fingered Pianist." *Woman's Home Companion* 54:12 ff. (September 1927); 8 ff. (October 1927).
"The Migratory Executive." *Saturday Evening Post* 202:10 ff. (March 15, 1930).
"The Mind of Coolidge." *Collier's* 74:6 ff. (December 26, 1925).
"Moscow and Emporia." *New Republic* 96:177-80 (December 7, 1938) [Reprinted 131:183-85, November 22, 1954].
"Mr. Howe's New Novel." *University Review* 10:111-13 (December 1888).
"Mr. White Comes Back." *Saturday Evening Post* 187:25-27 (November 14, 1914).
"The Natural History of a Gentleman: Being the Autobiography of Herbert Spencer." *Saturday Evening Post* 177:13-15 (July 30, 1904).

"The New Congress." *Saturday Evening Post* 173:5-6 (January 2, 1902).
"Now We Eat It 'n' Like It." *Rotarian* 54:10-11 (February 1939).
"The Odds Against the U-Boat." *Collier's* 60:4-6 (December 8, 1917).
"The Old Order Changeth." *American Magazine* 67:218-225 (January 1909); 407-14 (February 1909); 506-13 (March 1909); 603-10 (April 1909); 63-70 (May 1909); 376-83 (August 1909).
"The Old Problem of the Dog and the Engine." *American Magazine* 71:517-20 (February 1911).
"Old Slugs," *Newspaper West* 2:93 (July 1899).
"On Bright Angel Trail." *McClure's* 25:502-15 (September 1905).
"One Year of Roosevelt." *Saturday Evening Post* 175:3-4 (October 4, 1902).
"The Other Side." *Sunflower Magazine* 3:8 (September 1905).
"The Other Side of Main Street." *Collier's* 68:7 ff. (July 30, 1921).
"A Page of National History." *Saturday Review of Literature* 7:261-63 (October 25, 1930).
"The Partnership of Society." *American Magazine* 62:576-85 (October 1906).
"The Passing of Reuben." *World Review* 7:21 ff. (September 24, 1928).
"The Passing of the Free Editor." *American Mercury* 7:110-112 (May 1926).
"Patience and Publicity." *World Tomorrow* 7:87 (March 1924).
"Payday in Politics." *Saturday Review of Literature* 18:10-11 (April 9, 1938).
"The Peace and President Wilson." *Saturday Evening Post* 192:15 ff. (August 16, 1919).
"Platt." *McClure's* 18:145-53 (October 1901).
"A Poet Came out of Tailholt." *Collier's* 54:3 ff. (December 25, 1915).
"Political Signs of Promise." *Outlook* 80:667-70 (July 15, 1905).
"The Politicians." *Saturday Evening Post* 175:1-3 (March 14, 1903).
"The President." *Saturday Evening Post* 175:4 ff. (April 4, 1903).
Proceedings, American Society of Newspaper Editors, April, 1938, 131-35.
"The Progressive Hen and the Insurgent Ducklings." *American Magazine* 71:394-99 (January 1911).
"Progressive Leader." *Saturday Review of Literature* 16:5-6 (July 10, 1937).
"A Reader in the Eighties and Nineties." *Bookman* 72:229-34 (November 1936).
"Ready Made Home Out West." *Saturday Evening Post* 174:12 (April 26, 1902).
"The Reorganization of the Republican Party." *Saturday Evening Post* 177:1-2 (December 3, 1904).
"Rights of a Columnist." *Nation* 126:607 (May 1928).

"Roosevelt, A Force for Righteousness." *McClure's* 27:386-94 (February 1907).
"Roosevelt and the Postal Frauds." *McClure's* 23:506-20 (September 1904).
"The Santa Fe Magazine." *Santa Fe Magazine* 21:39 (December 1926).
"Science, St. Skinflint and Santa Claus." *American Magazine* 63:182-84 (December 1906).
"Seconding the Motion." *Saturday Evening Post* 177:4-5 (July 23, 1904).
"The Sheriff and the Chaperone." *Saturday Evening Post* 173:14 (March 30, 1901).
"Shock Troops of Reform." *Saturday Review of Literature* 19:3-4 (April 8, 1939).
"Should Old Acquaintance Be Forgot." *American Magazine* 74:13-18 (May 1912).
"Simplifying the Business of Politics." *Woman's Home Companion* 51:21 ff. (November 1924).
"The Solid West–Free and Proud of It." *Collier's* 70:5 ff. (December 30, 1922).
"Some Personal Glimpses of Early Kansas Editors." *Kansas Editor* 18:1 (March 1933).
"Speaking for the Consumer." *Vital Speeches* 5:47-49 (November 1, 1938).
"Splitting Fiction Three Ways." *New Republic* 30:22-26 (April 12, 1922).
"The State Administration–A Weak Man in a Strong Situation." *Agora* 4:90-95 (October 1894).
"Storming the Citadel." *American Magazine* 72:570-75 (September 1911).
"Sullivan I and Roosevelt I." *Saturday Review of Literature* 19:3-4 (November 19, 1938).
"Summer on a Cattle Ranch." *University Review* 10:13 (September 1888).
"The Supremacy of Beefsteak." *Nation* 117:731 (December 26, 1923).
"Supreme Court–or 'Rule by Impulse'." *New York Times Magazine*, April 26, 1937, 3 ff.
"Swinging Around the Circle." *Saturday Evening Post* 175: 1-2 (June 27, 1903).
"Taft, A Hewer of Wood." *American Magazine* 66:19-32 (May 1908).
"Taft, T. R. and the GOP." *Saturday Review of Literature* 21: 3-4 (October 28, 1938).
"Tale that is Told." *Saturday Evening Post* 192:19 ff. (October 4, 1919).

"A Tenderfoot on Thunder Mountain." *Saturday Evening Post* 175:1 ff. ("The Trail," November 8, 1902); 3-5 ("The Foot of the Rainbow," November 15, 1902); 15-16 ("The Foot of the Rainbow," November 22, 1902); 3 ff. ("The Pot of Gold," November 29, 1902).

"Theodore Roosevelt." *McClure's* 18:40-47 (November 1901).

"A Theory of Social Progress." *Columbia University Quarterly* 12:408-20 (September 1910).

"There Were Giants in Those Days." [*Autobiography*]. *Scholastic* 52:18-19 (March 1, 1948).

"They Can't Beat My Big Boy." *Collier's* 79:8 ff. (June 18, 1927).

"This Business of Writing." *Saturday Review of Literature* 3:355-56 (December 4, 1926).

"Those Heartbreaks in Washington." *Collier's* 62:7 ff. (December 31, 1921).

"A Thought for a Great Occasion." *American Legion Monthly* 1:8 (July 1926).

"Thoughts and Thanks." *New York Times Magazine*, November 19, 1939, 4 ff.

"Three Years of Progress." *Saturday Evening Post* 84:3 ff. (February 24, 1912).

"Tinting the Cold Gray Dawn." *Collier's* 67:5 ff. (December 17, 1921).

"Turning Knowledge into Votes." *National Municipal Review* 23:85-86 (February 1934).

"Twelve Years of Mr. Bryan." *Collier's* 42:12-13 (October 1[illegible], 1908).

"Two Recent Kansas Books." *University Review* 10:199-202 (April 1889).

"Uncommercial Traveling." *Saturday Evening Post* 174:12 (May 3, 1902).

"The Unknown Soldier." *Collier's* 68:13 (November 12, 1921).

"W. A. White on the Kansas Court." *Nation* 115:718 (December 27, 1922).

"We Who Are About to Die." *New Republic* 24:36-38 (March 9, 1921).

"What About Our Courts." *American Magazine* 69:499-505 (February 1910).

"What Democracy Means to Me." *Scholastic* 30:9 (October 23, 1937).

"What Happened to Prinkipo." *Metropolitan* 51:29-30, 60-67 (December 1919).

"What Happened to Walt Mason." *American Magazine* 76:19 (September 1918).

"What Music Has Done for Me." *Etude* 56:779-80 (December 1938).

"What 1920 Holds for Us All." *Collier's* 65:7 (January 3, 1920).

"What the War Did for Old Brewer." *Yale Review* 8:243-51. (January 1919).
"What the West Thinks of Wall Street Now." *Collier's* 32:9-10 (November 28, 1903).
"What's the Matter with America?" *Collier's* 38:18 ff. (October 20, 1906); 16 ff. (November 10, 1906); 16 ff. (December 1, 1906).
"What's the Matter with America." *Collier's* 70:3 ff. (July 1, 1922).
"What's the Matter with American Cooking?" *Pictorial Review* 27:4 ff. (July 1926).
"When Clubwomen Are News." *Clubwoman* 8:5 (May 1933).
"When Johnny Went Marching Out." *McClure's* 11:198-205 (June 1898).
"When the World Busts Through." *American Magazine* 71:746-47 (April 1911).
"Where Are the Pre-War Radicals?" *Survey* 55:55 (February 1, 1926).
"Who Killed Cock Robin?" *Collier's* 58:5 ff. (December 16, 1916).
"Why I Am a Progressive." *Saturday Evening Post* 193:3 ff. (April 22, 1921).
"Why the Nation Will Endure." *Saturday Evening Post* 177:12 (March 4, 1905).
"Will America's Dream Come True?" *Collier's* 80:12 (February 18, 1922).
"William Allen White on Mr. Steffens' Book, 'The Shame of the Cities'." *McClure's* 23:220-21. (June 1904).
"William Allen White to F. J." *New Republic* 19:88 (May 17, 1919).
"William Allen White States His Own Case." *Outlook* 131:560 (August 2, 1922).
"A Woman of Genius." *Saturday Review of Literature* 9:235-36 (November 12, 1932).
"Woodrow Wilson." *Liberty* 1:19-23 (November 15, 1924); 22-26 (November 22, 1924).
"The Worthy Rich." *Saturday Evening Post* 178:12 (January 13, 1906).
"A Yip From the Doghouse." *New Republic* 93:160-62 (December 15, 1937).
"The YMCA Huts, 'Safety Valves' for Our Boys in France." *Touchstone* 2:344-50 (January 1918).

BOOKS AND ARTICLES ABOUT WILLIAM ALLEN WHITE

"Bill White's Own Record." *Newsweek* 29:92-95 (March 4, 1946).

Canby, Henry Seidel, "A Personal Tribute." *Saturday Review of Literature* 27:16 (February 5, 1944).

Clough, Frank C. *William Allen White of Emporia.* New York: Whittlesy House, 1941.

Commanger, Henry Steele. "Small Town Editor Whose Window Was the World." *Scholastic* 58:14 f. (April 25, 1951).

Davies, B. "Autobiography of William Allen White" [Review]. *Canadian Forum* 26:93 (July 1946).

Davis, K. S. "Wit and Wisdom by Will White." *New York Times Magazine,* April 20, 1952, p. 13.

Dilliard, Irving. *The Editor I Wish I Were: Eighth Annual William Allen White Lecture, Delivered February 11, 1957, William Allen White School of Journalism and Public Information, University of Kansas, Lawrence.* University of Kansas, 1957.

"Discovery in a Desk Drawer." *Christian Century* 70:133 (June 24, 1953).

Dubbert, Joe L. "William Allen White's American Adam." *Western American Literature* 7:271-78 (Winter 1973).

"Emporia Buries Distinguished Editor who Gave National Influence to a Small-Town Daily." *Life* 16:37-38 ff. (February 14, 1944).

Frederick, J. T. "William Allen White and Mark Twain." *Rotarian* 68:7, 47 (April 8, 1964).

Gannett, Lewis. "William Allen White." *Nation* 158:276-77 (March 4, 1944).

Geismar, Maxwell. "A Middle Class Folk Hero." [Review of Johnson, Walter, *William Allen White's America*], *Saturday Review of Literature* 30:17 (August 16, 1947).

"Great Citizen." *Survey* 80:53 (February 1944).

Groman, George L. "The Political Fiction of William Allen White: A Study in Emerging Progressivism." *The Midwest Quarterly* 8:79-93 (October 1966).

Hanson, Howard. "White of Emporia." *Survey Graphic* 34:478 (December 1945).

Hibbs, Ben. "Up Yonder the Trumpets Blew. . . ." *Saturday Evening Post* 216:100 (February 26, 1944).

Hinshaw, David. *A Man From Kansas: The Story of William Allen White.* New York: G. P. Putnam's Sons, 1954.

Hoover, Herbert. "World Peace and the United Nations: Address Delivered at the Dedication of the William Allen White Memorial." *Vital Speeches*

16:617-20 (August 1, 1950).

Irwin, Will. "One Man in his Time." *Saturday Review of Literature* 29:7-8 (March 16, 1946).

"Jo Davidson's Bronze." *Survey Graphic* 36:306 (May 1947).

Johnson, Walter. *The Battle Against Isolation.* University of Chicago Press, 1944.

______. "William Allen White: Grass-Roots American." *Selected Letters of William Allen White, 1899-1943,* pp. 1-22. New York: Henry Holt and Company, 1947.

______. *William Allen White's America.* New York: Henry Holt and Company, 1948.

Life 4:9-13 (February 28, 1938).

Lindley, Ernest K. "Clapper and White: A Personal Tribute." *Newsweek* 23:52 (February 14, 1944).

Long, J. C. "Good Editor, Good Citizen." *Saturday Review of Literature* 28:42 (November 10, 1945).

Mencken, H. L. "The Last of the Victorians." *Smart Set* 29:153-160 (October 1909).

Obituaries: *Christian Century* 61:165 (February 9, 1944); *Current Biography* (April 1944); *Nation* 158:147 (February 5, 1944); *New Republic* 110:165 (February 7, 1944); *Publisher's Weekly* 145:700 (February 5, 1944); *Time* 43:82 (February 7, 1944).

Pemberton, Murdock. "Our Far-flung Correspondents: Town Without a Sage." *New Yorker* 23:58 ff. (July 5, 1947).

Pick, F. W. "Great American Journalist." *Contemporary* 171:27-31 (January 1947).

Rich, Everett. *William Allen White: The Man From Emporia.* New York: Farrar & Rinehart, Inc., 1941.

Rovere, Richard H. "Will White's Memoirs." *New Republic* 114:622 ff. (April 29, 1946).

"Sage of Kansas." *Time* 47:97 (March 18, 1946).

"U. S. and Emporia." *Newsweek* 30:90 (August 11, 1947).

Villard, Oswald Garrison. "A Long and Foolish Life." *Nation* 144:467 (April 24, 1937).

"War and William Allen White." *Commonweal* 41:74 ff. (November 3, 1944).

"W. A. White's Papers to Library of Congress." *Publisher's Weekly* 150:384 (July 27, 1946).

"William Allen White." *Newsweek* 23:77 (February 7, 1944).

"William Allen White Children's Book Awards." *Publisher's Weekly* 61:18, 53 (May 3, 1953).

William Allen White: In Memoriam. Contributions by Henry Seidel Canby, Dorothy Canfield (Fisher), Harry Scherman, and others not named. New York: The Book-of-the-Month Club [1944].

White, W. L. "The Last Two Decades." *The Autobiography of William Allen White,* pp. 627-649. New York: The Macmillan Company, 1946.

"W.L.W. for W.A.W." *Time* 43:44 (January 31, 1944).

"Young Kansas Editor." *Atlantic* 177:39-47 (March 1946).

BACKGROUND

Barck, Oscar Theodore, Jr., and Nelson Manfred Blake. *Since 1900: A History of the United States in Our Times* (rev. ed.). New York: The Macmillan Company, 1952.

Beard, Charles A., and Mary E. *America in Midpassage.* New York: The Macmillan Company, 1939.

Bryan, William Jennings, and Mary Baird. *The Memoirs of William Jennings Bryan.* Philadelphia: The United Publishers of America, 1925.

Croly, Herbert. *Marcus Alonzo Hanna: His Life and Work.* New York: The Macmillan Company, 1923.

______. *The Promise of American Life.* New York: The Macmillan Company, 1909.

Garraty, John A., ed., "T. R. On the Telephone." *American Heritage* 9:99-108 (December 1957).

Goldman, Eric F. *Rendezvous With Destiny: A History of Modern American Reform* (revised and abridged). New York: Vintage Books, 1956.

Hicks, John D. *The Populist Revolt.* Minneapolis: The University of Minnesota Press, 1937.

Langer, William L. and S. Everett Gleason. *The Challenge of Isolation: The World Crisis of 1937-1940 and American Foreign Policy,* 2 vols. New York: Harper Torchbooks, The University Library, Harper & Row, Publishers, 1964.

Lippmann, Walter. "Introduction," *Congressional Government: A Study in American Politics,* pp. 7-17. New York: Meridian Books, 1956.

______ *U.S. Foreign Policy: Shield of the Republic.* New York: Little Brown, 1943.

Morison, Elting E., ed. *The Letters of Theodore Roosevelt,* vol. III. Cambridge: Harvard University Press, 1951.

Mowry, George E. *Theodore Roosevelt and the Progressive Movement.* New York: Hill and Wang, 1960.

Norris, Frank. *The Responsibility of the Novelist.* New York: Doubleday Page and Company, 1903.

Parrington, Vernon Lewis. *Main Currents in American Thought,* vol. III. New York: Harcourt Brace and Company, 1930.

Pringle, Henry F. *Theodore Roosevelt: A Biography.* New York: Harcourt Brace and Company, A Harvester Book, 1956.

Roosevelt, Franklin D. *F.D.R.: His Personal Letters.* Elliott Roosevelt and others, eds. 4 vols. New York: Duell, Sloan and Pearce, 1947-1950.

Roosevelt, Theodore. *American Ideals and Other Essays, Social and Political.* New York: G. P. Putnam's Sons, 1900.

Wilson, Woodrow. *Congressional Government: A Study in American Politics.* New York: Meridian Books, 1956.

Wright, Ernest Hunter. "James Hulme Canfield," *Dictionary of American Biography,* III, 472. Edited by Allen Johnson. New York: Charles Scribner's Sons, 1929.

NEWSPAPERS

Bound volumes of *The Emporia Gazette,* 1895-1944. William Allen White Memorial Library, Kansas State Teachers College, Emporia, Kansas.

MANUSCRIPTS, CORRESPONDENCE, AND CLIPPINGS

The bulk of the William Allen White correspondence is in the White Collection in the Library of Congress. Some letters remain in the William Allen White Memorial Library at Kansas State Teachers College, Emporia, along with a mass of newspaper clippings and much manuscript.

The William Allen White Papers in the Library of Congress consist of 324 containers with about 3,000 items per container, arranged in the following manner:

Letterpress Books, 1899-1920, 24 containers chronologically arranged.

Personal Correspondence, 1909-1944, 261 containers, chronologically arranged with alphabetical series within.

Special Correspondence, 1914-1943, 37 containers, political, personal, miscellaneous.

Selected Correspondence, Presidential and other, 1897-1942, two containers.

BIBLIOGRAPHY

Johnson, Walter, and Alberta Pantle. "A Bibliography of the Published Works of William Allen White." *The Kansas Historical Quarterly* 15:22-41, (February 1947).

The Kansas State Teachers College. *A Bibliography of William Allen White,* 2 vols. Emporia: Teachers College Press, 1969.

GOVERNMENT DOCUMENTS

Biographical Directory of the American Congress, 1774-1971. Washington, D.C., p. 937.

"Population Growth of Kansas Counties, 1880-1972." *Kansas Statistical Abstract.* Topeka, 1973, pp. 5-7.

Index